INSIDE THE
DEATH
FENCES

*Memoir of a
Whistleblower*

CAROLINE
GIAMMANCO

Inside the Death Fences

Memoir of a Whistleblower

Caroline Giammanco

Publisher's Note: With the exception of public and/or elected officials, all of the people featured in these pages have had their names changed, or have agreed to have themselves identified.

Published by

**RhetAskew
Publishing**

a division of
Rhetoric Askew, LLC
15701 S. 257 E. Avenue
Coweta, Oklahoma 74429
United States

RHETASKEWPUBLISHING.COM

EDITORS@RHETORICASKEW.COM

CRITICAL ACCLAIM FOR
INSIDE THE DEATH FENCES

"Caroline Giammanco's book on teaching behind bars reveals not just the hierarchy of inmates in a maximum-security prison but the ones among guards and her fellow educators who she feared just as much. [. . .] Caroline's resolve is fierce as she fights to keep her job amid the recession even if it means dodging danger behind prison walls. A must-read chilling story rarely told by a civilian and one that rarely makes it out of a penitentiary."

— Dawn Fratangelo, NBC News and Dateline NBC

"A terrific read. This whistleblower doesn't tell us what she sees, but what we might miss, even standing next to her. Read Caroline Giammanco's book for a rare blueprint. She shows us how to find the courage to do what is right.""

— Bob Dotson, former NBC television journalist and New York Times bestselling author of _American Story, a Lifetime Search for Ordinary People Doing Extraordinary Things_

"An engrossing account of workplace bullying, harassment, and widespread corruption told by a courageous and exceptional woman. A wake-up call for our society; a painfully honest look at the inner workings of a prison. It is also a powerful account of the importance of using one's voice for good and how even in the bleakest of circumstances, love can give you the courage to stand up and be heard. Powerful and engaging."

— Lisa Regan, USA Today bestselling author

"Riveting. Inside the Death Fences is both a fascinating and horrifying glimpse into what goes on within a maximum-security prison when a union of love challenges authorities' deceptions."

—Parris Afton Bonds, New York Times bestselling author

"A tangled and intriguing read. The strength of character she and her husband exhibit serves as a lesson for all to never lose faith in what is right, no matter the obstacles."

— Deborah Ratliff, Administrator for <u>Writers Unite!</u>

"Prison reform advocates have a much stronger case to make today thanks to the mind-boggling revelations of daily corruption and prisoner abuse by a brave whistle blowing educator, Caroline Giammanco. She details an unimaginable picture of a broken system and pit of despair which tells America firsthand why the failure of our prison system is by design and destined to self-destruct without major reform."

— Tobin Smith, former contributor to FOX News

"[Caroline] keeps readers riveted as she subtly forecasts trouble in the system. Her description is chilling, [her] example of a guard commander using blackmail against staff members to prevent any complaints reads like a mob boss keeping his extortion victims under control. As we say, 'You can't make this shit up.'"

— Gary Jenkins, former Intelligence Unit detective
with the Kansas City Police Department,
and host of <u>Gangland Wire</u>

"Giammanco enters a world few of us are ever likely to experience. A world which makes clear why the world's oldest republic has built the most expansive prison system in the history of democratic governance and why racial disparities in criminal justice have worsened over the past forty years. What she reveals should shock us all—a web of corruption and deceit that goes to the very top of a state agency. Giammanco takes us inside the seldom seen underbelly of a flawed system where telling the truth can be deadly. "

— Steve Murphy, host of <u>Law Business Insider</u>

"Caroline Giammanco, the daughter of a deputy sheriff, grew up believing that those on the law enforcement side were the good guys. But, once she was inside a state correctional institution as a teacher, she soon became disillusioned by the conduct of her superiors and the guard staff. Giammanco describes her journey there, culminating with her courageous decision to identify the rule breakers with the hopes of effecting change. Her personal account makes me wonder how many others like her are out there."

— Beth Karas, Legal Analyst, Host of Oxygen's podcast, <u>Unspeakable Crime: the Killing of Jessica Chambers</u>

" . . . a courageous whistleblower tale. A former prison teacher and the wife of the 'Boonie Hat Bandit,' dares to take on the prison system at personal risk and reveals the blackmail, backstabbing, assaults and more—that come from the prison guards and staff as much as the prisoners. The inside story of corruption in corrections. You can't put it down. You can't help but be outraged."

— James Campbell, host of <u>Business Talk with Jim Campbell</u>, <u>Forensic Talk with Jim Campbell</u>, & Assistant News Director—WGCH 1490 AM, Greenwich, Connecticut

To Keith

*I love you, and I will
never, ever stop.*

FOREWORD

S ome events in our lives fundamentally shape and define who we become. Caroline Giammanco worked in a maximum-security prison, and her experiences within the dark underbelly of the system drastically altered her perception of crime and punishment. Like many middle-class Americans, she thought that the people kept in our nation's correctional facilities belonged there while brave corrections officers kept the rest of us safe from the criminals. The bad guys were locked away, and if you were locked up, you deserved to be.

My journey within the prison system is also a personal one. Those preconceptions Caroline had were the same thoughts people had about me when I was sentenced to 304 months as a first-time drug offender when I was twenty-two years old. Suddenly, my normal life was transformed by the events occurring behind those razor-wired fences. I witnessed the same corruption she describes. I experienced it as an inmate while she was an employee. My experiences were inside the federal system while hers were inside a state facility. The truth is the same, however, and she is telling the truth.

I remember meeting educators like Caroline who came into the facility to teach. They weren't custody staff like corrections officers were, but they were guards just the same to the prisoners. The working conditions and the personalities Caroline describes are accurate. Some teachers were as filled with hate, greed, and disregard for human dignity as corrupt custody officers were. Still, some staff members were different. They had compassion or saw the charade of prison for what it was.

Not that some prisoners don't deserve to be in prison; they do. I won't claim that all inmates are choir boys; they aren't. However, many are in prison under excessive sentences or are wrongly convicted in the first place. Regardless of what brought someone to prison, no one is served, not our communities, the victims, nor the government if inmates are left unrehabilitated or are turned into even worse people by those who oversee them for years on end. This book is a warning bell for those who have safely hidden behind their preconceived ideas of what prison is and how it works.

When I was in prison, I tried to speak to the prison staff to show them that they were making money off of other people's misery. A lot of them didn't understand or refused to. Some like Caroline, though, saw prison for what it was. She entered the netherworld of corruption and violence with one opinion, one that most citizens have, but left with another opinion. The simple fact is that prisons are corrupt. The greed and quests for power by authority figures within prisons must end.

I've written about the injustices of my case and the inhumanity of prison for years, both during my incarceration and now that I am free. A book like *Inside the Death Fences* is vital to understanding what our prison system has become, and Caroline is the perfect person to write it. Not only did she work in a prison, but she fell in love with an inmate in a prison. This is nothing she ever expected to do, proving that life is more complicated than most like to imagine.

It is possible to have a caring, respectable relationship while one half of a union is behind bars. It takes work and dedication, but it is possible. The power of Caroline and Keith Giammanco's love is undeniable and should serve as an inspiration for anyone facing what appears to be an insurmountable obstacle.

I also married while in prison.

My beautiful and wonderful wife, Diane, and I met when I was a fugitive at the age of twenty-one. I was sentenced to twenty-five years in prison at the age of twenty-two, but she stuck with me and we finally married at FCI Gilmer, a federal prison in West Virginia in 2005. I have been out since 2014, and we are still together living life and enjoying each other's company. It's my hope that Caroline can soon do the same with Keith.

Inside the Death Fences offers a perspective few Americans ever have: that of someone who walked through the bowels of the prison system and came out the other side. Not only did she survive, but she did so with determination to bring awareness to a broken and dysfunctional system that we all pay for, in one way or another. By telling her story and exposing the corruption happening inside prisons across the nation, Caroline adds valuable information and evidence to the national conversation on prison and sentencing reform.

— *Seth Ferranti, Writer*
Crime Contributor to
Rolling Stone, Vice,
and Penthouse

HOW DID A NICE GIRL LIKE ME WIND UP IN A PLACE LIKE THIS?

Truth has a hard time against a lie people want to believe. It's a lie that our prison system keeps us safe and that the good guys rehabilitate those who have committed crimes. People have been fed that lie for so long—and they want to believe it so badly—that they ignore the corruption within the correctional world. I believed the lie until my own experiences forced me to not only acknowledge the corruption, but fight it.

People want to believe the myth because it is comfortable and safe. We don't want to think the system intended to protect us is corrupt, that it produces more violence in our communities than it prevents in the long term, or that our tax dollars are spent on a system that cannibalizes those employees who want to do their jobs the right way.

Death threats, corruption, and retaliation—I faced them all thanks to the "good guys." What happened to me, and what I saw happen to others, is something I will not—cannot—forget. My life and my world changed forever once I stepped inside the death fences of a maximum security men's prison. My experiences inside the death fences crushed the myth.

For two-and-a-half years, I worked inside the South Central Correctional Center in Licking, Missouri, one of twenty-one correctional facilities in the state. The chain link and razor wire fences, charged with high-voltage electricity, posed certain death to anyone who dared escape. The twisted, deadly wires became a metaphor for the web of corruption inside them. My story is set in Missouri, but it is repeated daily in one form or another across our country. This is my chance to give others a look behind the secretive curtain of corrections.

As a college-educated, middle-class school teacher, and the youngest daughter of a small-town deputy sheriff, I made an unlikely candidate to be inside a prison. My family was law-abiding, and prison was far removed from my daily life. I grew up on a farm in southern Missouri, moved to Tucson to attend the University of Arizona, married, gave birth to two beautiful little boys, and then began my teaching career in northern New Mexico. For the most part, I lived a picket fence life.

So, how did I get inside a maximum-security men's prison?

A winding path took me there. After a meat grinder divorce from my sons' father, I remarried. In 2006 my family moved from New Mexico back to the Missouri Ozarks, an area often facing economic struggles. The economy tanked nationwide a few years after we settled into Mansfield and our sixty-acre farm. With the economic downturn, the tax base plummeted and families moved out of our area in search of employment.

The Great Recession, in full swing, affected southern Missouri much as it did other regions of our country. Foreclosures, job losses, and emotional turmoil drained the spirits of most communities. Decreasing student numbers crippled my school district's budget and, as the last teacher hired, the district eliminated my position to balance the school's finances.

Leaving the staff and students I loved broke my heart, and it felt more like a death in the family than a job loss. I faced an uncertain future while consumed by deep emotional wounds and fears. I worried about my family and whether or not my teaching career was permanently derailed. Small districts across rural Missouri faced the same financial distress as Mansfield. Jobs disappeared, and prospects were bleak. I wasn't sure where to turn to find employment. This is where my journey into prison began.

My husband, also in search of a new job, suggested that we both apply with the Missouri Department of Corrections. He wanted to become a corrections officer while I only applied for teaching positions. I had no interest in becoming a prison guard. Having taught at alternative high schools, dealing with inmates wasn't far-fetched to me, but working at a prison wasn't on my bucket list, either. Still, I felt desperate. I held my breath, took a gulp, and sent my application through the state employment website.

I waited. Then I waited some more. Discouraged, I substitute taught at area schools to keep money in the bank and food on the table. Substitute teaching filled a gap, but it wasn't the same as having my own classroom. It didn't pay as well either.

One day in mid-May, I received a letter from the Missouri Department of Corrections, offering an interview for a teaching position at the South Central Correctional Center in Licking, Missouri. A long commute, an hour and a half one way, worried me, but desperation for a steady paycheck and benefits overruled any concerns. Neither the commute nor squeamishness over working in a maximum-security prison overruled my need for a job.

I answered the letter right away and set-up a date in late May to interview. As that day approached, my anxiety grew. When the day of my interview arrived, I was deep in thought. The long drive to the prison gave me time to weigh the advantages and disadvantages of the job.

Will I be safe? Can I dare pass up a steady paycheck?

My nerves lengthened the drive, or so it seemed, as I made my way along an unfamiliar route. I pulled into Licking, turned left at the only stoplight in town, then followed the signs directing drivers to SCCC. Arriving at the prison parking lot, I sat in my car for a moment staring at the stark prison buildings. Surrounded by massive chain link and razor wire, the compound sobered me. I grew up around our hometown sheriff's office, but the prison projected a far more imposing image than any county jail.

As I walked across the parking lot, I couldn't miss a large white sign with red letters announcing, "Danger! High-Voltage Electricity!" Pausing a moment, I read the sign and its warnings, then I stepped onto the sidewalk leading to the main doors of the administration building.

No one gets past those fences alive.

Nothing welcoming greeted me as I pulled open the doors. A metal detector took center stage, and a wall of post-office styled staff mailboxes lined the eastern side of the room.

It felt institutional.

Behind a glass partition stood the officer on duty, a pretty brunette, professional but friendly.

"Hello, how can I help you?" she asked with a smile.

"I'm here for a job interview at 11:00."

"Your interview will be upstairs. See that metal door?"

I turned around, noticing a solid steel door leading to a stairwell.

"Next to the door is a button. Push that and wait for the door to click. That means it's unlocked and then you can go on up. I will call the officers upstairs and let them know you are on your way."

I followed her instructions, and the secured, solid metal door made a loud "clunk" signaling me to pull it open. As I climbed the stairs, the echoing slam of the door behind me confirmed that this wouldn't be a normal teaching experience.

After passing through a second metal door at the top of the stairs, I made my way through the security checkpoint. Having arrived early, I sat for twenty minutes as guards came and went. Some talked and laughed with their coworkers. Others stood glumly, leaning against the beige walls waiting for their shifts to begin. No one spoke to me as I anxiously drummed my fingers on the arm of the chair.

Finally, they called my name and motioned me toward a woman waiting in a doorway. I picked up my briefcase and followed her down a hallway with rooms to each side.

"Hello, Caroline. I'm Eleanor Heath, the assistant warden here. We're going to the conference room where we will join Mary Castor, the regional education manager.

After introducing me to Mary, she motioned for me to sit in a leather office chair across the table from the two of them.

Eleanor began the interview by saying, "I see you went to college at the University of Arizona. That's a very good school, but I also see you graduated from high school in Ava, Missouri. How did you end up going from small-town Missouri to Arizona?"

"My oldest sister went to graduate school at the U of A and she still lived in Tucson when I graduated high school. I had my heart set on attending Mizzou, but my sister offered to let me live with her for free if I moved to Tucson instead. It was too good to pass up, so I changed my plans."

"That's quite a change from southern Missouri," Mary Castor added.

"Yeah, it took some getting used to, but it was a great experience and it gave me the chance to see a different part of the country. I never dreamed it would take me so long to get back to Missouri, but I'm here now."

"Your resume says you taught on the Navajo Reservation in New Mexico for several years. That must have been interesting. You've also taught in large metropolitan schools. Both Arizona and New Mexico have large Hispanic populations. How did you adapt your teaching to reach diverse classrooms? In the prisons, we have a mix of people. What did you do differently when teaching other races?" Eleanor asked.

"That question comes up often in interviews, but my answer isn't what most administrators expect."

This caught their attention, and both women adjusted themselves in their seats then leaned forward.

"While it's politically correct to say each racial or ethnic group must be approached in a different way, that's not really the truth. What does it take to effectively teach a Hispanic child or a Native American child or an African-American child? The same thing it takes to effectively teach a white child: Treat each student as a valued individual—as a person with his or her own abilities and interests—and he or she will want to learn."

Mary and Eleanor looked at one another in surprise. That wasn't the pat answer they expected.

"I'm not saying you should ignore cultural nuances. I don't recommend bringing an owl into a Navajo classroom, for example, because owls have a cultural taboo attached to them. But as far as teaching content goes, I treat each of my students as a person and that breaks down the differences society imposes on us."

"Wow, I never thought about it like that before," Mary said. Eleanor nodded in agreement.

Eleanor added, "Prison isn't homogenous. The department needs someone who can relate to the black population as well as to the growing number of Hispanics serving time in the prison system. The changing demographics of America are apparent, even in the rural prisons of Missouri."

"What do you consider your strengths as a teacher?" Mary asked, switching gears.

"I know my subject matter very well, and I have excellent classroom management skills."

"As you can imagine, classroom management is extremely important in a prison setting," Eleanor interjected.

"I can see where having control of your classroom is a top-priority here. Good classroom management requires firm but fair expectations and the willingness to enforce the rules. I have a lot of experience doing both."

Eleanor then asked, "I see you have extensive experience working at alternative high schools. How do you see that helping you in the prison system?"

"It's an advantage. I've worked with difficult students before, many of whom had probation and parole officers. There isn't much difference between a sixteen-year-old who commits a violent crime and a twenty-two-year-old who commits the same crime. One goes to juvenile hall while the other one ends up in a maximum-security prison. Their personalities are the same. One is just in a bigger body."

Mary Castor and Eleanor Heath gave a subtle nod to one another.

The interview continued for a few more minutes as we chitchatted about the commute and my availability if hired. I left the prison that day confident that the interview went well.

I sure need the job, so I hope Mary and Eleanor viewed our conversation as positively as I did...

As the days ticked by, though, the phone never rang. For three weeks, I heard nothing.

Well, Caroline, it looks like they went with someone else.

Just when hope faded, my luck changed. One afternoon, while I sat on my front porch enjoying a mild June day, my phone rang.

"Hello, Caroline? This is Mary Castor, the DOC regional education manager calling from Jefferson City."

"Hello, Mary, it's good to hear from you."

"Are you still interested in the teaching position you interviewed for?"

"Yes, I am." My voice gave away more eagerness than I wanted to show.

"I apologize for taking so long to get back to you, but I want to offer you the position."

"I accept it, Mary. When do you need me to start?"

"Well, it is going to take a few weeks for us to get the paperwork processed, and then there's the 4th of July coming up. How about we set your start date for July 5?"

"I'll be there!"

A job! I have a job!

"Before you can officially be hired, we need you to come in for a pre-hire drug screen," Mary added. "Is that something you are comfortable with?"

"Absolutely, Mary. I've never even smoked a cigarette. I'll gladly take any drug test you need me to."

"I'm glad to hear that, and welcome to the Department of Corrections. You will get a call telling you when to go to SCCC for your test."

A tremendous weight lifted off my heart. The anxiety that hounded me since my unemployment melted and I wasn't concerned about the location.

I had a job!

WARNING SIGNS

A few days after Mary Castor's call, I received another one, this time from the prison human resources office, to arrange the drug screening. As I made my way to the prison, the long commute didn't bother me.

I have a steady paycheck in my future.

Scorching summer weather hadn't arrived yet, making it a picture-perfect June day in the rural Ozark Mountains. With the window down, I soaked in the beauty of the day.

Arriving at the prison, I parked and made my way to the front entrance. A familiar face greeted me as I came through the doors.

"It's great to see you again! I take it your interview went well. Welcome to SCCC (known as S-Triple-C to those in the system). I guess you're here for your drug test?" asked the smiling officer at the desk who I'd met on the day I interviewed.

"I'm happy to see you, too!" I replied. We exchanged names and visited for a moment. Tracy Parr and I instantly hit it off.

"Do I follow the same instructions to get upstairs? I'm not quite sure where I'm going."

"Yep, just push that button and go on up. I'll call the officer at the desk and they will tell you what to do from there. You'll probably have to wait a few minutes, but just hang out in the lobby and someone will come get you for the drug screening."

I still jumped a bit when the metal door slammed behind me as I made my way up the stairs. At the top of the landing, I pulled open the door and stepped into the bustling lobby area. Approaching the officer behind the reception desk, I introduced myself.

"Have a seat over there and I'll let the officer who handles the tests know you're here."

After a five-minute wait, Corrections Officer Lonnie Duncan met me in the lobby and escorted me to a room down a winding hallway. Once in the testing area, we chatted as Officer Duncan opened the clear plastic bag containing the urine capture cup. He explained the process and sent me into the bathroom with orders to not flush the toilet.

When I emerged with the sample, we continued visiting as he labeled the container. My spirits were high in anticipation of my new job.

This is nothing more than a formality.

What Officer Duncan told me, however, concerned me.

Duncan looked me squarely in the eye and said, "You will have people tell you to beware of the inmates. They can be silver-tongued devils who will try to manipulate you—and some will try. I'm telling you right now, though, that you need to be just as worried about your coworkers as you are the inmates. There are plenty of employees who will do and say things to you that they shouldn't."

A bit shocked, I nodded. "Thanks for the heads-up."

Duncan continued, "The only difference between some employees and the inmates is the color of the uniform they wear. You seem like a really nice lady, and I feel like you should know this going into the job."

"I'll keep that in mind."

He smiled warmly as he finished sealing the samples, then took off his gloves and shook my hand. "Good luck to you."

What have I gotten myself into? What did he mean the employees are just as bad as the inmates? I understand there are bad cops, but aren't the people wearing the badges the good guys?

I'd grown up believing we could trust the law and the courts. Television shows and movies portray the criminal justice system, including the prisons, as institutions designed to keep us safe. Duncan's warnings rolled around in my mind like a piece of hard candy. I tried to digest what I'd learned.

I'll keep his warnings in mind, but I need a job, and now I have one. This is no time to look a gift horse in the mouth.

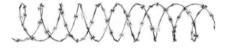

Welcome to Prison

W ith a negative drug test on record and a forewarning by Officer Duncan, my real initiation into the prison system began on July 5. My official title of Academic Teacher III meant my years of teaching experience placed me on the top rung for teachers in the prison system. My salary brought in slightly more than an entry-level corrections officer made.

The State of Missouri required any inmate who didn't have a high school diploma or equivalency to attend GED classes. SCCC was the only maximum-security facility with a fully staffed education department, while the other maximum-security GED programs utilized inmate tutors as instructors. The medium- and low-level prisons had paid teaching staffs, mainly because lower level inmates integrated into society sooner than those at the maximum-security level.

My first few days at the prison began mundanely enough. The normal start time for teachers was 6:30 a.m., but Mary Castor told me to arrive an hour later on my first day since the human resources director wouldn't get to work until 7:30. I arrived at the prison as scheduled, said hello to Tracy in the visiting area, then buzzed my way into the stairwell.

At least I'm getting the hang of how to get in the place.

After going through the metal detector and security checkpoint, I stepped up to the reception desk, informed the officer of my arrival, then I took a seat. The waiting room bustled with activity. Corrections officers, some going into

13

work and others leaving from their shift, crowded the area. They talked, joked, and milled around waiting for their turn through security or to make their way down to the prison grounds.

As a new employee, an escort accompanied me everywhere. While I waited, I fiddled with my rings, a nervous habit of mine, and struck up a conversation with the clean-cut man in his mid-forties who sat next to me.

"Hi, my name's Caroline. Have you worked at the prison long?"

"It's nice to meet you. No, this is my first day at work. They told me I had to sit here until they send someone to meet me. My name's Randy, by the way."

"Hey, it's my first day, too! I'll be teaching here."

Smiling, Randy said, "No kidding? I'm the new educational supervisor. It looks like you just met your new boss." He reached over, and we exchanged a friendly handshake.

"I've never worked in a prison before, have you?" Randy inquired.

"No, before this, I taught in Mansfield."

His eyebrows went up. "I used to teach in Mansfield."

Randy, it turned out, taught there three years before I began at Mansfield. We joked that we shared common friends and common enemies. Humor broke some of the tension that first day. As we talked, we exchanged basic information about ourselves. Randy, an officer in the Army National Guard, was a high school principal before his last deployment.

"When I returned from active duty, I found out my job was eliminated. My wife says the school district broke federal law by firing an active duty service member, but

I don't want to go through a legal battle. It's better to just move on, so that's how I ended up here."

I'm not surprised he's military with his short haircut and military bearing. With so many family members in the services, I can spot them a mile away. One thing's for sure: Randy knows how to run an organization.

Before long, our escort arrived, and we wound through the hallways until we reached Human Resources. There we met Sheila Stokes, the director of all things personnel at SCCC.

Our first two days consisted of filling out mundane paperwork, having photo IDs made, and going on a tour of the prison. Eddie Lee, the training officer, was average height with brown hair and a continuous smile. He joined us during our orientation. Eddie, quite the comedian, kept conversations light and entertaining, even if we were up to our eyeballs in forms and insurance paperwork. In the early afternoon, Eddie took us to the training trailer for a short briefing on policy. Then he led us on our tour of the facility.

Randy and I were shown everything from the kitchen to the carpentry shop to the inside of administrative segregation, more commonly known as "the hole" or "ad seg." Each housing unit, including the hole, consisted of four wings. Eddie walked us through one wing of the hole as men yelled perverse invitations to look at their genitals, giving us a crash course in prison culture. While I was the intended target of much of what they yelled, we all tried to ignore the crude comments, which was difficult.

One man screamed over and over, "Honey, come on over here and look at my dick!"

Turning to Randy, I said, "Hey, I think he's talking to you."

Randy, Eddie, and I broke into laughter. By the way they looked at me, I could tell they thought I was all right.

They're relieved I have the gumption to not let prison behavior intimidate me.

While Randy and Eddie talked with a guard, my curiosity got the best of me and I ventured into one of the padded isolation cells used for suicide watches. As I stood in the middle of the cell, checking out the padded white interior and noticing the cramped conditions, the door slammed shut behind me. Of course, I jumped at the loud clang and whirled around to face the doorway. Randy and Eddie stood smiling and snickering through the 6 x 9-inch window, proud of their prank. I gave them credit for giving me a scare, and we all had a good laugh.

Having a sense of humor made the prison surroundings a little less daunting, but there's no doubt about it—they were daunting. Even a few seconds of captivity inside the isolation cell jarred my senses.

It must be an awful existence to live in a space this small.

Granted, the ugly comments hurled my direction by ad seg inmates moments before kept my sympathy level low.

Next, Eddie walked us across the camp to a regular housing unit where the general prison population lived. Housing units were loud, but the men behaved better than those in the hole. More memorable than the sounds, though, was the smell inside the housing units. I will never forget the aroma: one part sweat, one-part industrial chemicals, one-part anger, and one-part desolation. It didn't matter which housing unit we entered, the smell remained the same.

We went by the carpentry shop where the air filled with the sound of tools and the pungent scents of varnish, acetone, and paint. Sanders and drills buzzed in the background. Hammers banged against furniture in the making. By the time we left the shop, a migraine hit me, the result of the noise and chemical aromas. Relieved to leave the sounds and smells behind, I headed to the education wing on our final stop of the tour.

The buildings lining the sidewalk were identical to each other. The school was adjacent to Housing Unit 1, where one wing contained the most violent inmates in solitary confinement. The medical facilities were located in another wing of Housing Unit 1. On the other side of the school, the Major's Hallway, containing the barber shop, chapel, and prison major's offices, stood indistinct from the surrounding buildings.

Entering from the walk—prison lingo for sidewalk— we passed through a metal detector as we walked into the school. On the right was the library. To the left was the education administrative area, including Randy's new office. A guard station with an L-shaped countertop blocked off the office area which was also comprised of the secretary's office, the storage room, the janitor's closet, and just beyond that, the teacher workroom.

Past the office area and the library was a hallway. On the left was the staff bathroom and, next to it, the inmate bathroom. Double doors led to ten classrooms and a testing room at the end of the corridor. The place had a sterile institutional feel to it.

Nothing inside this place is bright and cheery. That same sense of desolation we felt in the housing unit flows down these halls too.

As we made our way down the hallway, teachers came out of their classrooms to meet their new boss and coworker. Randy and I were not prepared for the cast of characters. The rapid fire of introductions was confusing.

"Hi, I'm Doris. It is so good to meet you." She smiled, but a wild-eyed look about her set both Randy and me back on our heels.

We shot each other glances as another woman approached. She boisterously shook our hands. "I'm Sandra, and we are just thrilled to have you here!"

Before we finished shaking hands with Sandra, another woman chimed in. "Nice to meet you. I'm Christy and I teach the upper division classes. I get the students ready for the GED." Something in her tone of voice screamed, 'I'm better than the rest of these people.'

And so, it went as we met all the teachers and staff. Randy and I gave each other more "What the hell?" looks as we met some of the more peculiar members of the staff.

At the end of the day, with my migraine flaring even worse, Randy and I shook hands in the parking lot and exchanged a quick conversation. "If first impressions mean anything, we're going to need to stick together. Let me give you my cell number." He reached into his pocket for his cell phone, and once in hand, I gave him my information.

"That's not a bad idea at all. Here's mine. Get some rest and get over that headache. I'll see you here tomorrow for Day Two."

The next day, Thursday, we spent observing in the education wing. Normally school ran on a Monday-Thursday schedule, but since that week began with the 4th of July holiday, teachers reported on Friday.

"How does that work? Teachers still have to work four days and don't get a holiday? That seems wrong," Randy asked.

Michael Vaughn, a veteran teacher at the prison told us, "Teacher workdays are ten hours long, and holiday pay is only for eight hours, so during holiday weeks teachers work shortened hours, but still four days a week. We complained about it, but Jefferson City said we'd all have to give up two hours of vacation time to get the holiday off. Most of us don't like the sounds of that, so, this is what we do instead."

Randy pulled me aside. "I want to get to know the staff and make some general announcements. I'll get an idea of who these people are, aside from the introductions we've had." He scheduled a faculty meeting for 9:00 a.m. on Friday.

When Friday arrived, we met in a classroom midway down the education hall.

He began the meeting by saying, "Thank you for the warm welcome you've given me since I started a few days ago. Working as a team is important to me."

Everyone smiled and nodded their heads.

"In order to work as a team, I'm designating the Fridays we work on holiday weeks as mandatory professional development days. I know some of you have used those as vacation days, but I think we need to focus on PD."

Hell broke loose.

"Oh, no we won't work on Fridays!" bellowed one staff member from behind me.

I don't know them well enough to know who said that, but oh my God.

"I'm not giving up my Fridays off! You can't tell us not to use vacation time we've earned!" yelled another.

"Actually, I'm the one who signs off on leave requests, so I can deny leave time if it interferes with a planned meeting." Randy stiffened in his chair.

A chorus of complaints arose.

"You can't do this!"

"You can't make us!"

"It's never been like this before, and you aren't going to change it now!"

"I've worked here five years and we have always been able to take Fridays off!"

To our surprise, teachers turned to Barb Mason, the secretary, for approval instead of listening to the boss for direction.

They expect her to overrule him. Since when does the secretary run the school?

"I feel strongly that our department needs professional development, and everyone needs to be here for that to happen," Randy said adamantly.

"What about Kelly Rainer?" Doris McGeehon bellowed.

"What about her?" asked Randy.

"She'll never stand for this! She always takes Fridays off. She's not here today, but you are going to hear about this from her. She will quit if you try to do this to us!" Doris huffed.

"Well, I guess she will have to make that decision, but we're going to meet on Fridays during holiday weeks." Randy spoke quietly, but his clenched jaw made it clear he wasn't budging.

People yelled, sighed, and glared at Randy. Faces flushed, eyes bugged, and lips pursed.

If this is the way they react to the new boss, Randy is right: This place needs professional development.

Randy and I looked at each other. We'd found ourselves inside a dysfunctional version of the Island of Misfit Toys.

Later that day, I told Randy, "I think you need to give Kelly the opportunity to speak for herself. She may not be as bad as Doris is making her out to be."

"You could be right."

On Monday, I recognized Kelly Rainer as the polite, friendly blonde woman we met on our tour of the school.

She's not the battle-axe Doris described. She's not even close to it.

Bubbly, fun, and lighthearted, Kelly didn't strike me as the type who raised hell over coming to work.

Based on first impressions, Kelly is one of my favorite people here so far. What was Doris trying to pull? Should I say something to her about Friday's debacle?

She deserved a heads-up. I stuck my neck out and told Kelly what happened at the meeting.

"Quit? I'm not going to quit! I've taken Fridays off to spend time with my grandkids, but it's not something I'm going to quit my job over. If Mr. Turner wants me to work on Fridays, I'll work on Fridays!"

"Doris shouted that you wouldn't stand for it." Kelly rolled her eyes.

Kelly and I are going to get along just fine.

"Let me tell you, that's the way faculty meetings are around here. You and Mr. Turner shouldn't feel like this is new or because of him. These people can be crazy. I swear they look for something to fight about. Just ignore their drama."

After such a horrible beginning, is every day going to be chaos?

Thankfully, that wasn't the case. The first three weeks of my employment at SCCC passed uneventfully. I treaded water as I waited to go to the Academy—the name given to the mandatory three-week training all custody and non-custody employees, such as teachers, secretaries, and cooks, must attend. Corrections officers attended an additional week of training to learn take-down tactics and other physical force methods. The Academy was held in Jefferson City, Missouri, the state capitol. I couldn't be assigned my own classroom, or even go anywhere in the prison unchaperoned, until I completed training. So far, no start date for training was assigned, so Randy and I made ourselves useful by helping whenever and wherever we could in the classrooms.

We acquainted ourselves with the staff, observed classes, and basically filled time. Randy familiarized himself with paperwork, and I spent most of my days in Kelly's room. I pitched in by working with students and paid close attention to how she ran her classes. In spite of a decade of prison experience, she still managed to keep a positive outlook on life.

Kelly's tutor, Marty Josephson, threw himself into his job.

"He's really good at this," I told Kelly.

"Well, he should be. He was a teacher before he went to prison. Now he's teaching in the only capacity he can, or ever will, have."

As a rule of thumb, I had begun looking up the inmates I worked around on the department website. To protect myself, I decided it was a good idea to know who I was dealing with. I already knew Josephson was in for pedophilia.

I don't even want to think of what his crime was.

"Josephson sure goes above and beyond." I added, trying to change the subject in my head.

"He puts time and detail into lessons that most teachers can't devote to their prison classrooms. We aren't allowed to bring in materials or to take work home, but Josephson works on ideas for the classroom even during his off-hours. I'm glad to have his teaching experience in here to help me, and he enjoys it."

As a teacher, it would kill me to not be in a classroom again. What a waste of talent for someone who ruined his life and career.

Kelly's room was a great place to learn the logistics of the job. Teaching at a prison wasn't the same as teaching in public schools. Security measures and constant situational awareness were primary, not secondary, considerations throughout the day.

Know where the exits are. Don't let inmates walk behind you. Where are that inmate's hands? Don't let them steal anything. Be careful, pencils can be weapons.

Every moment, my eyes scanned my surroundings in an effort to stay safe. In a normal junior high or high school, teachers didn't worry about rape, stabbings, or becoming a hostage during a riot. Kelly handled herself expertly, and I soaked up every example she set when it came to running a prison classroom. Still, sometimes no matter what an employee did, danger lurked inside those death fences.

THE CAST OF CHARACTERS

O n-the-job training gave me the opportunity to size up the work environment—both the students and the staff. Most coworkers lived up to my first impressions. Surrounded by an eclectic group of misfits, my head swam with the quirky behavior many displayed. There's no other way to describe the atmosphere inside the prison school than to give a rundown of the characters who worked there.

A few, like Kelly Rainer and Michael Vaughn, came across as solid professionals and decent people. Kelly, Mike, and I developed fast friendships. Mike lived in a town along the way on my commute, and we became carpool partners. Kelly, a country girl and devoted mom had an upbeat personality and a great sense of humor. Our group insulated us from the rest of the staff.

"Before you came here, Caroline, I thought I was going to pull my hair out. When my friend, Donna, retired last year, I was afraid I was going to have to work until I retired with no one to talk to," Kelly said.

Some personalities in our hallway do make it difficult to warm up to them.

Doris was "high-strung." She blew up at inmates over minor issues. One day, while I circulated between classrooms, I witnessed Doris in action.

"Mr. Williams, go to the board and tell me which one of those is a participle."

Her student slowly stood.

"I said get to the board!"

The man faced the board. "Ma'am, I don't know which one it is."

"You do too! Which one is the participle, Mr. Williams?" Doris yelled.

"No, Ma'am. I really don't know."

"Stop acting like you don't know what I'm talking about. Just do it!"

"Ma'am, please. I don't know." He looked uncomfortably around the class. Men held their breaths and tried not to make eye contact with Doris or Williams.

Doris looked at me smugly as though she knew she was setting an example for me. "You tell me what the participle is or I'm writing you up."

"Ma'am, I just don't know, please."

Doris screamed, huffed, and furiously wrote a conduct violation for Williams, claiming he caused a classroom disruption.

"Get out of my room! You're going to the hole!"

Williams and I caught each other's gaze for a second. He looked defeated, and I lost a lot of respect for Doris in that moment. Her outbursts were daily or weekly spectacles everyone, staff and inmate, dreaded.

Farther down the hallway, Sandra Jennings, a widowed farming woman who wore men's clothes—primarily the same parachute pants with a plaid shirt—every day taught mid-level classes. She kept her hair short and used the prison barber shop. Her sudden bursts into song while she skipped down the hallway of the school set her apart from anyone I'd ever known. Thankfully, Sandra's voice was beautiful, but I'd never seen a fifty-plus-year-old woman skip then shuffle down a hall while singing gospel songs—in a maximum-security prison no less.

Hopelessly addicted to the television show NCIS, Sandra greeted everyone each Tuesday with an enthusiastic, sing-song, "It's NCIS Tuesday!" Avid television viewers may remember the insurance commercials that featured a camel asking his coworker, "Hey, Mike! Mike! Mike! Do you know what day it is? It's Hump Day!"

The commercial was funny at first, but after a while it got on a person's nerves. Sandra's weekly ritual was just like that annoying camel. Each week Sandra interrupted classes with her NCIS announcement, and then she skipped down the hall to the next room to repeat the ritual.

She's a sweet Christian woman, and she doesn't harbor a malicious bone in her body, but she is a unique character.

Additional staff members included Richard Blake, a perpetually nervous middle-aged man who laughed a little too boisterously, often at his own jokes. He taught a re-entry class and a few mid-level courses. While eccentric, he seemed harmless.

Preston Hubbard was a special education teacher temporarily covering the regular classroom vacancy I filled.

"Caroline, I was hired just eight months ago. I'm still learning the ropes, too, but if you have any questions, let me know."

"Thanks, Preston. I appreciate any help you can give me."

"Before I came here, I worked at a juvenile delinquent boys' school. I was a special-ed teacher there, too. That's where I met my son. I adopted him two years ago."

"That's a great thing for you to do, giving him a chance at a real home."

"Thanks. I always wanted to be a dad. He still struggles with some behaviors, but I'm glad I adopted him. You know, I dropped out of school when I was a sophomore. I earned my GED and then went on to college. I like teaching special-ed because I can relate to the struggles these guys go through because school wasn't easy for me."

Preston hung out with Kelly, Mike, and me, so I got to know him pretty well as time went by. He reminded me of the cartoon character Dilbert, both in looks and disposition. Most conversations with him centered around his juvenile delinquent son and his own health issues. On some days, he came to work with bruises. "Dominic had a bad night last night," he'd tell us to excuse his son's physical assaults. We wondered at, but admired, Preston's willingness to love a difficult child. Not everything I learned about him was positive, though. Kelly, Mike, and I visited one morning before school, and topic number one was Preston Hubbard.

"I don't know what to think about him," Kelly said.

"It sure is suspicious that if any of us gripe about something, Jefferson City knows right away. It's almost like he's a pipeline for anything he hears," Mike said.

"Preston also has an unlimited number of sick days he takes off." I said.

"Yeah, what's up with that?" Kelly asked. "If we can get past him ratting on us when we complain, Preston isn't a bad coworker, but I think we need to be careful about what we say around him."

Christy Massey, the woman with the condescending attitude I met on my first-day tour, taught the advanced classes, just like Mike Vaughn did. Once other teachers brought student skills up to the point they qualified for the GED, students transferred to the advanced classes. There they received academic fine-tuning before the big testing event. Christy, upbeat and friendly on most days, also carried her own personality baggage. On some days, the rest of us avoided her at all costs.

"She is a complete know-it-all," Mike said.

"Oh, heck yes! She's one of the reasons I thought I was going to pull my hair out before you got here," Kelly added. "Just watch her for a while, and you'll see how she believes everyone is racist against her husband. He's a white shirt (upper level officer) here. It's not Tom who's the problem. Everyone likes him. She's the one people don't like."

Kelly was right. Tom Massey, a sergeant (which gave him a little more influence and pull than the run-of-the-mill corrections officer) never bothered people. Christy, however, used Tom's position as a club. She perpetually campaigned for a promotion for Tom.

"Tom was the best qualified for that lieutenant position."

"But wasn't Martin a sergeant longer, and hadn't he done two years working in ad seg, which was a requirement?" Sandra asked.

"Tom wasn't given the position because he's black." Christy countered, undeterred by facts.

I told Kelly and Mike, "Christy's a bit of a stage mom with her husband."

"You aren't kidding," Kelly replied.

"She's a stone around his neck. She gets under everyone's skin with her superiority complex. No one wants a know-it-all around," Mike added. "It's not that he's black. The other officers probably don't want to put up with Christy."

Thankfully, not everyone came across as abrasive as Christy, as eccentric as Sandra, or as volatile as Doris. Melanie Foster taught mid-level classes. Petite, well-groomed, and attractive, she embodied everything Sandra wasn't in dress and mannerism. Melanie displayed the epitome of prim and proper behavior, almost to the extreme.

During a break between classes one day, she complained about how badly her neck hurt. I mentioned the amazing massage I received over the weekend. I suggested she give my masseuse a call.

Melanie gasped. "I wouldn't have to take my clothes off, would I?"

"Well, only if you want to get a massage."

"Oh! I could never do that!"

No, Melanie won't skip or sing down the hallway. She's wound a little tighter than that.

Nearing retirement from the system, she bid her time until her separation date. Her husband Jack served, like Tom Massey, as a mid-level officer on the camp. Melanie, however, lacked Christy's sense of entitlement. She did her job, remained professional, and tended to stay out of the prison limelight.

Martha Tennant taught the low-level classes, meaning her students struggled to read and calculate simple math problems. A short brunette, she lived with her elderly parents and seldom socialized with the rest of the teachers.

"Martha's okay, but she's very rigid," Kelly told me.

If another teacher called her "Martha" instead of "Ms. Tennant," hell was paid. A former kindergarten teacher, she decorated her classroom with primary posters and her room more closely resembled an elementary room than a space for adult education in a maximum-security prison. Never outgrowing her kindergarten experience, she treated students and staff like her five-year-old charges.

"She is stiff, but Martha sticks to her own classroom and doesn't involve herself in drama or gossip. Those traits are hard to come by," Mike added one morning as we discussed the different personalities in the hallway.

Mike's right. I respect Martha for minding her own business. No one accuses her of stirring the pot or meddling.

Last, but not least among the teaching staff, was Shannon Rafferty—a force of nature, as unpredictable as a tornado and as difficult to navigate around as a flooded roadway. Shannon brought drama and strife to the education hallway. In her early thirties, she was the youngest of the staff members. Shannon was in charge of the testing room. The state required periodic testing of student skills to check their readiness for the GED.

A fiery redhead and a self-professed witch, she gleefully told everyone, "I cast spells and work my magic."

She's a bit of drama we can't avoid, though. She controls when our students test, so I better learn how to deal with her.

"Shannon was put in the testing room because she couldn't run her classroom," Kelly confided. No lost love lingered between Kelly and Shannon, and Kelly never held back what she really felt about her during our private conversations.

"Shannon sees her new role as a promotion. A test administrator proctors exams. Bless her Wiccan heart, she thinks it means she is an administrator for the department," Kelly continued.

"Her delusions of grandeur, along with her other quirks, sure stir up trouble in our hallway," I added.

"Try to keep your distance from her. I know it's hard because we need our students to test, but stay away from her as much as possible," Kelly warned.

Believe me, I don't want anything to do with her. That girl is trouble.

Barbara, the school secretary, seemed great. Early on, however, inklings of trouble appeared. Mike brought her up in conversation one night in the carpool. "How has Barb Mason treated you?"

"She's been really nice. I was kind of worried after how she acted at that first staff meeting, but she's always asking me if I need anything."

"She thinks she's the head honcho of the school. She's short-tempered and crass."

"Really?"

"Oh, yes. Barb runs the place. Nearly every decision has her fingerprints on it."

"How did that happen?"

"Barb's been in the system for a long time, and over the years she's increased the number of duties under her control. Most of these are things the educational supervisor should handle, but Barb has slowly but surely made them her responsibility."

"And the bosses just let her?"

"Well, a couple of ed sups ago, we had a guy who just didn't care if Barb ran everything. He wasn't much of a leader. Then we had Dan Chambers who was a great boss, but as you've heard, he came down with cancer. Before Randy Turner was hired, we went a whole year with no educational supervisor, but really, we went without a leader for longer than that. Dan missed a lot of work, and his cancer treatments made him ill. Sometimes when he was at work, he still wasn't working, if you know what I mean. It wasn't his fault, but Barb used every opportunity to grab control over what should have been Dan's duties."

Kelly also gave me a heads-up about Barb. "She's a snake. Don't trust her—at all."

"So far, she's seemed really nice to me."

"Oh, she can be nice, but she has a vicious side. She knows you're friends with Randy, and she always sucks up to the new boss. Just hope that doesn't change. I've been here a long time, and I've seen her in action when she chooses to unleash on someone."

Even in these first few weeks, I've seen her explode, Doris style, at inmates. And her attitude at Randy's first Friday meeting is enough reason for me to take Mike and Kelly's advice to heart.

Barb's role as a fixture of the prison system was a reality. She was ingrained as a member of the in-crowd of corrections.

One day, Barb shared with me how she first came to work at the prison. "When I was in high school, we had to write a paper about what we were going to be when we graduated. That was an easy paper for me to write."

"Really? What did you want to be?"

"I wanted to work for the prison, of course! What else would I want to do?"

I can't imagine a high school girl's goals reaching no further than a prison.

Barb considered the prison system her Alpha and Omega, though, and her roots in the system ran deep. That kind of connection bought her all kinds of leeway to behave however she wanted to.

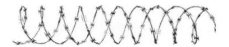

THE INDOCTRINATION

After getting my feet wet in Kelly's classroom in early August, the Department of Corrections finally scheduled Randy and me for the Academy.

"It sure did take a while," Randy said.

"Let's get this over with. It's one step closer to us being able to do our jobs."

While relieved that the ball was rolling, training at the Academy in Jefferson City was more complicated than attending classes during the day and then going home. It was an upheaval of normal life. I considered myself lucky. My youngest son was nineteen and had moved to Tennessee. My oldest was already in the military. I didn't have to worry about childcare. Employees with small children faced a real struggle.

Trainees coming from prisons hours away, like the South Central Correctional Center, stayed in state-provided hotel rooms at the Capitol Plaza Hotel, Monday-Friday, for the duration of the training. Home life took second place to the demands of the prison training sessions.

Five SCCC new hires went to the Academy during that session—two corrections officers, one locksmith, Randy, and me. Each week we met at SCCC and used a state vehicle to drive the three hours to the Department of Corrections headquarters.

Once in Jefferson City, we met other corrections employees from across the state.

Not everything I learned about my fellow trainees was flattering. Many spent their evenings out on the town, drinking and hooking up with sexual partners. Married or single didn't matter for some once the drinking and partying began.

Maybe I shouldn't be surprised by their behavior, but I am. We're considered law enforcement, and we should be setting a better example.

On our first night at the Capitol Plaza Hotel, a few classmates asked my roommate, Jean, if we'd like to go out drinking. Jean considered it and she invited me to come along.

"You can go if you want to, but I don't want any part of it. It sounds like a good way to get in trouble."

"What do you mean?"

"We're here at taxpayer expense, and of all the places for a state employee to go out and get drunk, the capitol is probably the worst choice ever. There are eyes—important ones—all over this town. I came here to have a job. I don't want to jeopardize that."

Jean paused. "I hadn't thought about that but, boy, are you right!"

"Let the others think I'm a stick in the mud. I'm fine with that. I don't see the sense in risking trouble just to spend time with a bunch of people I don't really care to hang out with."

"Exactly! We can visit and spend time watching television—and sleep well at night knowing no one can blame us if something does happen."

"I don't know what you like to do, but I was thinking some night we could go to Hobby Lobby. I crochet and would love to get some yarn, so I can work on a project."

Jean's eyes lit up. "You crochet too? Hot dog, girl! Let's go get some yarn tonight!"

Over the course of three weeks, we spent hours talking, laughing, and working on crafts.

"We may not seem very exciting to others, but we won't need to worry about answering difficult questions if trouble tracks down the partiers," I told her one night.

"Staying in is the smartest thing we could do," Jean agreed.

Every night after training, the five of us from SCCC, along with several of the other forty-eight new employees going through the Academy, returned to the Capitol Plaza Hotel. The next morning, we met in the lobby and traveled the short distance down McCarty Street to the multi-storied beige Department of Corrections Building. At 8:00, we assembled in the large conference room.

Our days busily filled with information to absorb. Classes consisted of the dos and don'ts of prison employment taught by rotating instructors. Most trainers, veterans of the system, taught us no nonsense policy, restraint techniques, and tips on how to conduct ourselves when interacting with inmates.

Some lessons and instructors bordered on the ridiculous, however. For example, they instructed us to never say "please" or "thank you" to inmates. We couldn't say, "I appreciate your help." To show gratitude or to ask them to "please" do something supposedly put a staff member in an inferior position. I didn't buy it.

We are supposed to rehabilitate inmates. Teaching common courtesy through example should be part of the job. Apparently, it isn't.

In an absurd twist, the system allowed us to say, "I 'ppreciate that," if an inmate did something we asked them to do.

Excuse me? How is dropping the "a" going to make it any less of a gesture of civility or gratitude? Can someone please explain that to me? I'd 'ppreciate that.

Learning the mountain of rules demanded our full attention. Hours of lecture kept us superglued to our chairs. As a teacher, I was used to occasional staff training days at school. The Academy, however, meant day after day of sitting in the same room, taking notes on required minutia before the final exam. It was more monotonous and tedious than any college lecture or in-service I'd attended as a teacher.

Three instructors, Tom Berring, Rod Clements, and Karen Forsyth stood head and shoulders above the others. They did their best to provide fair and consistent advice, training us according to policy.

Karen's lectures were all business with an emphasis on doing the job right. Tom and Rod included humor and insight gained from years of DOC experience, always focusing on professionalism.

One instructor, however, wasn't what I expected. Stan Baker, a veteran of the department whose career began as a corrections officer at one of the two women's prisons. regaled us with "humorous" anecdotes. Those stories revolved around bending rules and finding ways to aggravate the inmates. He used examples, by name, of inmates he intentionally harassed over the years. He bragged that he poked and poked until they blew up, opening the door for him to send them to the hole.

"It's great sport," he said with a twinkle in his eye.

Stan's mission is to mentor us on how he thinks employees should behave—and policy be damned.

He sprinkled lessons with examples bypassing proper policy and protocol, completely undermining the integrity of the rules we needed to learn.

Stan stood before us saying, "Policy says, 'x,y,z.'" He read from the DOC handbook in a stilted voice. "But this is how you really do it," he'd say with a wink. "You know what I mean?" Wink. Wink.

Finding methods to irritate inmates is entertainment for Stan. He's teaching people to pick at an inmate until he or she explodes. How is that helpful?

For example, Stan told us if we wanted some real fun to single out an inmate on his way to the chow hall, then radio other staff members to search him and take his inmate ID as he walked across the camp. Stan told us how enjoyable it was to "accidentally" not open a man's cell, so he missed a medical appointment, knowing he'd receive a violation for failure to arrive at medical on time.

Oh, yeah, Stan Baker knows how to have a good time, and he's more than willing to share his methods with impressionable new hires. Is this what we are being trained to do? Is he really paid by the state to teach us how to antagonize easily angered people in a volatile environment?

Astonished by his lectures, I looked across the room at corrections newbies who drank up every one of Stan's stories with their eyes and ears. Twenty-one-year-old men and women sat starry-eyed, indoctrinated into a system which said one thing according to policy but then did something underhanded in real life. Cruel, deliberate acts of abuse on inmates, powerless against the authority of a corrections officer, were encouraged by Stan Baker.

Excessive force reports, we learned, could be written to disguise a beating as "assisted offender to the ground."

How euphemistic.

Stan salivated while telling how satisfying a good inmate beating felt.

These kids don't even know they are being brainwashed into behaving unprofessionally.

New employees left Stan's lectures tinged by a model of skirting rules in order to inflict pain and aggravation onto the people the department supposedly "corrected." Groomed to make working conditions inside the prisons even more dangerous for other staff members, they couldn't comprehend the subtle insidiousness of Stan's lessons. The fresh faces listening to him idolized Stan, whom they viewed as "telling it to them straight."

Doesn't anyone else notice this? I see what is happening, and so does Stan.

Bending and breaking rules, legitimized by a seasoned officer who worked his way up the food chain, became the focal points of his seminars. Sadly, Stan trained year after year of employees who, in turn, spread the same mentality in facilities throughout the state. If the indoctrination didn't stick with new hires when Stan told them directly, peer pressure effectively sealed the deal once work began inside the institutions. The ripple effects of Stan's training were immense.

We're going to work around dangerous and easily agitated inmates. Staff holds all the power and authority, and staff always wins an argument with an inmate—but inmates can strike back.

Impulse control issues landed many inmates in prison in the first place. The combination of Stan's lessons and the violent nature of prison created a bad mix.

Stan's telling us to poke sticks into the lion cage.

My anger built as I considered the long-range effects. The young recruits didn't realize the perils of antagonizing inmates.

Tom Berring taught us that the vast majority of prisoners eventually release back into our communities. He said over 97% of all offenders, as the state referred to them, ready or not, returned to our streets.

Men who've been used as entertainment for years by guards aren't likely to become good neighbors for the rest of us.

With age comes wisdom, and I was far older than most new employees in that room. I envisioned scenarios their young hearts and minds couldn't. I imagined an unsuspecting employee encountering an angry inmate—an inmate driven to the edge by Stan's tactics.

Asking an inmate to take off his hat, to pull up his pants, or to verify why he was at that location might ignite fury from an inmate who tired of the games played by Stan's minions, putting the innocent staff member, unaware of the inmate's earlier experiences, in danger.

It's doubtful any of the impressionable twenty-somethings in the room are thinking so far ahead. Their star-struck expressions prove they don't know to be troubled by Stan's lessons.

Stan Baker knew what he was doing, and he recognized that I did too. He didn't care for me, and I knew it. I asked questions and Stan didn't like accountability, especially from a woman who, in his opinion, couldn't possibly understand how prison worked.

The problem is, I'm beginning to understand exactly how prison works.

I was a bug in Stan's ointment that he barely tolerated. Tom, Rod, and Karen didn't spew any agendas other than teaching us the rules, how to follow the rules, and how to keep ourselves alive in the prison environment. Stan, however, didn't like his tactics questioned.

A role-playing exercise called "Alligator River" deepened the growing rift between Stan and me. During the skit, two lovers are separated by a river filled with ravenous alligators.

Bob calls to Mary, his lover stranded on the island, "Oh, Mary, I love you so much. I need you to be with me. Please cross the river!"

Mary tearfully pleads with him. "Oh, Bob, I can't cross the river. There are too many alligators and I have no way to get to you. I love you, but please understand there is nothing I can do. Help me!"

This scene repeats itself until Bob demands that Mary find a way to cross the river—any way—if she wants to prove her love to him. Otherwise, he will leave her.

Desperate and afraid of losing Bob, Mary considers a deal with the devil. Okay, not with the actual devil, but with a shady man on the island named Dave who owns a rowboat.

Dave's tactics and motives are clear. He listens to Mary's sob story. "I'll give you a ride across the river in my boat, Mary, but first you have to have sex with me."

Mary doesn't like the sounds of Dave's bargain. Troubled by this dilemma, she begs Bob to give her more time to find a way to reach the other shore. Bob, however, won't relent.

"Mary, if you don't find a way to join me, I won't love you anymore," Bob yells back at her. "Isn't there some way you can get to me, so I know you love me?"

"Well, there is this one way, but—"

"I don't want to hear any excuses. If you have a way to get to me, you must do whatever it takes. Otherwise, I don't believe you love me.".

Caught between her love for Bob and her revulsion toward Dave, Mary eventually chooses to sleep with Dave, the lecherous boat owner. Bob, after all, says he will doubt her love forever if she doesn't use every method available to join him.

Once across the river, Mary runs to Bob's arms crying, "Oh, Bob! I made it to you. Do you see now that I truly love you?"

"But, Mary, I have to ask: how did you get a ride in Dave's rowboat?"

Mary explains the deal she made with Dave, and Bob is furious. That little whore Mary slept with another man! Bob storms off the stage and leaves the hussy Mary crying in a heap.

Stan asked the class of forty-eight new hires to choose which character was the most immoral person in the skit. In the final tally, forty-seven class members selected Mary.

I'm the lone holdout.

Stan Baker said to the rest of the class, "I'm proud of you. You got it right." Then he turned to me. "Caroline, I don't understand you at all. Can't you see the obvious truth?"

"No, Stan, Bob was the most immoral character because he told Mary he didn't want to know the details and that she had better join him or he was leaving her. He told her to do 'whatever it took' to be with him. Then he wasn't willing to accept the terms of his own demands. No one should make demands and then not be willing to live with the results."

"I can't believe that's the way you see this. Can any of you believe Caroline feels this way?" Forty-seven sets of eyes looked at me, and none of them showed a flicker of support.

I said, "Mary wasn't deceptive. Even Dave was honest in his own sleazy way. While Dave was a perverted jerk, he never changed the rules of his agreement. Bob did. Therefore, Bob was the most immoral person."

My Bible Belt cohorts couldn't get past Mary having sex with Dave and continued to stare at me. Stan did more than stare. He glared.

I get it, Stan. I'm not buying your line of bull, and you think publicly "shaming" me is going to make me change my mind. It won't.

Days dragged on, and Stan used every opportunity to make me seem like an outcast. I continued to ask him difficult questions. Ironically, on the last day of the three-week training, a lesson called "Anatomy of a Set-Up" gave me a chance at vindication.

We listened to scenario after scenario of ways inmates manipulate staff into breaking the rules. Some warnings were simple, such as the importance of never overlooking an infraction, no matter how small. Otherwise, inmates used lapses in consistency to blackmail staff into committing progressively worse acts out of fear of losing their jobs.

Escalating scenarios went as far as not falling for promises made by inmates about love, protection, or money because inmates made unreliable allies. Once a staff member fulfilled a demand or need, they were no longer useful, and the inmate tossed the employee aside. The moral of the story was "Don't be the good person who becomes a victim to seemingly sincere but manipulative tactics by worthless inmates."

That makes sense to me. Not falling victim to manipulation is good advice, in or out of prison.

While he didn't conduct the lesson, Stan Baker was present for the Set-Up training session. When I raised my hand during the question-and-answer phase, Stan sighed in exasperation.

"What?"

"So, what today's lesson teaches us, is that we are the good guys, right?"

"Yes."

"And the inmates are the people we should never trust because they will tell us one thing and then leave us to take the fall, right?"

"Yes, that is the lesson."

"That's interesting, Stan."

"Why?"

"Well, isn't this just like 'Alligator River'? Aren't we all Mary and the inmates are Bob? Mary fell for Bob's demands and manipulations, but then he was the one who left her holding the bag. Isn't that why we did a role play in the first place? But you said Mary was the immoral one?"

Anger flashed across his face. "I don't want to hear another word about 'Alligator River.' Don't bring this up again!"

The lessons he teaches have nothing to do with what we are supposed to learn. How dare I bring that to light?

One more sweet moment of vindication came during the afternoon session on the last day of the Academy. The DOC expected even non-custody staff to undergo pepper spray training. Corrections officers didn't carry guns inside the prison, but all employees were capable of carrying spray. We practiced with a non-hazardous imitation, but the instructor, Rod, taught us how and where to aim the canister in case we ever needed to disable an aggressive inmate.

Standing in line, each student waited his or her turn. Looking behind me, I noticed Stan staring at me, snickering and grinning.

He's certain I'm a girly-girl who will spray myself or some poor onlooker. Look at that smirk!

A sense of satisfaction crept through me.

I listened to the instructions Rod gave me as Stan eagerly watched in the wings.

Occasionally, I looked his direction. Giddy and leaning forward with his elbows on his knees, Stan waited for me to miss. When my turn arrived, I fired off three bursts of spray, as instructed by Rod, each landing direct hits on the bulls-eye.

Rod smiled approvingly and told me, "Great job!" as I turned to leave.

I beamed triumphantly as I nodded at Rod and said, "Thanks!"

Stan shook his head in disbelief. I savored the moment.

I didn't grow up in the hills of the Missouri Ozarks without knowing how to shoot a gun or hit a target.

The comprehensive final exam happened that afternoon as well. It consisted of general knowledge questions as well as scenarios we reacted to. Could we diffuse dangerous situations? Could we navigate our way out of a set-up?

Randy earned the highest score in class. I landed in the top three or four. While not the most difficult test I ever took, it wasn't easy either. Some employees didn't make the cut. Trainees who spent three weeks in Jefferson City, upending their daily lives and families, now went home without jobs. None of us accepted a position in the Department of Corrections on a lark. Jobs were hard to come by, and the pain on the faces of the men and women sent home jobless broke my heart.

For me, the three weeks weren't a waste. Yes, I tired of the drudgery of class. I tired of sitting on hard plastic chairs and tired of weeks away from home. I tired of Stan and his methods. Nevertheless, I learned a lot, met people from across the state, and developed lasting friendships.

No major mishaps occurred during those three weeks for any of the trainees, except for those who failed the test at the very end. The partiers lucked out, and no authorities caught them in compromising positions. What happened in Jefferson City, stayed in Jefferson City. Trouble did, however, find its way back there in the months to come.

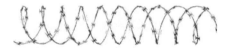

SETTLING IN

A week passed at SCCC after my return, and I still didn't know which classroom I'd be in. Randy hadn't made up his mind. I was getting antsy.

"Have you decided which room will be mine? I assume it'll be Preston's."

Randy paused. "I need to think about it for a while."

Kelly and I wanted to team teach, but sharing a classroom wasn't realistic. We voiced not-so-subtle hints about the idea to Randy.

"You two know that's not likely," he said good-naturedly.

"Darn!" we said in unison.

For one last week, however, Kelly and I worked together and caught up on life after my three-week stint at the Academy. Finally, Randy decided to put me in Preston's room, Classroom 10.

As a GED teacher, my plate filled with the laborious task of developing curriculum. Preston wasn't exactly a ball of fire, and he didn't leave me many materials to use when I took over his classes. Each teacher taught every subject, and even though my fields of expertise were English and social studies, I taught math and science too at SCCC. While I loved science, I always struggled with math. With a little practice, though, I was ready to go.

Finally, the time arrived for me to do the job I loved. I missed having my own classroom. I was ready to settle in and get down to business.

In total, ten classrooms filled the wing. At any given time, 150 or more inmates attended classes. Most people assume guards remained in the rooms with us, but they didn't. We were alone and in charge of our classrooms, and we all hoped everyone maintained discipline on his or her own. In the event of a riot, only our wits protected us. At most, two officers were on duty each afternoon, with only one on duty in the morning. The corrections officers' desk, which they stayed at 95% of the time, sat at the end of the hall next to Randy and Barb's offices. If trouble erupted in our classrooms, too many ticks of the clock passed before help arrived.

Psychologically, it helped knowing that Mike, next door to me, carried a can of pepper spray, but it provided minimal protection if violence broke out. Even though every teacher trained to use pepper spray, most of us didn't carry it, and it wasn't automatically assigned to all staff. Most teachers didn't volunteer for it.

Our jobs required constant mental awareness. We were responsible for the behavior of fifteen inmates, and we were fully engaged in teaching students of varied abilities. Pepper spray could be taken from us if an inmate overpowered us, and teachers had enough to focus on without having to worry about keeping it out of the hands of inmates. Carrying it also required wearing a cumbersome belt around our hips that inmates might use to grab ahold of us. Overall, we viewed pepper spray as more of a negative than a positive.

Instead, teachers wore body alarms around our necks or in our pockets. These alarms chirped like birds when engaged, and they presented their own issues. The string we pulled in case of emergency easily caught on chair arms and false alarms were common—so common that we sometimes wondered how seriously an alarm would be taken in the event of a real emergency.

Thankfully, while I worked there, only a few fights broke out in the education hallway. The worst occurred in Mike's room, and the disturbance almost spilled into my room as the two men fell into the accordion wall separating Classrooms 9 and 10. I jumped from my chair and headed toward the door as the wall bulged towards my desk. A few inmates laughed.

"What's wrong? Are you afraid of the fight, Ma'am?"

"No, I know Mr. Vaughn has pepper spray, and if they fall through that wall, that pepper spray is going to go off."

Their eyes widened, and all fifteen men walked backwards, away from the wall.

Other than scuffles and shoving matches, I never witnessed a violent emergency in the education wing. Nevertheless, Mike remembered a day when the prison first opened in which one inmate nearly killed another in the hallway between the library and the inmate bathroom. We couldn't lull ourselves into a false sense of security.

Even though a prison isn't the best teaching environment, I was excited to begin in Classroom 10. My enthusiasm wasn't shared by the students. Preston forewarned me.

"I was pretty lax, and you might face some resistance from the students. They're used to visiting."

Boy, he wasn't kidding. My class wasn't going to be a social hour or story time. I was there to teach them, and they were there to get an education. With it, they stood a better chance for success upon release. I took my job seriously.

The students, chips on their shoulders and glints in their eyes, wanted to run over the top of the new teacher, and they tested me to see if I would fold. As a woman in the chauvinistic world of a men's prison, the transfer of power in the classroom was even more difficult. I overheard their comments.

"That little woman isn't going to make me work. This is our classroom, not hers. I wish Hubbard was still here."

Well, guys, you are going to work, and I'm here to stay.

After a lot of grumbling and a battle of wills, most of the students settled into the new routine. Months later, one student, Robbie Franks, confided how much he hated me at first. He called me "the devil in a dress" as he recalled the early days of my employment. We laughed about it, but he and others gave me headaches during my first weeks in Classroom 10.

Franks eventually earned his high school equivalency, as did many of my students who fought me in the beginning.

Dustin Johnson, another student from my early days in Classroom 10, admitted that he, too, was angry in the beginning. "When Hubbard was our teacher, we just kicked back and socialized. You expected more, and we didn't like it."

Johnson, a twenty-five-year-old man from Springfield, Missouri, grew up only an hour from where I lived. Serving a ten-year sentence for a drug dealing charge, Johnson was personable and still employable (he hadn't disfigured himself with face and neck tattoos). He was roughly the same age as my own sons.

"You've got a lot of potential, Johnson. I hate to see people waste their lives."

"Thank you for believing in me. I wasn't always like this," he said, as he pointed to his gray prison uniform. "When I was a kid, I enjoyed school and earned good grades. I even played sports. Then, during my sophomore year, I started using drugs. Nothing big at first. Just pot. But it got to where all I wanted to do was smoke pot in our basement."

"I bet you were good at sports."

"I was. I threw it all away. One of my friends got me into harder drugs. As time went by, I quit going to practices, quit the team, and then just stopped going to school altogether."

"Life started to spiral, huh?"

"It did. It was a slow spiral, but I stopped being me. My mom and I fought all the time, and she said if all I was going to do was sit at home that I needed to get a job."

"I can see her point."

"I can too, now. I didn't want a job. So, to make money, I started selling drugs. I figured the hours were flexible, and the money was good. It seemed like a plan—until I was arrested. Now here I sit."

"You can use this time to better yourself, though. That's why I push you in class."

"You do, and you're right. I hated it when you first got here, but then I got to thinking. All you want is for me to do better for myself. Why would I be mad at someone who wants me to be a better person than I have been? You didn't have to care. You could have let us just sit there and talk like Hubbard did, but that's not you."

"No, that's not the way I am. In the past few months, I've seen you come a long way. You're only a few points away on your TABE tests to move up to the advanced classes."

"I can do it. I just wanted to say thank you for not letting me waste my time."

Within eight months, Johnson earned his GED. The last time I talked with him, he was determined to get his life back on track once released from prison. He still had years left on his sentence, but I hoped when he returned to Springfield that he pulled his life together.

Since we can't have contact with former inmates, I'll never know if he succeeds, but I sure hope he beats the odds and makes it on the outside.

The hope that my students rehabilitated themselves, to some degree, gave meaning to my job. It took effort, like that put in by Johnson, for it to happen, though.

In addition to unmotivated students in Classroom 10, I also inherited the two tutors Preston hired, Brandon Parks, and Arthur Smith. Much like the students, they weren't overjoyed by the changing of the classroom guard. They'd had it easy and were known for their laziness.

Often, other teachers told me, "Oh, yeah, that's right. You have Parks and Smith. Sorry."

My tutors begrudgingly accepted the fact I expected them to work, but I dragged the horses to water every day. Getting them to work with students or to grade papers— their jobs—was a struggle. The students picked up on their lack of motivation, making my job more difficult.

I get not wanting to work for the system that imprisons you, but come on, guys. You were hired to help.

Brandon Parks, a forty-year-old originally from Colorado, served his sentence in Missouri under an interstate agreement. I never asked him the details of his crimes, but it was uncommon for Missouri to house out-of-state inmates. I figured it was a sleeping dog I should let lie. Imprisoned former law enforcement officers were generally housed out-of-state. Maybe he turned state's witness, and they moved him for his own safety.

I don't know, and that's okay.

Parks stayed upbeat with a good sense of humor, and I didn't push or pry into his past.

Arthur Smith, a man in his sixties, had spent years in prison serving a life without parole sentence for first degree murder. He spoke of his children and grandchildren often, sharing stories about their visits. Before transferring to SCCC, Smith tutored at the prison in Potosi (where Missouri houses death row inmates), and he celled with Richard Blake's tutor, Reese. They transferred from Potosi together, and rumors flew about the nature of their relationship.

I don't care about his personal life. That's his business. I just want him to work in my classroom.

Smith, not the happy-go-lucky type, had a penchant for criticizing others. He considered himself an expert on how schools and individual classrooms should run. Too many times he said, "When I was at Potosi, we did it such-and-such a way." His complaints seemed endless.

"Mrs. Rainer lets her tutor have too much control in her classroom. He might have been a teacher in the past, but he needs to remember he's an inmate now."

"Mr. Vaughn shouldn't discuss politics in his classroom," or "Mr. Vaughn didn't handle that situation the right way. If he wants to get the students ready for the GED, he needs to do this or that."

"Mr. Turner needs to remember he isn't in the military anymore. That's not the way prison schools are run."

"That chaplain needs to stop with these special programs. No one is interested in them, anyway."

He complained about students as eagerly as he did staff members.

"Carter has been working on math too much lately. He needs to do more grammar if he ever wants to get his GED. Back in Potosi..."

"We never would have allowed students to work together on their assignments at Potosi."

"That young man looked at me funny. At Potosi he would have been..."

And so, the laundry list of complaints went on.

Even with his grumbling, Smith was easy to coexist with during the ten-hour days in Classroom 10. With his beard and stories of his children, he seemed like a kindly old grandpa figure, except this grandpa committed first degree murder.

Since he talks about his children and grandchildren, but never mentions his wife (or even ex-wife), I'm pretty sure who his victim was.

As frustrating as his lack of enthusiasm and his negative outlooks were, Smith never behaved aggressively in my classroom. However, his dark storm clouds rained on the parade I tried to create in Classroom 10.

Within a few weeks, I established a routine and students understood the expectations. The initial grousing subsided and talking minimized.

Within a few months, students arrived at class, collected their assignments, and worked without a fuss.

Inmates, even maximum-security ones, weren't the unruly beasts most people envision. They were people who made bad decisions in life. Nothing more, but nothing less for most of them.

Few inmates sought mayhem and most followed the rules.

I didn't threaten or harangue my students, and we had times of good-natured humor. I expected positive behavior and hard work, and for the most part, my students didn't fight getting an education. I created a pleasant learning environment in Classroom 10, and the students appreciated it. Trouble wouldn't hit until October.

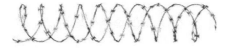

You Don't Wear Blue

T he school day at the South Central Correctional Center was divided into three class sessions, each three hours in length. Teachers reported to work between 6:15 and 6:30 in the morning, and students arrived by 6:45 for the first session. Lunch time divided the second session in half with a forty-five-minute break. Third session, the last of the day, began at 2:00 and ended at 4:45. Each class consisted of fifteen students, so throughout the course of the day, each teacher worked with forty-five inmate students, give or take a few as people went to the hole or transferred in and out of the prison.

When I took over Classroom 10, my second session class filled, for the most part, with young men fresh from serving administrative segregation, or "the hole." They were a difficult bunch to deal with, and poor attitudes oozed from their pores. I made them work, but nearly every day I dealt with resistance from that group.

Barb, along with her other powers, placed students in classes. As the newest staff member, she assigned me the less desirable students, and she primarily put them in my second session. I wasn't upset by it, but I understood why the newly released hotheads from the hole landed on my roster.

Reggie Ellison, an outspoken man in his early twenties, embodied every quality of those hotheads. He fancied himself a future movie star. So good-looking, charismatic, and talented—according to him—he inevitably he was destined for greatness.

"Someday Halle Berry is going to be my wife," Ellison said.

Only one thing stood in his way: Ellison was serving a seventy-year sentence in the Missouri prison system.

Frequently, he burst into rants during class, and each time I told him to stop disrupting other students. He usually stopped, but not on one October day. Wound up when he came back from lunch, Ellison spewed words of hatred towards law enforcement. Something outside the classroom agitated him, but his words within Classroom 10 were dangerous.

"We need to kill all law enforcement, all police officers, all corrections officers. We need to kill them all!"

"You need to stop—right now!" Two, three, four times I told him to quit.

"I'm just expressing my free speech and my opinion."

"You need to keep your free speech and your opinion to yourself in this class."

Ellison, partially out of his eagerness to appear defiant in front of his classmates, and partially because he really believed he was something special, continued his threats against corrections officers and law enforcement.

"We need to do something. We need to kill all these motherfuckers. All police, all corrections officers, all law enforcement! We need to kill them all!"

A new arrival from the hole, Rodriguez, chimed in, "Yeah, we should!"

That's it. Ellison's words are tantamount to inciting a riot.

I sent him to the education officer while I wrote the conduct violation (CDV). Inciting a riot, a major violation, carried serious consequences, and I wasn't going to let it slide as a mere "classroom disruption." He was threatening to kill people.

A guard marched Ellison off in handcuffs to Housing Unit 2, the building designated for the hole. Since I wrote the conduct violation, the prison required that I go to the hole when the guard read Ellison's CDV to him. Randy found someone to cover my class while I walked the two hundred yards across the prison grounds to Housing Unit 2. I had no idea what was in store for me.

The screaming and shouting from the hole were deafening from the moment I walked into the building. Many of the men in it behaved like animals.

If you think I'm an out-of-control badass, I'll show you what a badass I can be. That was the mindset of most ad seg inmates.

Some yelled and screamed for entertainment's sake. Some unleashed anger by pounding on their doors. The hole looked and sounded like a madhouse. Men shouted disrespectful and lewd comments my direction. I ignored them as the officer in the housing unit bubble directed me to where they held Ellison in D wing. Passing through a series of doors, the officer motioned me to go to my right.

There, Sergeant Tyler Coats lingered next to the holding cage where Reggie Ellison, stripped down to his underwear, stood. Approximately the size of a telephone booth, the cage was made of metal small-gauge mesh paneling. Coats waited for me before he read the CDV. Training required me to stand silently by. Ellison, visibly angry, glared at me the entire time. Coats finished reading the violation and Ellison screamed at me.

"You better go home and tell your children goodbye because I'm going to kill you, bitch! I will find you on the walk. I will find you in your classroom. I will go wherever I have to, and I will kill you, bitch!" Spit flew from his mouth.

Oh my God.

Fear rocked through my heart.

"Sergeant Coats, what are you going to do about Ellison's threats? He just threatened to kill me."

"You can go into the office and write another CDV for threats against staff." He shrugged as he walked away.

That's it? You shrug your shoulders and walk away while this man threatens to kill me?

I tried to remain calm, but I couldn't stop my hands from shaking. I clenched a fist to hide my trembling.

Ellison's threats sounded in the background as I went to the administrative office of the wing where I filled out another violation. After handing the paperwork to Coats, we walked back into the wing for round two.

Ellison didn't slow down a bit. He ranted at a fever pitch and inflamed other men in the wing. From all corners, threats rang out of, "You're gonna die, bitch!"

I turned to the sergeant. "What now? What's going to be done about this? He's threatening to kill me. You heard that, right?"

"Yeah, I heard him. You can write another CDV for threats if you want to, but it's not going to do any good." He turned and walked away once more.

Ellison's scream fest continued.

Two write ups, one for threats against staff and one for inciting a riot, should be God's plenty to get results.

I couldn't leave Housing Unit 2 quickly enough. Ellison's screams echoed through the building and were audible even after the wing doors closed behind me. I made my way across the prison grounds into the somewhat safer confines of the education wing.

When I told Randy what happened, he reassuringly said, "Don't worry too much. It will blow over. Angry people say a lot of things in the moment, but over time Ellison will calm down."

I hope you're right, Randy.

Barb told me, "They will transfer him from this camp immediately. Threats against staff are taken seriously. Why, a few months ago Officer Stafford was threatened, and the inmate was gone in three days."

"He won't be here long, Caroline," Sandra Jennings said.

Mike told me, "They aren't going to let a guy like that be anywhere near you. He'll be gone."

"Just for good measure, let's get it in writing so the higher ups know what's going on," Barb said.

I wrote an in-house memo to everyone in the chain of command, from the warden to the housing unit manager in administrative segregation, requesting Ellison's transfer from SCCC to another facility for my safety.

I went back to class shaken but relieved I was back in familiar surroundings. For the rest of the day, and for the next several days, I worried about Ellison's threats.

The prison will handle it. I need to keep my mind on other things.

As luck had it, two weeks later another write-up caused me to return to the administrative segregation unit. The offender in this incident also came from my second session class and the prison also assigned him to D wing in the hole. As soon as I walked into ad seg, an explosion of voices rang out from the wing.

Ellison energized his colleagues as they yelled disgusting insults at me. Above the fray, however, Reggie Ellison's voice bellowed. Calling me by my first and last names, Ellison raged against me. He literally bounced off the walls of his cell during his frenzy. His message was clear.

"Bitch, I am going to rape you and kill you!"

Once the officer read the CDV to Offender Jeremy Prince, whom I just sent to the hole, I marched to the wing office and completed another CDV against Ellison.

A second write-up for threats against me will seal the deal for his transfer.

While in the office area, I talked to Greg Miller, the case-worker for the unit. A longtime employee, Miller, medium height, in his thirties, with short brown hair oozed an aura of lazy smugness.

"I want you to come with me when this is read."

"Sure, I'll go."

The two of us followed Sergeant Stuart out into the wing, walked up to the top tier of cells, and stopped at Cell 216. Stuart read Ellison the CDV.

I'm certain Ellison will deliver.

He did, with fireworks. Ellison became immediately unhinged at the sight of me, so much so that he drowned Stuart out.

"I'm going to kill you, bitch! I'll find you on the walk! I'll find you in your classroom! There is no place you can hide. I will kill you! You think you can do this to me? You are going to die!"

He banged his body against the walls and door of his cell in a frenzy. Saliva flew from his mouth.

Walking back to the office area, I turned to Miller. "Did you hear that?"

"Yeah, I did." He grinned.

"I've put in a transfer request to remove him from the camp, but nothing has happened yet."

"It probably won't."

"What?"

"Well, we can't just transfer him. He hasn't actually done anything to you." Miller shuffled paperwork at his desk.

He doesn't care.

I was hot by this point. "He hasn't done anything? He's threatening to rape and kill me! If he kills me, are you going to transfer him then?"

Miller laughed as he sorted more paperwork.

"I don't think there's anything funny about this."

Ellison's threats and lack of concern by other employees disgusted me. Coats hadn't cared. Stuart didn't care. Miller didn't care, and the wardens still hadn't said a word about my transfer request for Ellison.

"I wrote Ellison up because he made generalized threats against corrections officers, but he specifically says he's going to rape and kill me and none of the custody staff is going to do a thing to protect me?"

"Just let it go," Miller replied as he busied himself at his desk.

I left. On the way back to my classroom, I mulled over the inaction of the prison. Other employees assured me that threats against staff led to the rapid removal of an inmate from the camp. The prison, they said, didn't mess around when it came to protecting staff members.

So far, I don't feel protected. I feel alone. Why haven't I heard anything back from the powers-that-be?

A few weeks went by and no one at any level on the chain of command responded. I immersed myself in teaching during the days ahead, so I wouldn't dwell on the threats, but the fear was always there.

A few weeks later, a familiar face entered my classroom. I'd gotten to know Emilio Valdez when he was a student in Kelly's class before I went to the Academy.

Valdez, a twenty-four-year-old who grew up on the streets of Kansas City, and his best friend's brother went to prison for a vigilante killing. Gang members gunned down Valdez's best friend, Antonio Cruz, outside his house after a basketball game in the neighborhood park brought Cruz and Valdez into conflict with the gang. When the police did nothing, and the murder didn't even make the evening news, Valdez and Cruz's younger brother, Felipe, sought revenge. They killed Cruz's murderer, but Valdez and Cruz ended up with twenty-year prison sentences. Both men went to SCCC.

While I was at the Academy, Valdez went to the hole and, like most new releases from ad seg, Barb assigned Valdez to Classroom 10.

The moment he entered the classroom, he smiled and approached my desk. He sat down, and we struck up a conversation while I put his assignments together.

"Well, Valdez, it's good to see you again. How was the hole?"

"Crazy as usual, Ma'am. I sure enjoyed Mrs. Rainer's class, but if I have to be in any other room, I'm glad it's yours."

He had worse options.

Everyone knew about Doris McGeehon's screaming sessions. We listened to her tirades down the hall, and men dreaded placement in her classroom because of her volatile and unpredictable nature. Sandra Jennings had a reputation for teaching incorrect information to students. She'd even come to Mike or me in the middle of our classes to find out how to teach a concept.

Suddenly, Valdez's smiled vanished and his face turned somber.

"Ma'am, I need to talk with you. There's a guy in D wing of 2 House who wants to kill you. It's all he ever talks about. I'm worried because I think he means it. I wasn't sure if I should say anything to you, but I think you should know."

My heart stopped beating for a second and I caught my breath.

Obviously, Ellison isn't calming down. I've tried telling myself the issue will blow over like Randy said, but it hasn't.

As if Valdez's concerns weren't enough, two days later my anxiety rose even more. Lamont Beecher entered my classroom after a brief stint in the hole. When I first took over Classroom 10, Beecher was on my roster. He never caused me trouble but, unlike Valdez, he never spoke with me unless he had to. He picked up his assignments, worked, and then left when class ended. He treated me as no more than a piece of furniture in the room. I was just another part of the DOC keeping him from the outside world.

That afternoon, Beecher returned to Classroom 10 from the hole. As soon as he entered my room, he walked up to my desk and sat down in the chair across from me.

Hesitating at first, Beecher said, "Ma'am, I need to talk with you. There's this man in 2 House—"

"Yeah, he's in D wing, right?"

"Yes, Ma'am. He's off the chain and talks about nothing but killing you. I think you should know. He does nothing but yell and scream all day long, twenty-four-seven, that he's going to rape and kill you. Some of us tried telling him to stop—that yelling crazy things would only get him in more trouble—but he won't stop." Beecher shifted in his chair, but he kept direct eye contact with me.

"He's made it clear he's not a fan of mine." I listened closely to Beecher's warning, trying to remain calm. My guts churned, and my heart raced.

"He's got a long sentence, Ma'am, and it won't make him no difference to kill you. He's not getting out of prison either way. I'm afraid he's going to follow through on his threats."

"Mr. Beecher, thanks for letting me know, and thanks for being concerned. I knew he was yelling threats anytime he saw me, but it's not good that he's still making them even when I'm not there to hear them."

"No, Ma'am, it's not." He surprised me by looking genuinely distressed.

I gave Beecher his assignment, and he went back to a table to begin his work. My mind was in a jumble.

Between classes, I headed for Randy's office. Ellison's threats weighed heavily on my heart and mind.

Randy is just as green as I am to the system, and neither of us know if this is normal or if it's something out of the ordinary. Am I blowing this out of proportion? Should I be afraid?

The education department held periodic professional development in-services across the state. The next day I was supposed to attend a training in Jefferson City at the DOC headquarters. The class dealt with computer learning programs, which seemed like a waste of time since our classroom computers didn't have internet access.

Still, I was scheduled to go, and go I would.

I need to run something by Randy.

I knocked on his office door, and he motioned me in. I filled him in on what Valdez and Beecher told me.

"Do you think I should talk to Tom Berring while I'm at the in-service tomorrow? Tom gave us an open invitation to contact him if we ever needed guidance and do I ever need guidance right now."

"I think Tom would be the perfect person to ask. I'm at a loss for what to tell you right now. Tom's been around a long time and he'll know what to do."

"I thought I'd better check with you first. Tom can tell me if I should just ignore it and go on, or if I should be worried. He may even know how to fix this situation."

"I agree. Let me know what he says."

It was settled. I made it through the rest of my work day, nerves shot, but hopeful that relief could be found the next day.

Why won't SCCC help me? Since my first run-in with Ellison, I've received no support from the wardens or the guards.

My fear level escalated. Compounding my stress, my husband, a corrections officer at SCCC, never said a peep to anyone in my defense.

Granted, our marriage has deteriorated in recent years, but he could at least say something to his supervisors—or even to his coworkers—demanding action, but he hasn't. His world is intact, and as long as his applecart remains upright, he isn't going to do or say anything in my defense.

I wasn't asking for much. I simply wanted Ellison removed from the camp. Inmates transferred in and out every week.

How hard can it be? Maybe Tom will have some answers. Maybe it seems worse than it really is. Maybe I need to be even more afraid.

My emotions were on edge while my mind kept racing. Try as I did, I couldn't relax or stay calm. I vacillated from panic to anger as I wondered why no one helped.

I'm a nervous wreck, but at least now I have a plan. Tom will have some answers for me.

The next morning, as I drove to Jefferson City, I worried.

I don't want to look like a wimp to Tom. I respect him and his opinions. At the same time, Ellison is threatening my life. Not just once, and not just twice. Inmates are even afraid I am going to be assaulted or killed. No, I need to put aside my pride and just ask Tom for advice.

Once there, I attended the morning session of the in-service, but my fears preoccupied my thoughts. I had bigger concerns than computer programs I couldn't use in my classroom. With nothing relevant to focus on during the seminar, the events of the past few months formed the playlist constantly running through my mind.

Distraught from weeks of threats, I hoped a change of scenery would ease my frayed nerves. Getting out of the prison for the day, unfortunately, hadn't improved my emotional state. I was a frazzled mess. Once we broke for lunch, I headed for Tom's office. I hadn't made an appointment with him, and I wasn't sure if he was available.

I hope I haven't built this trip up in my mind only to miss him.

Tom Berring, in his mid-fifties, reminded me of a young Colonel Sanders with his mustache and polite southern ways.

He was a favorite of nearly everyone who went through DOC training.

Thankfully, Tom sat at his desk in his office and his face lit up when he saw me at his door.

"What brings you here today, Caroline? Come on in and have a seat." He motioned me to an easy chair across from his oak desk.

"I'm here for an in-service, but I was wondering if I could talk with you for a few minutes. I've got a problem at the prison, and I'd like to hear what you think." I slipped into the room and sat in the chair.

"Sure, what's going on?"

I explained the events of the past weeks, beginning with the initial write-up and ending with my conversation with Randy the day before.

Tom listened intently but said nothing. I couldn't read the expression on his face, but he listened carefully to every word I told him. He rested one hand on his chin while he twiddled the pen on his desk with the other. His eyes focused on me.

"Am I overreacting, or should I take this seriously?"

Tom's face took on a look of deep concern. "You should take this very seriously. You are not overreacting. And the wardens haven't responded to your transfer request at all?"

"No, they haven't."

Tom raised his eyebrows as he let out a deep exasperated sigh. He leaned back in his leather office chair. "I know all the wardens at SCCC and can't for the life of me figure out why they haven't jumped on this, Caroline."

He reached in his desk for a notepad. "Can you give me this guy's inmate ID and his name?"

"I sure can, Tom. Believe me, I've memorized his information." I then scribbled Reggie Ellison's name and ID number on the paper and handed it back to Tom.

"I'm sorry you're going through this. It's not supposed to work this way." He stood to walk me to the door.

I rose. "Thank you, Tom. It's been terrible, and I feel like I've been abandoned by the prison. I can't tell you how much it means to me that you want to help."

Tom shook my hand and patted my shoulder. "I promise you I will get to the bottom of what the hold-up is. We will get this guy transferred. I'd like to know what's going on down there at SCCC."

I made it through the afternoon session, still finding it difficult to focus on the class, but hopeful. Before I left Jefferson City, I texted Randy to bring him up to speed.

"Tom says this is a big deal and he's going to look into it. He said Ellison needs to be transferred."

"Good! I'm glad he's going to be able to help."

Relief is on its way.

The next morning, Kelson, Sandra Jennings's tutor, knocked at my classroom door. "Mr. Turner wants to see you in his office."

I bet he wants a face-to-face conversation about my visit with Tom.

I briskly walked to Randy's office. "Hey, Randy. What's up?" The look on Randy's face was troubled and tense.

Uh oh. This doesn't feel like a casual call to his office.

My stomach dropped when Randy said, "Come in my office— and shut the door." I quietly closed it. "Have a seat," Randy said as he pointed to the wooden chair across from his desk.

"What did you want to talk to me about?"

Randy didn't look me in the eye right away. He tapped the pencil he held against his left knee. Slowly, he turned to face me. "I just got off the phone with the wardens. They aren't happy with you."

"What? Why aren't they happy with me?"

"Someone told them you spoke with Tom when you were in Jefferson City yesterday." Randy appeared visibly uncomfortable with our conversation.

"I asked you if you thought it was a good idea before I talked with him. You agreed that Tom would be the person to talk to for some advice."

"Yes, I did. The wardens don't, however. I hate to even say this to you. It makes me sick to be the one to say this. The wardens told me I needed to give you a message from them."

"What message is that?"

Randy paused. "I was told to tell you that if you ever go 'out of house' with anything ever again, it's going to be your job."

"You can't be serious? They haven't done anything about transferring Ellison, but now they're threatening my job?"

I'm glad I took Randy's offer to sit down. My head is spinning, and I think I might throw up.

Clearly, Randy didn't agree with the wardens, but they put him under orders to get me in line with the prison. He was at a loss for words to justify any of this. Without even having to say it, the look on his face told me he felt nearly as terrible as I did.

"I'm sorry, Caroline."

"Welcome to the DOC, huh, Randy?"

Stunned and weak-kneed, I walked back to Classroom 10.

Not only is a crazed inmate threatening my life, but now the wardens are gunning for me. My life is threatened, my job is threatened, and no one is fighting for me. How is this even possible—all because I wrote someone up for making threats against officers? Where is my protection?

I wanted to quit on the spot, but I knew I couldn't. I needed the job. After a year of subsistence living on substitute teacher wages, I couldn't walk away from a paycheck. With a rocky marriage, I couldn't risk not having an income with an uncertain future ahead of me.

Instead of quitting, I kept pressing for Ellison's transfer, but I kept my comments within SCCC. Whenever possible, I talked to the manager of Housing Unit 2, Gary Rhoads, asking about any developments. Gary, a lumberjack of a man, began his DOC career in the education department. He watched this fiasco unfold and seemed exasperated by the lack of action by prison authorities. Days and weeks passed, and Gary shook his head time after time apologizing for the delay.

I never received any acknowledgement from the prison administration about Ellison's transfer. My days darkened because of the threats on my life and my job. I was terrified. Nearly every day plagued me with anxiety and headaches. The stress made me physically ill.

Then, one early December morning, as I entered the administration building, I spotted Gary Rhoads standing by the staff mailboxes near the entryway of the administration building.

"Good morning, Gary," I said as I stepped up to my mailbox.

Gary leaned in quietly. "I have some news for you. The transfer paperwork for Ellison finally hit my desk. I've already signed it, and while I can't tell you when the transfer is going to happen or where he's going, it is going to happen."

"Thank you, Gary. I know your hands have been tied."

"Thank you for understanding. If it had been up to me, I would have transferred him on the first day he threatened you. I couldn't do anything until the paperwork reached me, but as soon as it did, I signed it and sent it on."

"Why has it taken so long, Gary?"

Hesitating for a second, he replied, "It's because you don't wear blue."

I stared blankly at him, unsure how to take what he just said.

Gary said, "You aren't custody. None of the guards really care about what happens to non-custody staff. You didn't hear that from me, but it's true."

My mind reeled for a few seconds then I found my voice. "So, I wrote this guy up for threatening custody staff in general, but the guards don't care when Ellison wants to rape and kill me because I'm a teacher and not a corrections officer?"

"I hate to say it, but that's what it amounts to. I'm sorry it's taken this long, but I promise I will make this transfer happen as quickly as possible now that it's been approved."

I thanked Gary and walked away with a better understanding of how the prison worked—of how it really worked.

Now I know no guard has my back in any situation, and my husband's lack of concern is living proof of that. It's no big deal if my life is on the line. No warden will make sure I am safe. I don't wear blue.

THE IMPROPER FRACTION

R egardless of the threats by Ellison and the intimidation by the wardens, I had a job to do. Three times a day, groups of students arrived in my classroom; some willingly and some grudgingly, but they arrived nonetheless. At that time, I taught my classes using an individualized curriculum. Based on test scores and the content area, students, worked at their own pace. In any given class, fifteen students worked on three different levels of language arts, math, science, and social studies.

During statewide meetings, education department managers told teachers we should walk around our classrooms, monitoring student progress and helping students with their questions. At the prison level, though, guards and supervisors told me to limit the amount of time I walked among the inmates. In fact, I was told to stay behind my desk altogether.

Education Officer Craig Underwood, anytime he "caught" me walking around my room, loved to remind me, "Something bad is going to happen to you." He smirked as he said it.

Underwood is a little too interested in me and my classroom. He goes from acting like a stalker to acting like he's trying to find some way to get me in trouble. Either way, the guy gives me a bad feeling.

"You should stay behind your desk. Don't you know those men are just drooling over you? You're going to get hurt if you don't do what I say," he'd tell me.

With the way he watches me from the hallway, I'm just as worried that he will assault me. He acts like I'm a piece of meat.

Even my students commented. "What's up with dude? He's creeping on you."

I didn't have a good answer for them. I'd just shrug and continue teaching.

At a statewide education meeting, I raised my dilemma to Mary Castor. Did I mingle, or did I stay behind my desk?

"It's your job to work with students. Period," she flatly told me.

"I realize that, but the custody staff at SCCC doesn't agree."

She gave me a frustrated look and sighed. I tried to explain my plight. "There's no way for me to keep both sides happy."

"Do your job and figure it out." End of discussion.

I am trapped between two opposing forces.

Custody officers didn't like teachers or anyone else under the rehabilitation arm of the Department of Corrections. Mike Vaughn had told me more than once about custody officer attitudes.

"Custody staff thinks prisons exist to punish inmates, not to make them better people. Teachers, counselors, and medical personnel are the bastard stepchildren of the department."

We don't wear blue, after all.

After the meeting with Mary Castor, I approached Randy. "Mary made it clear that I'm supposed to walk around my classroom, but Underwood constantly harps at me to stay behind my desk."

"Funny you brought this up. Sergeant Cook was just telling me that you spend too much time talking to students at your desk. He said they're just trying to leer at you. You need to stay behind your desk and not have students work there either."

"What? So, I'm not supposed to walk around my room, I'm not supposed to work at the board, and now I'm not supposed to have students come to my desk either? Come on, Randy. I guess I'm supposed to sit in my classroom all day and just collect a paycheck instead of teach."

"No, I want you to teach. Just don't mingle with students or be at the board or let students come to your desk."

"Randy, this is ridiculous. How am I supposed to teach and not do those things? Mary tells me to do one thing, and you're telling me to do another. I can't win."

"I see how that puts you in a bind. Just go back to your classroom and do the best you can, but don't do anything that causes the custody staff to complain about you."

"None of the other teachers have those restrictions."

"Just go do your job. Figure out a way to keep everyone happy."

Meanwhile, I fielded daily comments from Underwood. "I'd hate to see you get walked out." Getting "walked out" meant a staff member was fired and unceremoniously marched out of the prison.

His comments have ugly undercurrents. Are they veiled threats? Am I targeted because I made the wardens angry?

Boxed in, I couldn't win for losing.

I tried to split the difference between the demands made by Mary Castor and the custody officers at SCCC. During this time of uncertainty, an incident in my classroom brought together both sides of the vise tightening around me.

Some students appeared "needier" than others, and that happened in classrooms regardless of their age or where the school was. In a maximum-security prison, some needy students had perverted ulterior motives. Inmates got more attention from female teachers if they constantly asked questions. The more questions they asked, the more time they spent with the teacher. It was weird and annoying, but it happened.

As my students quietly worked, one perpetually needy student, Jeremy Prince, pestered me for help with his math. Multiplying fractions confused him and he whined for assistance. He was baffled by every problem, even though it was calculated just the same as the previous ten problems that I'd already helped him with. He sat at a table in the back of the room, but instead of walking to my desk for help, he asked me time after time to go to his table.

"I can't do every problem for you."

"Oh, no Ma'am. It's just this one I really need your help on. It's the last one I'll ask you for help with." Of course, the very next problem repeated the pattern.

I made a few quick stops as I circulated around the room, checking on student progress and answering questions at other tables.

"Can't you stand here for just a minute to make sure I'm doing them, right?" Prince pleaded one more time.

I gritted my teeth and made my way to where he sat. I stood, watching him write the multiplication of fractions problem on his paper.

Isn't he right-handed? Why is he using his left hand to work this math problem? I'm not sure I want to know. Oh, God. I don't want to, but where is his right hand?

Rocking a half step back, I found my answer. His right hand enthusiastically gripped his penis, completely out of his uniform, underneath the table.

"Get out of my classroom now!" I pointed at the door and walked to my desk to fill out a CDV for inappropriate sexual behavior.

"What? What did I do? Did I say something?" He remained in his seat.

"I said to get out of my class. Now! You know what you did!"

"Ma'am, if I said something, I'm sorry. I won't say it again."

He isn't leaving.

"Prince get out of my classroom or I'm going to have a guard come in here and drag you out! You know what you did!"

"I promise I won't say it again."

The scene dumbfounded the entire class. What happened at Prince's table? Fourteen other men, nose-to-the-grindstone on their own assignments, missed the spectacle. Everyone was so used to his whining that they ignored him most of the time.

Suddenly, everyone in the room stared wide-eyed at me. What caused their calm, non-hysterical teacher to become anything but calm and non-hysterical?

"Get out or I'm calling a guard in here!"

Prince finally realized that life only became worse for him the longer he lingered in my classroom. As soon as he walked out the door, I faced a roomful of confused men.

Finally, a few of the students spoke up. "What did he say?"

"He didn't *say* anything."

I could almost see the question marks hovering in the air above their heads.

"You know how he kept wanting me to go back to his table? Well he was writing with his left hand." I paused. "He's right-handed." Knowing looks swept the classroom.

"Oh, Ma'am, you don't mean he was—"

"He was."

Prince whined all hour about his math, so what he was working on was no secret.

"Prince was working on an improper fraction."

Laughter erupted in Classroom 10. According to students who were there that day, for the remainder of his time at SCCC Prince was known across the camp as the "Improper Fraction."

Jeremy Prince's write-up sent me to Housing Unit 2 a few weeks after Reggie Ellison went to D wing, setting the stage for Ellison's second round of threats and the prison's inaction.

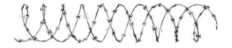

TROUBLE AT THE
CAPITOL PLAZA HOTEL

I mentioned earlier that trouble found its way back to the Capitol Plaza Hotel after we finished the Academy. It did, and in a big way. Dave Harmon, one of the corrections officer trainees, drove our carpool from SCCC to the Academy. Just months after we stayed in Jefferson City, tragic circumstances drew Dave back to the same spot.

During training, Dave asserted himself as an expert on policy—and practically any other topic related to law enforcement. In the past, he worked as an officer in a county jail.

He freely expressed his professional and personal opinions in class.

As far as the rest of us knew, other than being a little conceited, Dave Harmon was the devoted father and husband he appeared to be. His wife also worked at SCCC and he spoke lovingly of her and his five children.

During the long drives to Jefferson City, Dave told us stories about the little boy named Wade that he and his wife, Connie, adopted. A drug addict at the county jail gave birth and the baby had no family to care for him. Alone and orphaned at the hospital, little Wade needed a home. Dave and Connie made the decision to adopt him. Their children adored the baby.

What stand up people they are for taking on the responsibility of raising a homeless child. Dave's large doting family is the perfect fit for a little boy who needs love.

Months after the Academy ended, Randy Turner called me on a Saturday afternoon while I visited my oldest son at Whiteman Air Force Base.

"Have you watched any news?"

"No, I'm at Rick's and we haven't been around the apartment much today."

"Turn on the television. Get ready to be shocked."

Is there a national emergency? Are Rick and Randy being activated for war?

"Are you okay, Randy?"

"Yeah, I'm okay, but you aren't going to believe this."

I hung up the phone and switched on the news. On live television, a police chase played out after a double murder in the Ozarks. Along with the rest of Missouri, as live feed of the drama rolled, we learned the dark secret behind Dave and baby Wade.

Dave isn't the man we thought he was.

According to the reporter, Dave had an affair with an inmate at the jail and filling in the blanks wasn't difficult. He conceived Wade with her. Dave and his wife hadn't stumbled across a hapless orphan. He insisted that Connie accept and raise the child he created with another woman. Stunned, I watched the events unfold.

This puts a whole new spin on the loving Christian father we thought we knew.

The love triangle turned ugly when Wade's mother and her new boyfriend decided to fight for custody after she was released from jail. In a fit of rage, Dave shot his son's mother and her boyfriend to death in front of her other children.

Dave took the baby back to Connie who was unaware of the murders. The victim's older daughter ran to a neighbor's house for help, and she identified Dave Harmon as the shooter. Soon, police knocked on Connie Harmon's door.

Dave had fled, taking police on miles of high-speed chase. For a time, authorities feared he headed for SCCC with a weapon. The prison went on lockdown as a precaution, but Dave didn't stop there. For a few tense hours, he took officers on a pursuit ending at the Capitol Plaza Hotel. Like something out of an action movie, a shootout erupted in the lobby. Those of us watching the chase, the shootout, and the arrest were shocked. Dave survived the gunfire but would likely spend the rest of his life inside the Department of Corrections. This time, however, it would be as an inmate and not as an employee.

How many more surprises are out there?

DUTY CALLS

E xcept for the death threats by Reggie Ellison, behavior problems were rarely an issue in my classes. As tough as the maximum-security inmates were, and regardless of how vehemently some bragged that they weren't afraid of going to the hole, few men wanted to spend time in administrative segregation. When faced with a write-up, most men in prison cooled their jets.

My class wasn't paradise, but I didn't look for ways to "free case" them. Free casing, the term for employees writing CDVs based on trivial or nonexistent reasons, did happen. Few prison employees, including teachers, treated inmates as human beings. Doris McGeehon screamed at students, just itching to send them to the hole. At times, her outbursts caused us all to sit in silence, holding our collective breaths, until the episode ended.

When this happened, some inmates shook their heads and said, "It's not going to be me, but someday that woman is going to get hurt yelling at people like that. Eventually, she's going to do it to someone who won't put up with it."

Doris wasn't alone. Barbara Mason went off on inmates as well, and everyone feared the day when an inmate reached his breaking point and became violent because of her caustic ways.

The last thing a maximum-security prison needs is unnecessary hostility. Violence already spreads easily in a volatile environment. Egging it on is foolhardy.

As ugly as she was to inmates, Barb desperately tried to impress Randy. Since I was friends with him, she treated me like gold. I wasn't looking for special treatment, but she made sure I had the supplies I needed. She made a point to go the extra mile for me. I took it with a grain of salt.

"She can be vindictive. I've seen her drive teachers away," Mike confided on the drive home one night. Mike, an original staff member of the prison, knew everyone's backstory. He'd seen a thing or two during his years there. When he gave advice, I listened.

Doris and Barb weren't the only sources of drama at the school. Shannon Rafferty became even more demanding in the testing room. She deluded herself that she ran an empire. She rarely spoke directly to the rest of the staff. Instead, she posted a weekly testing schedule in the workroom. Some days she left blank, letting us know she wouldn't entertain visitors at that time. Those days she devoted to basking in the glory of her realm.

"I can't believe her behavior!" Kelly fumed.

"Considering none of the rest of us are delusional..." Mike added. We laughed.

Sandra Jennings stopped in the workroom as we complained, adding, "Talking to her is like holding a conversation with Don Quixote. There's a genuine prison diva in our midst."

The rest of the staff made Randy and me shake our heads, too.

"Did you hear what Christy Massey told everyone at lunch? Her son had breast reduction surgery, and she's bragging about it—at lunch while the rest of us are trying to eat," I told Randy one night as we walked out of the prison.

My sons would kill me if I ever told people they'd had that surgery.

"Yeah, but what about her next story—the one where her cousins stopped by the house and found her hanging laundry in the nude? That's enough to blind a person."

"What about Doris talking about her bladder surgery with students?"

"What about Sandra's dance she does in the hallway?"

The list was endless. Having a boss, I could vent to, was a mental health bonus. Randy's head spun as mine did by the behaviors of our coworkers. In public school systems we encountered occasional odd ducks, but we found ourselves swimming in a sea of them at SCCC. Randy shared his frustrations with me, and we relied on each other during the ever-evolving conditions of the education wing.

The odd working conditions provided a bizarre backdrop, but life developed a routine, and I finally felt comfortable in my job. I had a handle on curriculum and procedures, and my classes made progress. For the most part, I ignored the craziness once inside Classroom 10. Just as I settled into my new job, though, a bomb dropped in December. Randy called an impromptu faculty meeting.

"I brought you all in here to tell you some news. As you know, I'm a lieutenant colonel in the Army National Guard. I've been activated and will take a leave of absence for the next six months."

Everyone gasped.

"Where are they sending you?" Preston wanted to know.

"I won't go overseas, but I'll lead a readiness training program at Camp Clarke. My job will be to prepare units for deployment."

That's good news for Randy and his family. He'll be on active duty, but he won't be in harm's way. It's bad news for the rest of us, though.

"When are you leaving?" asked Sandra.

"Soon. My last day here will be December 11. I know that's quick, but everything will be okay."

"Who are you leaving in charge of the education wing while you're gone?" Preston asked.

"Well, I've done a lot of thinking about that. I'm going to leave Richard Blake in charge as acting educational supervisor until I return."

I breathed a sigh of relief with the assurance that some of the other personalities weren't given power. Richard was off-beat but seemingly good-natured. Still, I worried. Randy and I had formed an alliance since our first day at the prison, and he kept the unstable elements in our department from going off the deep end. Without him there, I feared chaos and power trips in the days ahead.

At the end of the day, Randy and I spoke for a few moments, just the two of us. Standing in the doorway of my classroom, I looked at Randy. "I know you don't have any choice about this, but I'm not sure what's going to happen here while you are gone."

"I *will* be back. Just hang on until I can get here."

In the week before Randy left, he tied up loose administrative ends and gave as many instructions as possible. He called a few people into his office, asking for their input and giving them guidelines on what he expected while absent.

When I met with Randy, he said, "I need you to keep me updated on what's going on here. We both know things could go haywire at any time with these people. I'm counting on you to let me know what's happening. I need to know what I'm walking back into in six months. I trust you to give me a heads up."

"I'll make sure I do that. I'm worried about what could happen while you're gone."

"I know that. I'll get back as soon as I can. Hang in there. You have my cell number, and I expect you to use it. I'm still here for you whenever you need to talk."

BE CAREFUL WHAT
YOU WISH FOR

L ife continued, both inside and outside the prison, as time
passed. The four ten-hour days we worked Monday
through Thursday were long and tedious, but the schedule
gave teachers three-day weekends to conduct personal business
and to connect with friends when our lives allowed.

With my home front becoming progressively lifeless,
and my sons now both away in the military, I relied on
my friends to fill in the emotional gaps. Given the long
hours I worked and my commute, I seldom socialized in
the evenings. The long weekends gave me my chance to
stay connected.

I taught Abby Lewis's son at Mansfield High School, and
through the years Abby and I became close friends. She
worked for the prosecuting attorney in the neighboring
county. Months went by since our last get-together, so we
planned to meet for a Friday afternoon lunch before Christmas.
After a few weeks, the day arrived. I drove the twenty miles to
the courthouse on a sunny, but cold, winter day.

As soon as I reached her office, she said, "My boss just
announced he wants to take the staff out to lunch today for
our holiday party. We can reschedule, or I can skip the party
and go to lunch with you. Or...you can come along with us
to the office party. I'm really sorry." Abby looked crestfallen.

We planned this for weeks. I'm going to be so disappointed if we have to reschedule.

"Let's go to the party! I'll pay for my own meal. I don't want to miss a chance to see you. It's been hard enough making today work for us."

"I was hoping you'd say that. Let me grab my coat and purse and we'll get going."

Along with her coworkers, we walked a few blocks to the restaurant, one of those hometown cafes where everyone knew everyone else. The waitress seated us in the back room set aside for large groups and parties. Everyone, including the prosecuting attorney, a former judge, and a prosecutor from another county who accompanied us to the restaurant, was fascinated by my work inside a prison. Only a table away, sat two local defense attorneys who joined in the conversation. All of them were clueless about how prisons ran.

"What's it like?"

"Why would you work inside a prison?"

"Are the inmates as dangerous as they show on television?"

"You have a guard with you at all times, right?"

"Do you carry a gun?"

How can prosecutors, who make their livings sending people to prison, know so little about them?

The most common question people in general asked me was "Aren't you afraid?" The prosecutors and the judge wanted to know the same thing.

"Anyone who isn't afraid to work inside a prison is crazy, but you can't act like you're afraid when you're in there or you won't last," I told them.

Kayla, the prosecutor's secretary, spilled lots of opinions about inmates into the conversation. Over and over throughout the meal she said, "I think we should save the money and just kill all the inmates!" She said this with a grin.

That's the holiday spirit. I'm sure Jesus is smiling when He hears that line at a party celebrating His birth. What is wrong with these people?

"I don't think they should go to school or have televisions either."

School rehabilitates inmates. Televisions keep them occupied so they aren't hatching escape plans or thinking of ways to attack a guard. She doesn't get it.

"Oh, and they get free medical. That's ridiculous. We should just let them die."

If she only knew how poor the healthcare is in prison. Guys with lung cancer are told they have bronchitis until it's too late. No matter what's wrong, medical gives them an allergy pill or an ibuprofen and sends them back to their housing unit.

Kayla spouted one bumper sticker quip after another. Reasons existed for every one of the items she complained about. Everyone nodded in agreement with her. With their iPhones and privilege at their fingertips, they relished in the thought of making inmates as miserable as possible.

They aren't choir boys, but society isn't helped by turning them into worse people because you think inflicting agony is enjoyable. Is that who you want coming back onto our streets?

By the fifth or sixth time Kayla said inmates should be killed, I'd had enough. I looked across the table at her, and in a loud, clear voice said, "Well, Kayla, that's all well and good until the DNA comes back and you find out you've killed an innocent man. What are you going to do then?"

The dining room went silent. My words hung in the air like cigar smoke. No one responded as they sat completely still, ducking their heads. No one brought up killing inmates again.

Most inmates aren't in prison for killing someone. Most are in for drugs, robbery, fistfights, burglary, and a slew of other crimes which, in the light of day, aren't death penalty offenses. Making mistakes should have a price, but breaking a law shouldn't be an automatic death sentence. We aren't a third world dictatorship.

The party goers found their voices once again and began asking me more questions about prison. Prosecutors and judges send people to prison, and my experiences reminded them of the gravity of their power. They showed me their utter ignorance about the system beyond the courtroom.

Prosecutors and judges should be required to go into prisons. None of what I told them today should be news to them.

The party ended, and we bundled ourselves up in our coats to face the biting north wind as we walked back to the courthouse. Abby and I had barely visited with all the prison talk.

"Thank you for coming along, Caroline."

"We'll get together soon. Maybe I can talk about more than my job then." We laughed.

Once inside the building, Kayla stopped me as I walked by her office. "I know you're right, and I don't know why I said those things."

"You aren't alone. A lot of people say the same things without thinking."

"I know someone who's probably going to prison soon. He's the son of family friends." She lowered her voice. "He's gotten into drugs and burglarized some houses around here. Now he's looking at doing hard time. His family is devastated."

"You don't want him to be killed just to save taxpayer dollars, right?"

"No, I don't. Now that you put it that way, I feel even worse for saying what I did at the party."

"Even if we don't like what they have done, every single one of those inmates is someone's son, someone's father or someone's brother."

"You're right. It's not as easy to say someone should die when they're your loved one." She cast her eyes downward.

How can the people who work so hard to send others to prison know so little about what happens once the conviction is in the books? It seems like most prosecutors only care about the next election. They don't care about what happens after they 'win' a case.

Kayla had no defense for the ignorance of her and her coworkers. I left the courthouse that day with a few questions swirling in my heart and head.

How can people who are otherwise good and kind become so heartless towards someone who made mistakes? Don't we all make mistakes? It's like Americans have a Puritanical urge to punish others.

After what happened with Ellison, I certainly didn't consider inmates misunderstood choir boys. At the same time, they didn't deserve to die because they broke a law.

THEY SAID HE'S FINE

K ayla complained about wonderful inmate healthcare, but the realities weren't so rose-colored. Neither medical nor psychological care were readily available to inmates. Mental health problems festered across the prison system, and with few mental health facilities accessible in communities, many mentally ill people ended up in prison—after they'd committed a violent act toward someone else.

Several of my inmate students took psychotropic drugs to control their emotions. If the people in my classes were any indication, the number of mentally ill people warehoused in prisons surprised me.

A month after Randy Turner left for military duty, Lester Albritton experienced a psychotic episode in my classroom. He stood in the middle of the room, in a trance-like state, as he talked about the colors of paint on the wall. "Green tells us to be angry, but brown tells us to be afraid. Have you ever heard what red says, Ma'am?"

Everyone came to a stop in Classroom 10. No one breathed. He grasped a sharpened pencil in his hand while he circled my room. He followed fellow student, Isaac Harrison, around the class, pencil in hand, muttering. No matter which direction Harrison turned, Albritton trailed him.

Everyone in the room teetered on the verge of freaking out. Killers and hardcore gangsters panicked. My heart raced, too. I quietly reached over and gripped the pen on my desk, sliding my arm to my lap with it.

In case I need to defend myself.

After a tense moment or two, concerned for everyone's safety, I slipped out of my room and alerted Officer Presley, the first education officer I ran across. Underwood was busy talking to Barb and Albritton needed immediate attention.

"A student is having a mental health episode in my classroom. Can you take him to medical? He needs help," I explained to Presley.

"Let me give medical a call to let them know I'm on my way over with him, and I'll be right down to your room to get him."

"He's walking around with a sharpened pencil, just so you know."

Presley sighed and reached for the phone.

I turned to go back to my room when Underwood blocked my way. "You were supposed to tell the *senior* officer about an emergency, not Presley." Underwood puffed out his chest. "Why didn't you?"

"I told the first officer I saw, and that happened to be Presley. There's a man having a medical emergency in my room." I tried to push past him.

Underwood once more stepped in front of me. "You should have told the *senior* officer, and you didn't."

"I'm guessing that's *you*? There's an emergency in my room. I don't have time for this. I have to get back to my class." I left Underwood standing at the guard station.

I hate to break it to Underwood, but he's a CO1, just like Presley, and he has no more authority than any other blue shirt.

Within a minute or two, Presley escorted Albritton out the doors of education. Everyone in Classroom 10 breathed a sigh of relief. We empathized with Albritton, but we also feared he might stab one or more of us with that pencil.

Ten minutes later, Albritton returned my room.

How can that be?

Collectively, we bristled and held our breaths when he walked through the door.

I popped out of my chair and went directly to Presley. "Why is Albritton back in my classroom?"

Presley shook his head. "Medical looked him over and sent him back. They said he's fine."

"He's not fine. I can't believe they sent him back to class."

"They asked him a few questions and there was nothing wrong with him."

"There's definitely something wrong with him. Take him back to medical."

As we spoke, second session came to an end and Albritton left with the crowd of students through the doors and into the yard full of general population inmates. God only knew what he might do—or what might happen to him.

"I want something done for Albritton's safety," I told Presley.

"Well, he's already gone, so there's not much I can do about it."

"Call someone who can do something. I want to talk to them."

Presley radioed to the lieutenant on duty. Both Lt. Fox and Sgt. Cook arrived a few moments later.

"If he was causing a problem, write him up for creating a classroom disturbance," Lt. Fox said.

"He wasn't willfully being a disruption. He doesn't need to be disciplined. He needs help. Writing him up will only send him to the hole. Albritton needs medical attention."

"That's your only choice, Ma'am, but if you don't write a CDV within the next few minutes, it won't be valid. Go ahead and write him up," Sgt. Cook chimed in.

DOC policy allows up to twenty-four hours to write a CDV. Just who do they think they are snowing?

I stood my ground. "You need to do something for him. He needs help. I'm afraid he's either going to hurt someone or be victimized himself out there on the yard."

"You can write him up or do nothing. We aren't taking him back to medical," Fox replied.

I refused to write him up, so they left. Albritton was out there, untreated, going through a breakdown.

Thankfully, he managed his way back to his housing unit and didn't harm anyone—no thanks to the custody officers, and no thanks to the medical staff who sent a psychotic man back to my classroom.

The Department of Corrections either medicated inmates into stupors, or it ignored mental illness completely. Unstable inmates, along with unstable coworkers, kept me on pins and needles all the time.

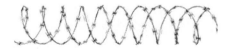

SECRETARY OF WAR

Kelly and Mike's warnings proved true. If Barb went out of her way to make me comfortable in Randy's presence, her engines thrust into full reverse once he left.

My friendship with Randy was never a competition with Barb, as far as I was concerned, and her jealousy blindsided me.

If I mentioned that I talked to Randy, her eyes snapped with fire. "Did you? Really, Caroline? Did you really talk with Randy, or are you just saying that because you think it makes you sound 'special'?"

"I don't know what you mean, Barb. All I said was that I talked to Randy and he wanted me to tell everyone hello. That's it."

"Sure, Caroline...sure."

I'm at a loss.

I turned to Kelly for advice. "I don't understand where her anger comes from."

"Oh, that's easy. She wants to be his only source of information about the school. Barb is territorial, and she thinks you're her competition."

"That's just ludicrous, Kelly. Randy and I have been friends since we started here, and he asked me to keep in touch."

"Barb doesn't care about any of that. As far as she's concerned, Randy is hers. Be careful around her. She's decided you're the enemy, and she has you in her sights."

I didn't like the sounds of that at all, but I quickly realized mentioning Randy around Barb set a match to a dynamite keg. As we spoke, Barb answered her office phone and she lit up because Randy was on the other end of the line.

"Look at that. She's like a schoolgirl with a crush." Kelly pointed at Barb in her office.

"If her hair was long enough, she'd be twirling it in her fingers saying, 'Oh, Randy,'" I said as we quietly chuckled on our way back to our classrooms.

"It's a good thing she gets a man's haircut at the prison barber shop so at least we don't have to see *that* happen."

"It's bad enough watching her glow and fawn while she talks to him."

Kelly and I, amongst ourselves, jokingly referred to Barb as "Randy's wife." His real wife was young, beautiful, and professional—all things Barb wasn't. At first, Barb's over reactions about Randy amused me. She became bent out of shape if anyone talked with Randy, but she became livid if I did. Kelly and I rolled our eyes at her childish pouts and then went about our days. As time passed, her fixation with Randy wasn't funny.

I don't like the feel of this. She looks for any opportunity to attack me, and I haven't done anything to her. She's nuts, and I'm in her crosshairs.

Barb became peevish and vindictive, and her years in the prison system protected her.

I'm new to the department and vulnerable without Randy. My best defense is avoiding contact with Barb as much as possible.

I tried to talk about her viciousness with Richard Blake. "Just let it go. I heard the way Barb talked to you, but you need to just let it go."

Barb viewed me as a threat—one she intended to eliminate. Her off-hand comments became full-blown onslaughts, beginning with a very public attack she launched during a staff training in February, just a few months after Randy's departure.

On-site training took place in the portable buildings located outside the prison fences, but still within the prison compound. The morning session began with an easy-going atmosphere. Trainer Eddie Lee did his best to keep us laughing while we slogged through the drudgery of bureaucratic details. In the high-tension arena of a prison, we welcomed time spent at the training trailer.

Lunch began well. Teachers weren't the only employees at the training. Outside of the education staff, I knew very few people at SCCC. People mixed, mingled, and shared stories while making new acquaintances and reconnecting with old ones. I enjoyed meeting caseworkers, clerks, and maintenance staff whom I never came into contact with while teaching. Then Barb took everyone by surprise.

"You think you're really something, don't you, Caroline?" A voice burned from across the room.

Barb sneered at me. All eyes turned my direction as I sat staring back at her, wondering where this attack came from.

It's bad enough that you act this way in our wing. Why do you have to make your hatred of me a public spectacle?

"Yeah, you're really something, aren't you? You think just because Randy talked to you last night that you're special," she spat.

People stopped eating. No one talked. No one laughed. Everyone sat silently and looked first at Barb and then at me as they tried to make sense of the block of ice that just dropped on our good time.

"I'm not sure what you mean, Barb."

Just how big of a scene does she plan on having? This is uncomfortable. I'm thrown onto center stage in a room full of strangers.

"Oh, you know. Just because Randy texts you sometimes, you think we're all supposed to treat you like you're hot shit. You think you have to be the one to tell him all the news, don't you?"

Randy hasn't even been a part of the conversation.

My communication with Randy struck a raw nerve with Barb, so I purposely hadn't said a word about talking to him the night before on my way home from work. Apparently, Randy talked with Barb and mentioned our conversation. She chose now, in front of all these people, to lash out.

Randy and I did talk the night before. He'd texted while I was on my drive home, asking how things were at school. We hadn't talked in a week or two, and he wanted an update.

There was news to tell. Drama with Shannon Rafferty headlined the day. The education department buzzed, and word spread across the entire prison.

"I'm sure Barb already filled you in on the hoopla," I'd written back.

"Is something going on?"

Uh oh. I thought Barb had called him today.

At that point, I didn't have a choice but to relay the information to him. Barb was too embarrassed to tell Randy what happened because part of the blame in the situation fell on her shoulders.

A combination of her jealousy and her own humiliation fueled her rage toward me. To Barb, my conversation with Randy scalded her wounded ego. She was supposed to tell him news—especially news that placed her in an unflattering light. She was supposed to decide what Randy knew and what he didn't.

I overstepped my bounds, in her mind, and I'm going to pay.

In front of twenty other employees and two trainers, Barb cut loose with one ugly comment after another. With wild eyes, she yelled as her rage rolled on. She hurled one nasty shot after another at me. Everyone sat still, stunned.

Please shut up, Barb.

She finally ended her tirade, red-faced and breathing heavily. The fun-loving atmosphere from before disappeared as quickly as my appetite. No one talked or joked for the rest of the afternoon. An introductory battle charge began in a war she outwardly waged against me for the next year and a half.

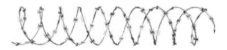

WITCHCRAFT IN
THE HELL HOLE

B arb Mason may have been angry and embarrassed because I talked to Randy about some education wing drama, but he needed to hear it. Shannon Rafferty, the self-styled Test Administrator Goddess, dove deeper into eccentricity.

Her superiority complex was over the top, she told outlandish stories to inmates, her appearance took on circus potential, and her interactions with an inmate raised eyebrows across the camp. Shannon touted herself as a witch and brought witchcraft books into the school where she whiled away her days reading them in the perpetually closed testing room. She used her witch status as a thinly veiled warning to not cross her.

Shannon oscillated from extreme friendliness to explosive wrath—with days of cold-shouldered indifference thrown in between—towards the rest of the staff. Edgy, unpredictable, and at times vicious, Shannon disrupted the entire school.

Worst of all, state mandated testing forced every teacher to interact with her. Our students tested periodically to assess academic growth. Shannon's behavior put us in the middle of an uncomfortable situation. Unbelievably, we walked on egg shells to test our students.

The stories Shannon told inmates left everyone, inmates included, shaking their heads. One day I passed by a classroom as Shannon talked to a group of students. Her appearance in a class surprised me enough. What she said downright shocked me.

"I'm black and love getting to know as much about our culture as possible," the pale-skinned and red-haired Shannon told a group of mainly African-American men.

Later, I asked her, "Why were you telling students in Sandra's room that you are black?"

"Because I identify as black. It doesn't matter where my parents came from. I feel black."

At other times, I overheard her bragging about how rich she was. "I drive a Porsche to work."

Staff members knew she bummed rides from coworkers every day. She didn't own a car of any kind, let alone a Porsche. Complicating her commuting problems, Shannon refused to associate with certain staff members, even if it meant she had no way to get to work. Mike was one of those people. As a devout Seventh Day Adventist, Shannon's pagan beliefs didn't impress him. Shannon viewed Mike as an enemy, so she never asked us for a ride even though every day we drove past her road. We dodged a bullet.

Sandra Jennings went out of her way to give Shannon rides; backtracking to pick her up and drop her off, making an already long day even longer.

Shannon expected, instead of appreciated, the taxi service.

Sandra didn't like being forced to give her rides every day, but she was too nice to speak up about it.

Shannon also claimed she had exquisite taste in clothing. "See these boots? I paid $250 for them at an exclusive boutique. Don't you just love them?" I over-heard her talking to another group of students.

I owned a pair just like them that I paid $30 for at Walmart. Shannon fooled no one with her claims. Granted, some of the men had been locked up for a long time, but even they knew Walmart merchandise when they saw it.

She had no reason to lie except for her obsessive need to be the center of attention. Most alarming was that she believed the lies she told. Looking her in the eye, clearly, she meant what she said. She was an administrator, she was black, and she was the other things she claimed to be. A full-blown sociopath walked around our school.

As her behavior worsened, so did her style. Desperate to get attention, Shannon went to any length to draw everyone's focus onto her.

"I'm not the fashion police, but did you see Shannon's makeup? I never knew eyeliner was supposed to wrap all the way up to your temple!" Kelly said as we walked out for lunch one day.

None of the lies, the makeup, or the constant talk of witchcraft mattered if Shannon did her job, but she didn't. Days went by when the testing room stayed closed. Richard Blake could have made her open-up shop, but he didn't. Weeks went by with very little testing taking place.

"It must be nice to get paid to sit in an empty room reading witchcraft books all day or to stand visiting in the office area," Mike vented in the carpool.

"Has she always been like this?"

"When she was a teacher in a classroom she had plenty of problems, but at least students had classes. Now that she's in charge of the testing room she doesn't work at all."

Students couldn't advance without proof their skills had improved. Tempers flared in the education wing as weeks passed. The state bosses weren't happy, students grumbled, and teachers were caught in between with no recourse. Tensions ran high when it came to Shannon Rafferty. Then she raised the stakes.

The school hired Offender Phil Greene as the porter after Barb fired the previous one. Porters took care of janitorial chores and provided office help. If we needed photocopies run, we filled out a request and Greene took care of it. Since teachers had limited preparation time, we used the aid of the porter quite a bit. Barbara was Greene's direct supervisor.

Somewhere along the line, Shannon and Greene became chummy. How it happened was easy to explain. She wasn't working, so she hung out at the office a lot. She was, after all, an "administrator" and felt it was only natural to spend long stretches of time in the office area supervising her realm. This amounted to sitting or standing around Greene, who was more than happy to ignore his duties. Shannon, it seemed, enjoyed playing with fire.

Kelly and I rolled our eyes as we ran our own copies. Meanwhile, Shannon and Greene spent their days visiting. Greene fed into her delusions of grandeur, and it was a visual wreck we couldn't help but watch. Shannon's fawning over Green both nauseated and somewhat entertained everyone in school.

"She just about makes me sick!" Kelly seethed.

"Too bad she spends more time 'supervising' Greene than she does testing our students," I added.

"She barely taught when she was in the classroom, and now she does nothing. Here she is cozying up to Greene. Where is Blake? Why does Barb let this go on right under her nose?"

Kelly asked good questions. Why did Blake and Barb let this continue? Barb and Shannon were tight, so she said nothing about her employee, Greene, ignoring his job. Blake, however, had no excuse for letting Shannon hang out in the office area instead of administering tests to students.

The situation impacted the entire school.

One afternoon I walked to the office area between classes. I asked Greene if the copies I needed were finished. I'd turned in my request a few days earlier. He sat behind the counter, reading.

"No, I haven't had a chance. I've been busy."

"Oh, hey, what are you reading?"

"I'm studying." He held up the book and pointed to the book cover. The title was *Ten Easy Steps to Witchcraft Mastery*, or something to that effect. I didn't wonder where he got it.

Over time, Shannon decided she needed help in the testing room. Greene now spent long spans of time with her there, only occasionally making an appearance in the office. Even when at his post, he read witchcraft books and mooned over Shannon while she leaned over the countertop, giving him a clear view of her cleavage. Our copy requests sat undone. The floors were littered with dirt and debris, and the bathrooms remained filthy.

"Just how much is there for Greene to do in Shannon's room when students are testing?" Even mild-mannered staff members like Melanie Foster asked.

"An even bigger question is just how much is there for him to do down there when students aren't testing?" Mike replied. Meanwhile, Greene increased the amount of time he spent in the testing room.

For our protection, policy dictated that the doors to our classrooms were left open and unlocked. Closed or locked doors made escape difficult should an inmate become violent or predatory. A closed door also drowned out calls for help or the sounds of a teacher struggling, making it more difficult for the corrections officer on duty to realize a crisis had erupted.

Teachers became so used to the inaccessibility of the testing room at the end of the hall that we blinded ourselves to its existence. Most of the time we were in our classrooms, unaware of Shannon's comings and goings. Slowly, however, we noticed the testing room was closed—and sometimes locked—while Greene was in the room with Shannon. Red flags popped up all over the place. Still, neither Richard nor Barb did anything.

It wasn't uncommon to find Greene in the staff workroom at lunch. "Is that your food in the microwave?" I asked Greene as he hovered nearby. Inmates weren't allowed to bring in food or to prepare it in the education wing.

"No, that's not my lunch. That's Ms. Rafferty's. It'll be just a minute more in the microwave. I want it to be just right for her." He searched through the refrigerator for condiments.

The microwave chimed, and he carefully picked up the plate and said, "Oh, this smells good. I think she's going to like it," as he traipsed out of the room on his way to deliver the meal behind closed doors.

Completely against the rules, it became a daily occurrence.

Teachers weren't the only ones left scratching our heads. "Just what are Ms. Rafferty and Greene doing all day in the testing room?" asked inmate tutors and students.

On the one hand, it provided a bit of drama in a dismally boring environment. On the other hand, some tutors envied the special treatment Greene received, and this caused increasing resentment. No one permitted them to slack off on their duties or to dote on a staff member.

Shannon's erratic behavior didn't win her any friends, staff or inmate. Richard and Barb were her only friends on staff, and they were the only ones with the authority stop her recklessness.

Shannon's behavior also had implications beyond the education hallway. She dated—and lived with—a lieutenant, Terry Richards, who worked at SCCC. In the middle of her budding romance with a prison employee, she became increasingly cozy with inmate, Phil Greene.

Shannon's need for attention knew no bounds, and she flaunted both her relationships. Tensions multiplied as she walked a tightrope between inmate and staff liaisons, and the custody staff wasn't happy. People across the camp buzzed with word of Shannon's antics.

Bombshell rumors circulated. Hector Ramos, one of Mike's tutors, was adamant that he witnessed lines being crossed by Shannon and Greene. "Ma'am, I don't even like to talk about this, but I have walked in on things I shouldn't have seen."

"What sort of things?"

"One day I had to take a testing roster to Ms. Rafferty. When I walked in, she was sitting with her legs spread apart—one leg over the arm of the chair—in skin-tight pants. Greene was sitting across from her, ogling her. Ma'am, it wasn't appropriate."

"What did you do?"

"I handed her the roster and left. She never even changed the way she was sitting." Ramos looked embarrassed.

He wasn't alone. Other tutors witnessed similar spectacles in the testing room. I personally watched Greene put Shannon's coat on her as he rested his arm on her back. Any sort of physical contact between staff and inmate was banned. I saw the cozy behavior, and so did every other employee and inmate in our wing. Barb Mason and Richard Blake remained silent.

I soon found myself in the middle of the theatrics. Kelly and I routinely left the prison for lunch.

While custody employees were paid for lunch, teachers weren't, so lunch breaks were our time. We enjoyed the short reprieve from the dungeon to catch some fresh air and to get in a quick visit with one another as we walked to the parking lot.

Kelly spent lunches with her mother at the local nursing home. Occasionally, her daughter and grandchildren joined her. I used the time to grab a bite to eat and to connect with my sons. Phones weren't allowed inside the prison, so I left mine in my car. During my lunch break, I caught up with messages from my boys and checked news headlines.

Leaving the prison was a multi-step process. Out the education doors, we walked down the long sidewalk then we buzzed in through a secured door where we entered our codes into the keypad. We also had to scan our fingerprint before the door would open. From there, we made a quick climb up the stairs to the administrative control center, or "bubble" as it's referred to by employees. There we showed our identification and punched our security codes in once more, opening the door that led to the administration area. Next, we made our way through a maze of hallways, passed through a metal detector, went down another set of stairs, walked through the front doors and then finally entered the parking lot. It was worth the extra hassle to get out into the sunshine. I took the same steps, in reverse, to return to work.

One day, James Clark, a prison investigator, stopped me as I made my way through the administration building to head to the bubble. "Excuse me, I need you to come with me to Olivia Hamilton's office."

Why am I being pulled into the lead investigator's office?

I entered Olivia's office and, as though she read my mind, Olivia reassured me. "You aren't in trouble, but I want to have a conversation with you. I understand there is some irregular behavior going on in the education department."

Relieved, I gave a little chuckle. "There's a lot of 'irregular' behavior that goes on in the education department. Just which behavior are you referring to?"

Olivia laughed because she was aware that the personalities in the education department were different.

"I understand one employee in particular has caused some problems in the education wing with her behavior."

"Yeah, things have been kind of stressful."

"I'd like you to tell me anything you know," Olivia explained as she reached inside her desk and pulled a tape recorder from a drawer. "Do you mind if I record our conversation?"

"No, I don't mind."

She set the recorder on her desk and pushed its red button. "Great, this will help me be accurate in my report. Could you please state your name, your position, and today's date?"

I did as she asked. "Do you want to know only what I have seen myself, or do you want me to tell you things I have been told?"

She leaned back in her office chair. "Both."

I filled her in on what I knew and suggested a few other people she might want to question.

"Caroline, thank you for being honest with me about what you know and for clarifying what you've heard but can't verify. I ask that you not share any of what we have discussed today with anyone—not even your friends inside the education wing. No one can know we've had this conversation."

"I won't tell anyone we've talked."

"Thank you. I'd like to know if you see or hear anything else, but I don't want to draw the attention of other staff members," Olivia added.

"I leave for lunch every day, so if there is anything noteworthy, I could stop by and see you as I'm coming through admin."

"That would be great. Since you come and go out of the prison on a regular basis, no one will be suspicious of you coming up here. I think this is a good plan." Olivia turned off the recorder.

I walked back to my classroom with my head racing. Now, dragged into the mess Shannon created, I wasn't comfortable with it.

I've only worked here for a few months, and I have my own problems with Barb. Now I'm in the middle of Shannon's investigation. I just want to do my job and go home at the end of the day. Period. I wish Randy was still here. None of this would be happening if he was here to stop it.

Randy Turner wasn't at SCCC, however, and I lived with that reality whether I liked it or not. I did let Randy know that Shannon raised questions and ruffled feathers at the prison, but I abided by Olivia Hamilton's request and told neither Randy nor anyone else about the investigation in motion.

Randy should be aware of the tensions circulating in the department, though.

"Keep your head down and try not to get caught up in any of it but keep me updated on what is going on. It sounds like a train wreck," Randy advised.

Events escalated. As weeks went by, we wondered when the axe would fall. The school sat on edge as tensions mounted. Kelly couldn't stand Shannon and made no secret of her feelings.

"I hope she gets walked out of here—and soon! She should have been fired before you ever started working here, but for some reason Barb talked Mr. Chambers into keeping Shannon on staff. He said he felt sorry for her. She brings all these problems onto herself. Now look at what she's doing."

I wasn't sure what transpired before my arrival at SCCC, but clearly Shannon created hard feelings with the rest of the staff before she began her reign as Test Administrator. Recent developments with Greene made Kelly's blood boil, and Kelly had a legitimate beef. The entire school was in turmoil.

"I want to be here when she gets walked out," Kelly mused. "It'll be my luck that I'm on vacation when it all goes down." Her long-awaited trip with her daughters to the Mall of America in Minnesota approached.

Meanwhile, Barb remained mum toward her employee, Greene. He spent nearly all his time now in the testing room. He followed Shannon around like a puppy whenever she ventured out of her castle.

Barb didn't hesitate to belittle me, but she kept her trap shut while her own employee neglected his job and doted on a staff member. Barb's silence was tantamount to approval of their behavior.

Two weeks later, while Kelly vacationed in Minnesota, guards walked Shannon Rafferty out of the prison.

When someone was escorted off the grounds, it was a spectacle, and people stopped working to watch the walk of shame.

Investigators were tight-lipped, and none of us knew exactly what amounted to the final straw, but items found in her desk and in Greene's cell sealed the deal—along with behavior caught on tape. Video cameras surveilled every square inch of the prison and, apparently, investigators spotted something as they reviewed footage of Greene and Rafferty's interactions.

Kelly was both thrilled and irritated when I called her at lunch to give her the news. "Damn! Why did I have to miss it? I just knew it was going to happen while I was out of town!" Still, she was happy and relieved that Shannon was gone.

I shared the news of Shannon's parade off prison grounds with Randy Turner on my drive home that night. When he learned the news, he called Barb. That conversation prompted her vicious attack during training.

When prison investigators finally brought the hammer to bear on Shannon Rafferty, people outside the education department began asking questions. We asked the same questions inside the education wing for months.

Why didn't Barb tell her inmate employee to stay in the office area and do his job? Why had she allowed Shannon to hijack her employee—an obviously bad scenario? Why did Barb allow a coworker to become so tightly involved with an inmate she supervised?

Barb didn't want to answer those questions. Part of the blame for the explosion that ripped through the prison with Shannon Rafferty's removal fell squarely on Barb's shoulders.

"People want to know what she was thinking," Mike said, shaking his head. "As a veteran employee, Barb knew better."

Barb understood that Randy would ask those same questions and she wanted to get to him first. Barb wanted to spin the situation in her favor by limiting what Randy knew and when he knew it. I blasted a hole through those plans when Randy and I talked the night of Shannon's downfall. I didn't talk to Randy to undermine Barb or to embarrass her. In Barb's mind, though, I purposely made her look bad. I had to pay.

Barbed Remarks

After the training trailer incident, Barb stopped ordering supplies for my classroom. If I asked her to place an order, she said I'd missed the deadline, or she'd already placed an order without me. "The next order won't be for three more months. I guess you're out of luck." She wore a self-satisfied smile.

Barb took any opportunity to harangue me, especially in front of others. With Greene gone, the school had no janitor. Barb used this as another excuse to jab at me. One day, in front of staff and inmates, Barb pointed toward the filthy bathroom and demanded that I "get in there and clean it!"

I ignored her order and continued walking down the hall. I was embarrassed when she ordered me around. Her bullying became a part of every workday for me, and some of her comments put me in danger.

Once, as first session students entered the building, I was in Kelly's classroom. Barb bellowed down the hall, "Caroline, where are you? Your students are looking for their baaaaby! They don't know what to do without their baaaaby! You'd better hurry up and get here. They miss their baaaaby!"

Mortified, I stormed up the hallway. "Just what do you think you are doing?"

"Oh, I'm just making sure you're here for your students. They didn't know where you were, and they were missing you." She used a sickeningly sweet tone of voice.

"Let's get something straight right now, my students don't refer to me as their "baby,' and you need to stop saying that!"

"Oh, I didn't know that would bother you. They were all asking for you, so I was just trying to help."

Sure, you were, Barb. Sure, you were.

Meanwhile, every inmate in the hallway observed and listened. The three students already in my classroom witnessed Barb's display and were shocked.

When I entered the room, Forbes said, "What on earth was she saying out there, Ma'am?"

"According to Barb, you guys refer to me as your baby."

Forbes, Crouch, and Jones, stood still, shooting frightened looks at each other.

They don't want to be dragged into Barb's accusations. Her insinuation is dangerous for all of us.

"Ma'am, I've never said that, and I've never heard anyone say anything close to that," Crouch said.

"What's wrong with her? Doesn't she know that kind of talk can get you and any inmate accused of saying it in trouble? She's gonna get someone sent to the hole with that talk," Jones said.

"Honestly, guys, I don't know what's wrong with her. I'm sorry this happened."

My students knew the truth, but what about the students in other classrooms? Those who didn't know me—did they believe what Barb yelled down the hallway? Undermining comments, like the ones Barb screamed that morning, did nothing to "enhance the safety and security of the institution," the catch phrase of the prison system. What she said put me in danger.

Any inmate who believed her might assume his sexual advances were welcomed by me. I might be assaulted because Barb planted a dangerous seed in the mind of an unstable man.

Ironically, Barb was the only one in the education department with an inmate who called her his "baby." Barb's longtime boyfriend, Jim Barker, was serving time in Colorado under an interstate compact agreement. He used to be an employee at SCCC and, for safety reasons, couldn't be imprisoned in Missouri. Barb drove out west to visit him from time to time and recognized no disparity between the viciousness she showed other inmates and her own love affair with one. Jim Barker was convicted of a sick crime, too.

The prison monitored and recorded all phone conversations, including those made by staff members. On prison phone lines, authorities caught Jim Barker apologizing to his daughter for molesting her. His own words condemned him.

Barb contended that Jim was set up, but no one voluntarily apologized for sexually abusing his daughter unless it was true. He did it, and Barb continued to stick by him. Barb, nasty and hateful to other inmates and staff members, was knee-deep in a relationship with someone who committed the unthinkable.

If she truly thinks the prison and law enforcement authorities set Jim up, why does she continue to work for the department? It doesn't make sense.

One thing was for sure, Barb enjoyed harassing me and using me as her designated scapegoat. She also screamed at inmates. Her volatility made the prison atmosphere even more dangerous for the rest of us.

I'm not sure how much more I can take, but I am trapped by the need for a paycheck. My husband doesn't care about my working conditions, but he expects me to keep the paychecks coming in.

Anti-bullying posters hung around the camp, including one right outside Barb's office. She wasn't the only harassing employee at the prison, but she was the one in my immediate world. The poster was a slap in the face to me. I lived with daily dread and fear because of her attacks.

What the department promoted and what it practiced were two different beasts. Those posters meant nothing, and they made a mockery of what I—and many others around the prison—endured.

Time after time, I approached Richard Blake, hoping he would help. He was, after all, our boss during Randy's absence. He bore the responsibility to keep the education wing running professionally. He overheard her nasty attacks against me but remained silent. Richard, I realized, was called the "acting" educational supervisor because he only pretended to be the boss.

Every time I asked him to intervene with Barb, he told me, "Don't file a grievance against her. It will only make her mad. You don't want to upset Barb because she's been here a long time. Nothing will happen to her and you'll be the loser. Just let it drop."

"Richard, her behavior is erratic and unprofessional. She harasses me."

"Yeah, I know. I don't think she's been taking her medication. She's bipolar and you don't want to get in her way when she's like this."

"Won't you talk with her about her behavior? You've heard what she says to me."

"I'm not talking to her. She'll make my life hell. You should just leave this alone."

How do you leave something alone that won't let you be?

I did everything I could to avoid the office area, limiting any encounters with her. She set her sights set on me, however, and the education wing wasn't big enough to avoid her altogether. With no administrative support from Richard, I did my best, but Barb never went long without another tirade.

FINDING BRIGHT SPOTS

O nce the drama of the Rafferty-Greene saga faded, the overall atmosphere of the school improved. After months of tension, everyone in the education wing relaxed. Richard Blake took over the testing room, so assessments happened regularly now. Students focused on their work, and teachers no longer dealt with Shannon's drama and difficult personality.

Months slipped by and life settled into a routine. I did my best to put the nightmare of Ellison's threats behind me, and I tried to ignore Barb's surliness and snide comments.

She never misses a chance to say something ugly to me. It's crazy that I dread prison because of her more than I do the inmates.

I needed my job, however, and accepted that it was less than perfect. I still felt vulnerable and on edge, but I plastered a smile on my face and concentrated on my job. It paid the bills, after all.

My friendships with Kelly and Mike grew, and we insulated ourselves from the more peculiar members of the staff. We avoided the staff workroom, and we spent most of our break time in Kelly's room, which became our safe-haven.

I love teaching and believe I'm doing my part to rehabilitate inmates. That helps me keep my sanity.

Many men in prison classrooms floundered in public school as children, and the GED program gave them the skills to function in society. As terrible as incarceration was, the prison school was the only way many inmates would become literate. Sometimes prison did more than educate them.

More than once I had conversations with inmates, encouraging them to turn prison into a positive. One in particular stuck in my mind. I spoke with Valdez, the same young man who had warned me of Ellison's continued death threats from the hole.

"Ma'am, sometimes it seems like these twenty years will never end."

"The DOC can't stop time from passing, Valdez. Every day you are closer to a life on the outside—a better life than you lived before."

"I know, but I feel like I've ruined my entire life. I always wanted kids and a family, but now here I sit." He motioned his hands at the classroom.

"What do you think would have happened to you if you were still on the streets?"

"I'd be dead."

"Right now, you still have a future, Valdez, and that means you haven't ruined your life."

"What do you mean?"

"How old will you be when you get out?"

"Thirty-five."

"I know it's hard at your age to understand this, but believe me, there is a lot of life left after thirty-five."

"I've never considered that."

"You'll still be young enough to have those kids and that family you want. You'll also be wiser—and the important thing is that you're still alive. You wouldn't have been if you were on the street."

"No, I'd be dead, and I think I see what you're saying."

"You need to look at prison like a cancer diagnosis. No one wants to be told they have cancer, and prison is an awful place to be, but if you survive—if you make up your mind that you are going to come out of this better than when you came in—then you will appreciate life so much more. You still have that chance, Valdez."

He smiled and said, "Ma'am, that's a great way to look at this. You're right. I need to do what I can now to turn my life around, so I can still have what I want in the future."

Adult education offered its own rewards for me as well. In my experience, children seldom showed gratitude for learning a new skill. In my prison classroom, however, the adults often thanked me for what they learned. Light bulbs turned on as they mastered the coursework.

Inmates would blurt out, "So that's how it's done! I get it!"

I didn't make an impact on all my inmate students, but I witnessed many "ah ha" moments. I did what I could to provide my students success that, hopefully, carried on beyond prison walls. It made a tough job rewarding.

I pushed past the agony of getting up at four o'clock in the morning for work to do my part in giving them better futures—and giving our communities a better chance at safety.

Getting up early to drive an hour and a half to the prison did get old. Conversations in the carpool took away some of the drudgery. Mike and I discussed our families, politics, religion, and the prison.

After ten hours at work, carpooling with Mike was a relaxing way to end the day. By the end of the week, though, I was exhausted. It took the entire three-day weekend for me to feel up to going to work for another grueling week.

I'd get another job if I could, but in this economy, I'm stuck.

Days and weeks turned into monotonous months, but I began to get used to the prison system, except for my encounters with Barb. Unfortunately, once at work, Barb's jagged comments became the wallpaper of my life.

I know I'm not alone. I've heard about others who've faced retaliation by other prison bullies. I can make it through this. She can't torment me forever.

Sinister behaviors became part of the daily ebb and flow of the prison environment. I, like others, sadly accepted much of what happened around and to us. Coping with these surroundings was difficult. Officer Lonnie Duncan warned me at my pre-hire drug screening that some of the "good guy" employees were hard to tell from the inmates they incarcerated. Barb and the corrections officers in the education wing proved his words true.

If the taxpayers had any idea what sick people I work around, I wonder if they would demand change? I had no idea my biggest fears in here would come from my coworkers.

RAISED EYEBROWS

Officers Presley and Underwood were the gatekeepers of the school who monitored the flow of inmates. They were not, however, a security force in the classrooms. Twice during the school day, the prison conducted an inmate count. At those times, Presley and Underwood went from classroom to classroom adding up a tally of those present. Count time was practically the only instance we saw custody staff at work in our rooms.

In case of an emergency, teachers need to think on our feet. No superhero in a blue uniform will rescue us if things go awry.

Situational awareness and safety were at the forefront of everything we did. For example, while one student called me "the devil in a dress," employees did not wear dresses to work. Women wore conservative shirts and pants with sensible shoes. We didn't wear revealing outfits because perverts were everywhere (including Richard Blake who stared at my chest, not my eyes, when speaking to me).

Dresses were impractical and showed too much leg. Shoes, also, had to be easy to run in. No one escaped a riot or a predatory inmate in heels. Safety won out over style every single time.

It didn't matter what a woman wore in the prison, though.

Unwanted stares and comments occurred regardless of how she dressed or her age. Inmates paid such close attention to me that they told me what color socks I had worn the day before. They remembered the exact day I wore the same shirt to work. Their attention to detail and their scrutiny unnerved me.

Twenty-year-old inmates hit on staff members in their fifties and sixties. It turned my stomach. Some inmates, young enough to be the sons—or even grandsons—of the women they pursued ogled them with ferocity.

This place is a freak show.

Inmates weren't the only ones who stared and made inappropriate comments. Guards and other employees said things that inmates couldn't get away with. Prisoners were written up and sent to the hole if they crossed certain lines. Employees, at least not ones "in" with the system, didn't worry about punishment. Sexual harassment served as the backdrop of the DOC.

I had my own ugly brushes with harassment. Unwanted innuendos, propositions, and crude jokes happened often.

Too many of these guys think that uniform makes them sexy. They're wrong.

One instance I'll always remember. On an early spring day, the weather turned bad. Heavy rains moved through the Ozarks, and my farm, located in the lowest spot in Douglas County, was flood prone.

I wasn't sure if I would get home or if I should get a hotel room in Licking to ride out the storm.

I'd better call home and see what the road conditions are like. If it's already running down the road, there's no sense in driving that far.

"What are you in such a hurry for today?" Lieutenant Davis asked through the glass of the administrative bubble.

"I need to see if my road is still passable and what the forecast is like. I don't want to be stranded."

"Now, darling, you don't need to worry about that."

"Yeah, I do. It'll be dark by the time I get home, and I need to know if the creek's over the road."

"You don't get what I'm saying. Forget about going home, sugar. You can come spend the night—all night—with me." He gave me a wink.

What in the hell?

"No thank you," I said as I rushed to enter my code into the keypad to leave.

Davis dates one of the nurses here. Why would he hit on me? Why would he think I'm interested? Until now, I thought he was a decent guy, but now he's just another DOC jerk. He did this just because he thinks he can get away with it—and, around here, he can.

Not everyone was as brazen as Davis, but employees whistled at women and looked them up and down like pieces of beef. Subtle and not so subtle come-on lines came from male employees.

Officer Underwood leers at me and makes comments outside my classroom. Even the inmates notice how creepy he is—and that takes a lot!

More than a few times I vented to Kelly about Underwood's unwanted looks and comments. I tired of his "I'd hate to see you get walked out of here" remarks.

At first, she didn't understand my anger.

"Oh, he's annoying and a little weird, but I don't think he means anything," she said, trying to cheer me up.

Then Kelly began receiving the same threats from Underwood. "Now I see what you're talking about! And

I don't like the way he stares at either one of us come to think of it."

"That's what I've been talking about all these months. He's weird and he's looking for some way to get us into trouble. Don't you think so?"

"I do, and it needs to stop!"

"Why do you think he's turned his attention to you?"

"He hates one of my tutors. Josephson was harassed by that guard, Freeman, over in 3 House—the one who kept making comments about him being gay. I don't know or care if he is, but apparently Freeman said some crude things to him every day in front of inmates and staff members. Finally, Josephson's dad called the warden. At first, the warden didn't do anything, but finally Freeman was fired. If his dad hadn't raised hell, nothing would have happened. Now all of Freeman's friends, like Underwood, are going after Josephson. I think my tutor does a great job, but now Underwood has decided to go after me because I'm not looking for ways to write him up. I hate it!"

Underwood eventually got the medical disability he vied for months to receive. Kelly and I were relieved when that day came.

At least one creep is out of our midst, but there are plenty of others to fill his shoes.

Officer Presley was one of them. On a professional development day, no inmates were in the building as I walked from Classroom 10 to the office. Presley happened to be in the hallway at the same time, and we walked side-by-side. I was always careful of doing anything that could be misconstrued as sexual, right down to yawning into the back of my hand instead of making a fist when inmates were around.

Since only staff was in the building, I yawned and made a fist to cover my mouth as Presley and I walked.

Presley stopped and faced me, then raised his eyebrows up and down several times. "You really shouldn't flirt with me like that." He winked.

I think I'm going to throw up. He's sick!

Satisfied that he had made his point, he grinned and raised his eyebrows up and down again.

This wasn't a one-time deal. Presley often made lewd comments about female teachers as they went in and out of the bathroom. He'd stand across the hall from the restroom with a group of inmates and rate women or make other crude jokes. His behavior made the prison even more dangerous for the women working there.

Far from them acting like good guys who protect us, Underwood and Presley are predatory and perverted. Officer Duncan is right: It's a good thing the officers wear blue, or I wouldn't be able to tell the difference between them and the perverts wearing inmate gray.

My experiences weren't isolated incidents. Men and their predatory behavior victimized women across SCCC.

THE GOOD OLD BOYS' CLUB

Paul Harvey once said, "If you want to see the worst humanity has to offer, go to a prison parking lot at shift change." Harvey wasn't a fan of the Missouri criminal justice system, and he paid close attention to crime and punishment in my home state. Bad employee behavior justified his comments.

Employees made out with other employees in the parking lot before and after work. Single or married, employees hooked up for sex after work and on the weekends with coworkers. It happened where I worked, and SCCC wasn't unique among Missouri prisons.

Some sexual activity was consensual, and some of it wasn't. Matt Carter, a utility officer, told me about a disturbing case of harassment. One of his carpool partners was Willie Roseman, a veteran corrections officer. Roseman, so at ease with his predatory behavior, bragged about it in the carpool. Willie described his exploits, and some of the events Matt witnessed himself while working in Housing Unit 5 with Roseman.

Well-established as a leader in the brotherhood of corrections officers, Willie worked at the prison, he said, for the insurance. His wife suffered from serious health issues and required extensive medical care. Working a dangerous job to provide insurance for his ailing wife seemed admirable, but Willie Roseman was also a sexist pig.

Over time, he found the DOC a great place to prey on women. Willie especially loved to victimize new employees, and Stacy McGraw, a recent hire, was vulnerable in Willie's eyes. Married with two small children, she was grateful for steady employment. Decent jobs with benefits were hard to find in the area. Even bad jobs weren't easy to find in the rural area surrounding SCCC. The $29,000 a year salary with insurance looked like a godsend for her and her young family.

After completing four weeks of training at the Academy, the prison assigned Stacy to the third shift in Housing Unit 5. It wasn't an honor house (where the best-behaved inmates lived), but it wasn't the hole either.

Shortly after Stacy arrived on the camp, the harassment began. Off-color jokes and sexually-charged comments flew around the housing unit bubble where officers sat for most of the shift. As a leader amongst his peers, Willie was accustomed to bossing people around.

"Stacy, take a walk around the wing. I like the way your ass looks in your uniform."

Crushed that her coworker said something so crude, she still wanted to show her willingness to do the job. From the looks on their faces, Stacy realized her coworkers didn't balk at Willie's remark. She shrugged it off, hoping it was a one-time event.

It wasn't. Night after night, Willie made the same sort of wisecracks. Her coworkers not only weren't troubled by his remarks, they laughed. They urged her to the door to make her rounds. At best, her colleagues turned their backs and acted as though they hadn't noticed Willie's behavior. At worst, they added their own two cents' worth. Willie's behavior progressively worsened.

Soon, he propositioned Stacy. "Why are you going home tonight? You need a real dick. I can give you what your husband can't."

Neither Matt Carter nor any of the other employees told Willie to stop. As a utility employee, Matt worked wherever the prison needed him to, and he was familiar with both Willie and Stacy because Housing Unit 5 frequently needed extra employees. Generally, a decent and caring person, Matt succumbed to the good old boy mentality of the prison system and said nothing. Willie emboldened and at ease in telling about the "fun times" he had with Stacy, continued the harassment.

Sometimes Willie leaned over Stacy at her desk or blocked her way through doorways, forcing his body next to hers. She tried to push past him. "Please, Willie, just let me go."

"What's the matter, little girl? I'm just trying to get to know you better. Don't you like me? I could be a really good friend, if you'd let me."

The abuse continued for months, and Stacy panicked. Her husband lost his income during a seasonal layoff, and her family depended on her paycheck. The working conditions around Willie, however, became intolerable. After months of crude encounters, Stacy filed a grievance against Willie, in hopes the harassment stopped. After all, the prison plastered anti-bullying posters in every building. Surely, the powers-that-be would intervene.

"I don't want Willie fired, but I want to be able to work without being sexually harassed," Stacy told her superiors.

Word spread about Stacy's grievance, and it didn't take long for her to face a new form of harassment. Guards turned icy shoulders to her, and the group clearly ostracized her. Willie's status didn't change a bit, and he remained a part of the DOC fold. Now, however, instead of cozying up to Stacy, he glared at her all evening in the housing unit control bubble. Every interaction between Stacy and Willie hinted barely contained aggression from him.

Two weeks after she filed her grievance, Stacy was notified that action was taken. Assuming a reprimand for Willie was in order, she was stunned when, instead, she was reassigned to work in the hole. Willie remained in Housing Unit 5. His job secure, his world intact, he was bolstered by his victory over Stacy. Willie bragged to Matt Carter and his other coworkers, mocking her. He laughed, rejoicing at how her complaint backfired.

"She works in the hole now! The bitch got what was coming to her. Who does she think she is?"

No one in the carpool, or anywhere else in the prison, stood up for Stacy—too afraid that if they spoke up, they would become the next targets. The supervisors who placed Stacy in the dangerous working conditions of the hole certainly didn't support her.

Willie gloated, "Let's see how she likes being with all the perverts. Maybe one of them will rape the bitch and she'll see what sexual harassment is. She could have been with a real man. Now she can try her luck with the inmates."

Stacy transferred two months later to a position on the yard which placed her in the middle of crowds of inmates, often alone. Relieved because she no longer worked in the hole, the new assignment, however, was an uneasy post for her. Still shunned by other officers, Stacy feared no one would come to her aid should an inmate become aggressive toward her. She had every reason to worry. She wouldn't be the first employee on the outs with the system set up for an assault.

One Thursday afternoon, Offender Christopher Thompson stopped to talk with her while she stood in the prison yard on duty. He lived in Housing Unit 5 and knew her from her time spent there.

"What are you listening to?" Stacy pointed at Thompson's CD player.

"It's the new Jason Aldean album. Have you heard it? It's pretty good." He handed her one of the headphones.

Stacy held it up to her ear and for thirty seconds listened, keeping an eye on the inmates playing handball on the courts.

"Yeah, that is pretty good, Thompson. I think I'll have to stop at Walmart on the way home and get it."

He went on his way, and she thought nothing more of it. The movement window was about to open, and she focused on getting inmates off the ball courts and back to their housing unit.

A few days later, Stacy was fired and walked out of the prison, escorted by two of her former coworkers who snickered at her. The prison charged her with "over-familiarity with an inmate."

That inconsequential event with Thompson, a short thirty seconds of sharing a headphone, was the prison's excuse to fire Stacy McGraw. She was devastated. After enduring Willie Roseman's daily sexual harassment, prison officials fired her for something trivial in comparison. When the system looked for a reason to fire an employee, it didn't take much. When it wanted to protect an abuser, it was almost impossible to get the wheels of justice to turn.

Women weren't the only ones targeted by retaliation and harassment. Men who witnessed too much, who wrote up the wrong inmate, or who questioned corrupt behavior faced retribution. The system made examples of those who spoke up as a clear message to the rest of the staff: "Keep your mouths shut or the same thing will happen to you. Welcome to the good old boys' club of the Missouri Department of Corrections."

I know how Stacy feels, too. I feel trapped and desperate. This place strangles the life out of good people and rewards predators. Everyone sees it, but no one does anything. We are all too afraid to speak up because they will go after anyone who tries to do what is right.

Remaining silent in the face of criminal behavior rankled me to the core, but it was difficult to fight back with the constant threat of unemployment. I understood why good employees turned blind eyes and kept sealed lips. As the days, weeks, and months went by, though, I tried to push the problems out of my mind. I had a classroom to run.

Still, the fear was real.

MAKING MY CLASSROOM MINE

Classroom 10 ran smoothly, and a routine was established until Brandon Parks announced, "Ma'am, I want you to know I enjoy working here. You're a good teacher and I don't want you to be upset about this, but I'm going to change jobs. I can make an extra thirty dollars a month by working in the carpentry shop."

"Thanks for letting me know, and I can't blame you. If you can double your pay by going there, I think you should. When will your last day be?"

"Next Thursday I start. Does that work for you? I don't want to leave you shorthanded."

"That works for me. Don't worry about it. I'm glad you've gotten a better opportunity."

His departure left me short-handed, but I understood his need for more money. Arthur Smith wasn't exactly a ball of fire, but I could manage with one tutor for a while.

At least now I can finally hire someone I want.

Smith wasn't thrilled that he'd be the only tutor in Classroom 10. He didn't tolerate the younger students very well, and his attitude only worsened with the increased workload.

It didn't take a mind reader to know he wasn't happy. Before long, the situation deteriorated.

A group of young white supremacist gang members caused Smith the most trouble. The men sported lightning bolt tattoos on their necks—dead giveaways to their white power gang affiliation—and rejoiced in making Smith miserable. Smith was white, but older and set in his ways. Lewis, Kramer, and McCreary took pleasure in pushing his buttons. Antagonizing an "old head" was good fun to them.

Smith exacerbated the situation by angrily staring at the three burrs under his saddle. Lewis and McCreary were rural kids who aligned with the gang for protection, Kramer was worldlier than the others, but not by much. Thanks to their tattoos, the mark of prison would be on them forever.

The prison culture divided people up by race, age, and level of fear. Everyone had to be on a side, and most young inmates joined gangs, even if they didn't belong to one on the street.

The three didn't threaten Smith in class. Openly confronting my employee wouldn't fly with me, and the three gang members were smarter than that. Instead, they found a number of little things to get under his skin. Smith glared at them, which only encouraged them to stop what they were doing to stare back. To annoy him, they tapped on their table with pencils. They asked for help with assignments but made it clear his help was unwanted. Only my help would do. Like high school kids looking for ways to test a new or substitute teacher, those boys found delight in pestering Smith.

More than once, I pulled the three into the hallway to reason with them. "Guys, why do you insist on bugging him? I know you think it's good fun, but you're wasting time in class. Just leave Smith alone."

"Aww, Ma'am, we know you're right. He asks for it sometimes, though. If he stares at us, we stare back. But you're right. We'll leave him alone."

After a week or so, we'd have another conversation. Sometimes they came to class looking to irritate Smith, and sometimes he stirred up tensions. The cycle continued for months. If he ignored them, they wouldn't have had as much fun with him, but he didn't ignore them.

Later, I found out they did more than pester him. They pressed (pressured) Smith on the yard to steal school supplies for them. That didn't come to light until after he no longer worked for me. By then, Lewis, Kramer, and McCreary were out of my class too.

When Parks left, Barb told me a few months might pass before we hired replacement tutors. "I don't have time to set up interviews right now. A few more teachers will need tutors soon, and you can all hire at the same time"

I'm not in any hurry, but I'm eager for the interviews to begin. I'll finally have a say over who works in my room.

Inheriting Smith and Parks was like wearing someone else's shoes. Life settled back into a routine in my classroom, but outside my problems continued to build.

THE NOOSE OF HARASSMENT

"**R**ichard, I need you to do something about Barb and her ugly treatment of me."

"Just leave Barb alone," he'd say.

I wish it was that simple. She has her sights set on me and any chances of that changing are slim. I feel vulnerable, and Randy's six-month absence just extended another six months.

Barb behaved with impunity. She grew bolder, and no one had the guts to tell her to stop. Before a faculty meeting, Barb stared right at me, and in front of everyone said, "I'm a vindictive person. If someone crosses me, I make them pay." People squirmed. People looked away. People did nothing.

I had no support.

Richard Blake's silence condoned her ugliness, and it took a toll on me. I dreaded going to work. I suffered from headaches, my stomach turned, and I faced constant anxiety.

Stress should stem from working around rapists and killers, but I'm as worried about Barb as I am the inmates.

Life was hell, and each day seemed worse than the one before.

A few weeks after Barb's "vindictive" remarks, Kelly and I returned from lunch early and went into the staff workroom. We nibbled on snacks while we waited for the second half of second session to begin. Kelly sat across from me at one of the long, brown tables, and we passed the time with good-humored small talk.

Barb walked in and plunked down in a chair next to Kelly, who shot me a look of worry.

"You like to have fun, don't you?"

Kelly and I tried to ignore Barb's comment, aimed at me, and continued eating our snacks.

"Yeah, I bet your nights are pretty wild."

I chewed my food in silence while Kelly and I gave each other nervous glances.

"There's no telling what you do on the weekends."

Kelly and I stared at each other in disbelief.

"I bet you have all kinds of stories you could tell, dontcha, Caroline?"

Finally, I sarcastically replied, "Oh, yeah. I'm really wild."

Wild? I get up at four o'clock in the morning, so I can drive an hour and a half to a maximum-security men's prison. I work ten-hour days with killers and people like you, Barb. Then I drive an hour and a half home, feed my animals, grab the quickest thing I can to eat, and crawl into bed by seven-thirty so I can get up and do this all over again. Yeah, I'm really "wild."

Barb leaned toward Kelly, tapping her on the shoulder with the back of her hand. Loudly, she said, "Why don't you just buy her a dildo!"

The clock stopped ticking for a second or two as Kelly and I tried to wrap our minds around what just happened. We stared, horrified, at each other and then sprang to our feet and left the workroom as quickly as possible.

I pulled Richard Blake aside and relayed what transpired moments before. Surely, he'd do something now. Barb crossed a line even he couldn't excuse away.

"You know how Barb is. Just ignore it. She probably hasn't been taking her meds."

"Richard, I don't care if she's taken her medication or not. She can't make sexually harassing remarks to me. This is serious."

"You really don't want to make a big deal about this."

"Why not? I'm sick and tired of her going after me, and this has to stop, Richard."

"If you report her, nothing is going to happen to her. She has too many connections. You're the one who'll lose her job, not Barb."

"Aren't you going to talk to her? You're my supervisor and I'm reporting harassment to you."

"Me? No!" He drew back from me in disgust.

"You're the boss. You're supposed to stop this kind of thing."

"Listen, I'm not going to say anything to her, and you shouldn't either. I'm not going to have her make *my* life hell, and that's what will happen if I say anything to her. You need to let this drop—now."

I'm on my own and, if I try to protect myself, I'll be in more danger. When does the DOC stand up for employees who are victims of bad behavior? I endured death threats, and I now am harangued by Barb. Maybe I should file charges, but everyone says that will just make it worse. If the Department of Corrections didn't care when Reggie Ellison threatened my life, they won't care if someone says something mean to me. The department is loud and clear: I need to keep my mouth shut.

Even Mike and Kelly warned me, "Just stay away from Barb. She's not going to change and all you can hope for is that she finds someone else to go after. Maybe this will all die down if you just ride it out."

I need my job and am trapped in a no-win situation. That's the way Barb and the department want it.

A noose tightened around my neck, and it was harder and harder to face the days at the prison.

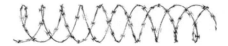

THUNDERCLOUDS

I f life at work was relentlessly miserable, conditions at home were no better. My emotions were jagged from a marriage that failed years before. The deterioration began on a hot summer day in 2009 when two catastrophic events set my life into a downward spiral. Two phone calls, within five minutes of one another, changed my life in ways I never imagined.

That morning I drove to Springfield to see my oldest son, Rick, who spent the weekend with my youngest, Kevin, in Tennessee attending a family wedding. Rick stayed the previous night at the condo Kevin rented in Branson before returning to Whiteman Air Force Base. Rick and I planned a fun day together, visiting and maybe watching a movie before he left the Ozarks.

I hadn't made it off my dirt road when my phone rang. Anna Marshall, a coworker from Mansfield High School, was on the other end. She cried so hard I couldn't even understand her at first. Finally, she calmed down enough that I made sense of what she said.

"It's just awful. Kristle Thomas was in a bad car accident."

"When?" My blood ran cold.

"Just a little bit ago. She's being airlifted to Springfield. I don't know if she's even still alive. Chuck Banks told me that he passed the wreck, and it was bad."

Kristle, the school counselor turned principal, was one of my closest friends. With a heart of gold and contagious laugh, she was beloved by the entire community.

"Anna, I'm headed to Springfield to see Rick already. I'll go to the hospital and I'll let you know as soon as I find out anything."

"I knew I needed to let you know right away."

Shell-shocked, I tried to process Anna's news. I called Rick.

"Honey, as soon as I get to Springfield, we have to go to the hospital. Kristle's been in a bad car accident and was air-lifted."

"Mom, this has to be the worst morning ever."

Something in his voice made me panic. "Rick, what do you mean?"

"I'll tell you when I see you. Right now, you just worry about driving up here safely."

"Rick, what's going on."

He paused. "Mom, I really don't want to get into it right now. Just drive up here and then we'll talk."

"If something's wrong, tell me."

We went back and forth, and then finally he said, "Mom, Kevin and Dylan were arrested this morning."

"Arrested? What for?"

"Distribution of drugs. It's not as bad as it sounds, Mom. Kevin didn't do it, but Dylan grew pot at the condo and he had a scale. When the cops raided at two this morning, they arrested Kevin because he lives there too."

"Dylan was growing weed in the condo?"

"Yeah, he had five plants he kept in his closet under a light. While Kevin and I were in Tennessee this weekend, Dylan got the bright idea of putting them out on the balcony to get sunlight. The neighbors must have called the cops. The cops found a scale, and they've arrested both of them for drug distribution. Mom, it's been the worst morning of my life."

Newly graduated from high school, Kevin had moved to Branson with Dylan, a friend I never approved of. Both worked summer jobs at Silver Dollar City, an Ozarks-themed amusement park. While I wasn't a fan of Dylan's, they paid their own bills and took their first steps into adulthood.

I didn't know Dylan has a drug problem. Kevin kept it a secret, knowing I'd never allow Dylan as a roommate. All these years I've spent raising Kevin to have a good life, and it's crumbling in front of me. He's going to end up in prison just like the guys in my classroom.

Rick and I met up at a strip mall parking lot on the east side of Springfield. Two broken and bewildered souls tried to wrap our hearts and minds around our new reality. Numb and hurting, we went to the hospital, where Kristle remained unconscious with fractured ribs, broken legs, a broken ankle, and a shattered pelvis. Her most serious injury, a bruise on the frontal lobe of her brain, occurred when her head struck a metal fencepost after she ejected from her truck. She wouldn't wake up nor respond to stimuli. We gave what support we could to her children before we left the hospital.

We knocked around Springfield like pinballs.

"Rick, I don't know what to do. Our hands are tied because today's Saturday and no attorney's offices are open."

He gave me a hug as I started to cry. "Mom call the jail and see if there's any way we can see Kevin."

143

I called information for the number to the Stone County Jail and dialed the number.

"There aren't any visits on the weekend. Monday night will be the first time you can see your son," replied the jailor when I called.

As the afternoon neared evening, Rick was forced to get on the road to Whiteman AFB. We parted ways as I faced a conversation at home with my husband that I didn't want to have.

His children, much older than mine, caused him a lot of grief over the years. Arrests, messy divorces, drug addictions, an unwed pregnancy, and homelessness—all challenges we faced with his son and daughter. My sons never caused us issues, and I hoped for support and understanding, but my gut told me to prepare for a blow-up.

Once home, however, instead of a blow-up, I met an icy silence. He didn't yell or scream. Instead, he said nothing. He acted as if nothing happened. My world collapsed, but he seemed oblivious to my pain.

I'm dying inside, and he won't hold me or tell me he loves me. I really need my husband.

Kevin tried calling me twice from jail that evening, but my phone service automatically rejected collect calls from correctional facilities, something I realized too late. As far as my son knew, Mom didn't want to talk to him.

What is he thinking and feeling? He's never been in trouble, and now he's in a dangerous jail cell thinking I've turned my back on him. I can't even breathe.

I laid in bed a broken woman. My heart ached for Kristle. My heart ached for Kevin. Immobilized by grief, into the darkness, I said, "I hurt so bad I can't even cry."

My husband stretched and said, "You know, I feel a little achy too. I wonder if I'm coming down with something."

I can't believe what I just heard.

"I'm talking about emotional pain." I turned to look at him

"Oh, yeah, that's what I meant too," he said unconvincingly as he rolled over to go to sleep.

I'm completely alone. I was afraid we'd fight, but this is worse.

In the days and weeks to come, he showed no concern or compassion for Kevin or me. Life went on for him.

"I don't want to hear about it," he'd say, when he said anything at all. "It's not my problem. What are we having for dinner?"

I'm an emotional wreck and he nonchalantly asks what's for dinner.

"He just doesn't have the emotional tools to deal with this," Rick told me as we talked over the phone.

"Rick, it's worse than that. He doesn't even have the drawers in his tool box where those tools should go."

Within two weeks, my husband stopped telling me he loved me. At the time, he worked out of town during the week, so most of our conversations occurred long distance.

"I love you."

"I'll talk to you later," he said.

When I need love and support the most, I'm given a cold shoulder.

No hugs. No kisses. No affection. When he did show an emotion, it was anger that was never directly aimed at Kevin's arrest. He threw fits about trivial things—a water bottle left on the patio; a pea-sized ding from months ago in the hood of the car. He refused to address the real problems our family faced.

Our relationship is one-sided, and I'm on my own to contend with my son's legal battle, my friend's injuries, and my own emotional pain.

His anger escalated. His mantra became "It's not my fucking problem! It's not my fucking fault! Stop fucking blaming me!"

No one ever said it's his fault, and no one is blaming him.

What hurt the most was that he didn't see it as his problem.

Don't we rally around each other in a crisis—a problem for one is a problem for all?

I stood by him through his daughter's unwed pregnancy. I oversaw his mother's medical care when she slipped into dementia. I never considered any struggle he faced as his problem and not mine. When tragedy struck from my side of the family, he vacillated between emotional deadness and rage.

Devastated on so many fronts, I stopped being "me." Depression hit hard. Rock bottom didn't have a bottom, and I slipped over the edge of a precipice. No matter what I did, I slowly dropped farther and farther into the abyss. I crashed into a depression so deep I couldn't pull myself out of it. Normally I was lighthearted and optimistic, but I couldn't find that version of me anymore.

I don't like who I've become, but I don't know how to stop my freefall.

I tried reaching out to him several times, begging him to please show that he loved and cared about me. On the Thursday before Thanksgiving, I called him a couple times after work, begging to hear the words "I love you, and this is going to be okay."

"Stop looking for a fight. I just want to know if the bills are paid. In this economy, we can't fall behind."

"I'm not trying to fight. I want to talk about fixing our relationship and our family."

"I'll talk to you later."

"We need to talk about this."

"It's this economy, money is what matters."

Why does everything come down to money with him?

"It's not the economy that we need to worry about. It's our family." Tears poured down my face.

"I'm worried about keeping a roof over our heads."

"It won't matter whether or not we own a house if we don't have a home anymore."

"It's not my fucking problem! It's not my fucking fault! Stop fucking blaming me!"

That night, I sat alone in agony, in the quiet darkness of our farmhouse. I stared at the .357 pistol sitting in my nightstand drawer.

I could just end it all now. All the pain would go away.

Suicide wasn't a plea for attention. It was a serious option. The only thing stopping me was fear.

What if I'm a quarter of an inch off and just injure myself? What if I end up like Kristle in a vegetative state, breathing but not out of my misery? I'd be stuck that way with no chance to finish the job.

At 3:06 in the morning, I called my husband to tell him what I almost did.

Broken and desperate, I made one last attempt to connect with him.

"Maybe you should talk to someone about that."

That's his only comment?

After that, he went on with his day, his week, and his month like I'd never said a word. As though baring my soul to him meant nothing more than if I'd said, "I think one of my tires is low on air."

If I'm going to get better, I have to help myself.

I sought counseling, but every office I called said I'd wait six to eight weeks for an appointment.

I'm not sure I have that long.

On January 19, I decided to do something drastic. I called into work and drove myself to Springfield where I checked into the emergency room at Mercy Hospital. By going that route, I fast tracked myself into counseling and care. In the past, I resisted medications, fearing they were a sign of weakness, but my options dwindled now.

I can either take anti-depressants and get therapy or follow through on my suicide. The pills are worth a try.

After my release from the hospital (which I shortened to a few hours so I could return to work the next day), I went to counseling every week for five months. My husband never asked if there was anything he could do, if he should go with me, or if I wanted to talk about what my counselor and I discussed during my weekly sessions.

I shattered into a million pieces.

I'm only going through the motions of life. The pills and counseling are aspirins for my pain, but I'm not whole. I can breathe again, but life isn't satisfying. I'm still completely alone.

Meanwhile, I kept working and the duties of farm life continued. Our livestock dog gave birth to a litter of puppies, and it was on my shoulders to advertise and sell them.

Arranging their transportation was also my responsibility.

At times, I had setbacks, and my birthday in 2010 was one of those days. A migraine, a failed effort to ship a puppy across the country (due to changes in airport policies), and the realization that I was another year older—yet more detached than ever from the ones I loved—drove me into depression once again.

Why is depression picking today to hit with a vengeance? It isn't worse than any other day I've had in months, but I am desperately low.

Returning unsuccessfully from the airport in tears with my migraine raging, I mumbled to my husband, who remained at home while I handled the dog business, "I've got a terrible migraine. I'm going to bed." I crawled under the covers hoping the world, or I, disappeared.

At some point, he came in the bedroom. "We'll figure out a way to ship the dog."

"I'm not upset about the dog. This has nothing to do with that." My head was splitting, and the depression was unbearable.

"I'm sure we can ship the dog sometime soon." He wouldn't shift gears. "I know you're upset about the dog, but we'll get the dog shipped."

"You don't understand. This isn't about the dog." Overwhelmed by the migraine, by the emotional pain, and by life itself, I didn't have the energy to repeat myself over and over again.

"We'll get the dog shipped. Don't worry about that."

"Stop about the dog. I don't care about the dog. I. Just. Want. To. Die."

"Well, I'd hate for you to do that. I wouldn't even know how to ship a dog."

Kevin's legal problems resolved after months of hearings and the draining of my retirement account.

Freedom isn't free, but it's worth every dime to know Kevin isn't going to prison.

Besides his proximity to the crime, there was no evidence of his involvement, and the court worked with us. His negative drug test saved him as well as my ability to hire a decent attorney.

If I left him to the mercy of the public defender system (and if I had kicked him out of the house like my husband said to do), he'd be in prison for years. I couldn't let that happen.

While not listed in his legal paperwork, the court encouraged Kevin to join the military. Before his arrest, Kevin planned to join the Air Force like his older brother. However, after his legal issues, the Air Force didn't want him. The Army did, though.

Have I worked this hard to keep him out of prison only to send him off to combat?

Kevin moved to Tennessee after the dust cleared to start anew. I understood.

He needs a fresh start and too many memories resonate here. I hate to see him go, but he can't stay here.

One more piece of my family—my world—drifted away from me as he left.

Rick was stationed only three hours away from me. Having him nearby kept my head on straight, and I drove to visit him every weekend possible. We leaned on each other through the ups and downs of those days. After I started working for the prison, I spent half my weekends with Rick until he transferred overseas to a base in the Netherlands.

At that point, my support was on the other side of the world.

Maybe my shattered emotions carried me through Reggie Ellison's death threats. I was so numb that his threats to kill me were nothing more than background noise.

In December of my first year at the prison, Kevin graduated from Army Infantry training at Fort Benning, Georgia. I saved up every bit of leave, so I was with him at the ceremony. Kevin's graduation gave me something to look forward to, and every day I checked another square off my calendar as December 14 drew nearer. For all the hell Kevin and I went through, his graduation was tangible proof that his life moved forward. Mine, however, was on autopilot.

My life remained one monotonous rerun. I went to work, endured whatever happened during the day, went home and endured whatever happened there. I slept in the extra bedroom, and I awoke the next morning before daylight to begin the cycle over again.

After the heartbreak of a failed marriage, I resolved to never let anyone else hurt me. My children mattered to me, but they were far away, living their own lives.

I'm alone. Maybe I'm supposed to be.

Then, one day, the clouds began to clear. My eyes, still so shaded by the pain of the preceding few years, didn't recognize the glimmer of sunlight at first. Somewhere, however, deep in my heart, I knew maybe there was hope after all.

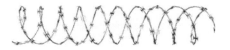

LIGHTNING BOLTS

After Phil Greene and Shannon Rafferty left the prison, the school kept porters on short leashes.

It's easier to run copies myself than to rely on Barb's employee. Avoiding her while I run copies is my main goal.

Some teachers let their tutors run photocopies, but I didn't like that idea. I ran my own copies for my employees' protection. Copy machines were famous for getting inmates in trouble. Whether to earn extra money, to pay a debt, or because they were pressed to break the rules, some tutors ran copies they shouldn't. Pornographic photographs, gambling sheets, and other contraband were worth money on the camp, so the temptation was real. If caught copying contraband, a worker not only lost his job but was written up and sent to the hole.

If my tutors don't have access to the photocopier, no one can accuse them of doing something they shouldn't on it. In public school, I ran my own copies, so it's not a big deal.

One afternoon in late January or early February, I stood at the copy machine mindlessly chitchatting with people as they passed by. I was tired and not in the best mood. I simply wanted to finish my copies and ride out the last few hours of the humdrum workday.

Standing in the doorway of the library, located directly across the hall from the office area of the education wing, was a man. Our eyes met, and the feeling was intense. I didn't even notice his face—his eyes captivated me. I stared into them and saw his soul. In that moment, he and I made a connection unlike any I'd ever experienced. A lightning bolt coursed through me.

I broke my gaze with him but was drawn to look at him once again. The lightning bolt returned. I shook myself loose one more time. He ducked into the library and was gone.

What if I just saw the man I'm supposed to spend the rest of my life with?

As certain as the lightning bolt, a voice within me repeated the question. I freaked out.

No way! You're going crazy, Caroline. You're in a maximum security prison. This is not happening!

The voice returned, more insistent this time.

What if I just saw the man I'm supposed to spend the rest of my life with?

I wasn't giving in to the voice.

You're too tired, too stressed out, or something, but you are in a maximum-security prison. You must be nuts because you're not going to spend your life with a man in prison. No! No! No!

I was unaware at the time, but the French have a phrase, "*coup de foudre*," meaning "love at first sight." It literally translates as "lightning bolt."

Standing at the copy machine, I refused to acknowledge what happened. Life had damaged me to the point that I was hardened to letting anyone near me.

What is this nonsense about a man I've never met before? He isn't even a man on the street. He's an inmate. Who knows what he's in prison for? He could be a rapist or a cold-blooded killer, and here I am committing myself to him for life.

I willed myself to ignore what happened at the copier. I forced it out of my mind, chalked it up to stress—and possible temporary insanity—and left it at that.

A few months later, Barb finally arranged a day for the four teachers without tutors (Kelly Rainer, Doris McGeehon, Melanie Foster, and me) to interview prospective candidates. Parks had been out of my room for a while, and I had scraped by with Arthur Smith long enough.

By this point it's getting ridiculous. He doesn't like to work, and I'm tired of constantly prodding him to get the job done.

A dozen men applied for these four jobs, and the school devoted an entire afternoon to finding new employees. I made my way through five or six interviews and hadn't found anyone who impressed me.

I looked at the name that was next on my list and stepped into the hall where a row of men sat in chairs along the wall. One, a handsome blond, caught my attention. Without taking my eyes off him, I asked, "Are you Mr. Giammanco?"

He smiled, and his vibrant blue eyes lit up as he stood to greet me at the door. As our eyes met, a recognition, a familiarity between the two of us, instantly formed and my heart swelled.

Turning to walk into my classroom, my mind spun. *Wow! There is something so familiar about this man. How do I know him?*

I sat behind my desk as Keith Giammanco took a seat across from me. We began with the normal questions.

"What's your educational background?"

"I graduated from high school in the St. Louis area. I admit that I was more into sports than I was academics during high school, but I did get a good education."

"What sports did you play?"

"Hockey."

Okay, there's some points for him already.

"You certainly are well-spoken. What are your strengths and weaknesses when it comes to classwork?"

"I'm interested in history, science, and literature. When I was in school, I didn't read much at all. I hate to admit it, but I didn't read very much as an adult until after I was arrested. Now I read a lot. I'm not as strong at math as I should be, but I'm a fast learner."

"Why do you want to be a tutor, and what are your plans for the future?"

"I'd like to help other inmates gain the skills they missed when they were in school. Many of them don't have what it takes to be successful on the outside, and I'd like to help in any way I can. I'm taking a college business module through Missouri State University right now, and I want the guys in here to make something of themselves after prison. When I get out, I want to get a job and then get back into trading stocks like I did before I went to prison."

As we talked, I wondered what this articulate, middle-class man did to end up in prison. Employees weren't allowed to ask what crimes inmates committed, and relief flooded through me when he volunteered the information on his own.

"I'm here because I robbed banks using notes. It was a mistake, and I regret it, but at the time I was trying to keep up the lifestyle my daughters and I had before the recession hit. We were going to lose our house, and I couldn't find a job. You know how it was back then. You couldn't buy a decent job, especially not one that would pay the mortgage and the girls' school tuition. If I could go back and change it, I would, but I can't, so I'm trying to do as much as I can to be productive while I am here."

A nonviolent bank robber? Whew! He isn't a child molester, a rapist, or an axe murderer.

As we talked, I learned he was a single father to twin daughters, a stock options trader by profession, who fell on hard times when the market crashed. I didn't have to ask him why he robbed banks. I'd never consider such a reckless move, but I related to the overwhelming stress of trying to raise children when money goes away. I'd gone through my own difficult times and understood his plight.

"Not many guys will admit what they're in here for. Thanks for confiding in me."

"I believe, should you choose to hire me, that you have a right to know who you would spend ten hours a day with in your classroom."

That's an incredibly noble thing to say.

Our conversation covered several topics: travel, the requirements of the job, and prison in general. We talked and laughed. He was different from any other inmate— or even staff member—that I had met at SCCC.

He was bright, interesting, and he engaged in an intellectual conversation.

"You're going to be just fine when you get out of prison."

"Thank you. Yes, I am. I know what I have to do to have a decent life when I'm released, and I've learned my lesson about breaking the law."

Melanie Foster popped her head in my door and tapped on her wrist. "Are you about to wrap this up?"

Who interrupts an interview?

Looking at Keith Giammanco, I could tell the same thought crossed his mind.

"Why?"

"It's already been an hour and you have other men waiting out here for their interviews."

Both of us looked at the clock, surprised to see the time since it felt like only ten or fifteen minutes had passed.

How did an hour go by so quickly?

"I'll be done in a few minutes." I said, crestfallen that our conversation was forced to end. I turned my attention back to Keith Giammanco. "How many more interviews do you have?"

"One more. It's with Mrs. McGeehon."

"How about you throw that interview? I really want to hire you."

"I'd like to, but I can't do that. It wouldn't be ethical."

Damn, what a respectable answer.

We bid each other goodbye as I walked him to the hallway. Shaking hands, we parted ways. I paused in my doorway.

Something monumental just happened. This thoughtful and intelligent man just entered my world.

I spent the rest of the afternoon going through the motions of interviewing other candidates. None of them compared to the bright, articulate man I met earlier that afternoon. After work, I compared notes with Kelly, Melanie, and Doris about their interviews. Keith Giammanco was my only choice for a tutor.

"What about you, Doris?"

"Oh, I don't want to hire him. He couldn't even pass the simple math quiz I gave."

Maybe he threw his last interview after all!

The news wasn't so good from Kelly and Melanie. They both placed him as their top pick. After I found that out, I approached Richard Blake.

"How did your interviews go today?"

"They went well, Richard. In fact, I know who I want to hire."

"Great. Who is it?"

"Giammanco."

"Sorry. That's not going to happen. I already talked to Melanie and Kelly, and they put him as their first choice too. I'm going by seniority, and you've only been here a year. You can choose from the people they don't want."

"Richard, you know I've gotten by with Parks and Smith while Kelly has Josephson and Melanie has Akers. Both of those are great tutors. I've been stuck with the laziest tutors in the school. Now I only have Smith. Can't I have a decent one?"

"I'm going by seniority, and I'm not changing my mind."

Great. I finally find a tutor I want, and there's no way I'm going to get to hire him.

As I went down the hallway, my face revealed my disappointment.

"What's wrong?" Kelly asked as she walked to meet me.

I filled her in on my conversation with Blake. She shook her head in exasperation.

"Hey, if you want to hire him that bad, I'll pass on him, so you can have him."

"Really? You'd do that?"

"Yes, really."

Melanie still wanted Giammanco as her tutor, though, which irritated me.

She's retiring soon. Why should she care who she hires at this point?

I felt a sting of resentment. Her tutor, Akers, was a staple in the education wing. For my first year there, I'd bitten my lip and endured with Parks and Smith. Fate, however, was on my side, and ironically Barb Mason played a major role. The next morning, Barb called me into her office.

"Smith wants to quit, but he doesn't want to leave you without a tutor. I mean, he wanted to quit yesterday. Have you figured out who you want to hire?"

"I know who I want, but Melanie wants him too. I don't even know who my second choice would be at this point."

"Who's your first choice?"

"Giammanco."

"I'll see what I can do."

"Thanks a lot, Barb!"

Barb had known Smith for years and was determined to help him leave quickly. I waited to see who won the battle of wills: Barb or Blake.

Within an hour, Keith Giammanco entered Classroom 10. I shook his hand and we exchanged big smiles. He sat at the empty desk Parks left behind.

He doesn't know how close we came to missing this opportunity.

Within fifteen minutes of my new hire's arrival, Smith, whose desk was next to mine, turned and said, "Ma'am, it's been great working with you, but my days in education are over. I quit."

I thanked him for his time in my classroom, and he walked out my door. Without hesitation, Keith vacated his desk and moved into Smith's. Arranging his pen, papers, and reading glasses on the desktop, he looked me in the eye and grinned.

"Welcome to my classroom, Mr. Giammanco."

My world just became a little brighter.

The prison, however, reminded us that no one should be too content. Shannon Rafferty's scandalous departure from the South Central Correctional Center left its mark on the institution. Given the hoopla spawned by Shannon and Offender Greene, the wardens at SCCC were edgy about staff-inmate relations.

They didn't like answering difficult questions from their superiors in Jefferson City and, as the saying goes, "shit rolls downhill." Nothing made that clearer than the meetings the administration ordered staff and tutors to attend that day.

The wardens rarely appeared in the education wing, so today was a special occasion. Every warden attended, and they called the teachers into the testing room at lunch for our lecture. Head warden, Kyle McMasters, who referred to himself as our "father figure," gravely warned us about the dangers of staff-inmate friendliness. We sat, biting our lips at the ridiculousness of their "concern."

The teachers knew Shannon never cared for Greene and that her involvement with him was purely attention-seeking.

Greene's only reward for his rendezvous with her was

a speedy transfer to one of the worst prison camps in the state. Shannon continued as the live-in girlfriend of Terry Richards which shocked everyone at SCCC.

After her shenanigans with Greene, we expected Richards to hastily toss her aside. However, he had a difficult time finding a girlfriend in the first place. Most likely he wasn't going to get rid of his only real prospect.

We sat in the testing room while the wardens warned us of the dangers of treating our employees as anything more than cardboard boxes—they were tools to utilize, but they weren't people.

Under the guise of "safety and security," they ordered us not to discuss anything even vaguely personal with inmates. Staff members routinely talked to their tutors (and even their classes) about their children, their grand-children, their farms, their home improvement projects, or their new cars. Teachers weren't alone. Custody officers often shot the breeze with inmates, sharing hunting stories and discussing sports.

Everyone in that room, including the wardens themselves, were in the habit of socializing with inmates. Among the five SCCC wardens present was Tom Starkey.

What a hypocrite Tom is! He's told me himself, "Some of these guys are friends of mine. I've known them for thirty years." So, you are going to tell us we can't even mention that we live on a farm, but it's perfectly okay for you to call inmates "friends"?

Stopping teachers from being cordial with their employees wasn't likely. Richard Blake and his tutor were especially close, and Doris McGeehon referred to her relationship with her tutor as that of "an old married couple." Barb Mason and a tutor from her hometown frequently swapped stories about people they knew.

161

It's unrealistic to work around other people—and that's what inmates are—without developing bonds.

The wardens were in our school for one reason: Shannon Rafferty embarrassed them. Safety and security had nothing to do with the lecture they doled out. The girlfriend of a lieutenant was marched out of the compound, splattering egg on the faces of the wardens, Richard Blake, and Barbara Mason.

The wardens are more worried about another scandal developing under their watch than they are about our safety. I hate to tell you, but plenty of scandalous behavior happens here that you ignore. How about the bullying, sexual harassment, and retaliation that happens every single day on this camp?

The faculty sat patiently and waited for the spiel to end. Then we went about our day. After lunch, the administrators summoned the tutors into the library for their own pow-wow with the wardens. Their meeting lasted nearly an hour.

I'm eager to compare notes with Keith when he returns.

"So, what did the wardens have to say in your meeting with them?"

"Oh, you know, the same old 'don't ask about their children, know their first names, or listen to them talk about their farm animals' line of bull."

"Sounds like we all got the same talk."

"Tutors wanted to know what constituted 'familiarity.'"

"What did the wardens say?"

"They didn't have a clear answer, so I said, 'Basically, you're using Supreme Court Chief Justice Rehnquist's definition of pornography: Don't ask you to verbally define it, but you'll know it when you see it.'"

"And?"

"Assistant Warden Starkey said that's exactly what he's talking about." Keith paused. "I can tell you one thing."

"What's that?"

"Nobody is going to tell me who my friends are."

Keith and I are already a team, and both of us need an ally in here.

WHO IS THIS MAN?

During our interview, Keith told me he robbed banks in the St. Louis area using notes. Other than my relief in finding out he wasn't a sexual predator or axe murderer, I didn't think much of it. A few weeks after he came to work in my classroom, though, I overheard a conversation that caught my attention.

"Come on, man. We all know who you are. Just admit it." A young student hovered around Keith's desk.

"No, I'm not. Now, just take your work back to your table."

My nerves were on edge as I watched the conversation go back and forth for a minute or two.

The last thing either of us need is a confrontation with a student. I don't know what this is about, but that kid needs to sit down. It's best if I let Keith handle it, though, so that he doesn't lose face in front of the other inmates.

Finally, Keith said, "Look, I'm way too high profile to lie about what I'm in here for. Have your family Google me. Go sit down and do your work."

The student walked away muttering.

I couldn't contain my curiosity. "What was that about?"

Keith rolled his eyes. "Oh, the kid thinks I'm a chomo (child molester)."

"Why on earth would he think that?"

He doesn't strike me as a pedophile at all. Where is that kid getting this?

"I get it a lot. I fit the profile."

"What profile?"

"I'm a middle-aged white man with no previous criminal record. Look around. Who are they?"

I scanned my classroom.

The child molesters are white, middle-aged men who look more like the guys down the street than hardened thugs.

"You're right. I hadn't thought of that before."

"It's something I have to deal with from time to time."

"So, are you really high profile?"

Keith let out a sigh. "Well, I was on the front page of, USA Today, and I was on, Good Morning America."

Suddenly, everything clicked into place. News stories during his year-long bank robbery spree flooded back to me. The single father of twin daughters, the middle-class stock trader who fell on hard times during the Great Recession, was my tutor.

"Oh my God! You're the Boonie Hat Bandit!"

A hint of embarrassment swept Keith's face. "Yeah, I am."

So much made sense now. Even the media hadn't vilified the desperate father who panicked while trying to provide for his daughters. No wonder Keith didn't seem like the "typical" inmate. He wasn't.

"Now that you know who I am, feel free to look me up on the internet. It's all out there. Read the news articles and you can ask me anything you want to if you have any questions."

"I'll do that."

The last session of class ended, and I headed home for the evening. As soon as I walked through my doorway, I went straight to the computer. I found scores of articles about Keith and his crimes, and only one negative stuck out. A former neighbor called Keith "odd" because he worked from home and frequently used his cell phone while working around his house.

If that's the worst thing anyone can come up with, considering he robbed twelve banks, that says a lot about this man.

The articles about Keith's twin daughters, Elise and Marissa, were the hardest to read. The pain and struggles they endured when their one functioning parent went to prison were nothing short of excruciating. Seniors at the time of their dad's arrest, the girls took different paths after graduation. Elise moved to Wisconsin for college, but Marissa developed a heroin addiction after she reconnected with her mother. My heart broke for Marissa and for the pain the family faced.

The next morning, Keith looked at me expectantly. "Did you look my case up?"

"Yes, I did."

"Do you have any questions?"

"One."

Keith subconsciously gripped the arms of his chair.

"How is Marissa doing?"

Keith's face flooded with emotion. Instead of judgmental questions about the crimes, or nosy questions about what he used the money for, I cared about his daughter.

"Thank you for asking about her. She still struggles. Marissa is such a wonderful, beautiful girl. It kills me that she's on heroin. Every day I worry that the caseworker will call me back to tell me my little girl is dead. I carry that worry every day and night."

"It must wear on you. I'll keep her in my prayers."

"Most people want to know about the crimes, but you went straight to the heart of what is going on here: the pain my daughters are going through because of my mistakes."

"Our kids are the centers of our universe. I couldn't help but be moved by what I read last night."

"Do you have any other questions?"

"No."

"You aren't going to ask why I robbed banks?"

"I don't need to. I get it. It's not something I'd do, but I understand what it's like to raise kids on my own. When there's no money and they look to us to make their world right, it's a lot to deal with. I understand."

"I appreciate that. You don't know how much it means."

"I know what it's like to have your world fall apart."

A student approached my desk needing help, so our conversation ended as another busy day began. We didn't ask each other about our personal relationships, but an unspoken bond developed between us.

I don't care in what capacity it is, but this man makes my universe brighter and I'm glad I know him.

My ACL Meets the DOC

Smith's departure on Keith's first day of work left me, once again, with only one tutor in my classroom. This time, however, Barb decided to speed the hiring process along. Within a few weeks, I interviewed several men who applied. I showed Keith the list of a few top candidates to get his input.

Keith knew these men, and I trusted his judgment. He lived with them, saw them on the walk, and heard how they spoke and behaved when they weren't trying to impress a staff member. Anyone can fake his way through an interview. Hiring someone who Keith got along with was important, too. Why bring unnecessary strife into Classroom 10?

After looking through the list of candidates, Keith suggested Joe Bryson. Barb campaigned for his hire too. During an interview with a different candidate, she barged in and introduced me to Joe. She made such a fuss over him that the man I interviewed, rightly, filed a complaint against her later.

Bryson and Keith were classmates in the college business module offered through Missouri State University. Barb, who included the college program as one of her many duties, knew him well.

He is by far the best choice because he is polite, industrious, and someone we will both enjoy working around.

Just as Joe Bryson began work, however, a twist of fate blindsided me.

I've always had a knack for hurting myself doing the simplest tasks. Once I dislocated my jaw playing Frisbee. Over the years, I've had more quirky injuries than I can count. On April 17, my klutzy nature caught up to me again.

Between second and third sessions there was a ten- minute break. It was long enough to run to the bathroom or to make a quick trip to another building on the prison grounds.

Preston Hubbard popped his head in my classroom doorway. "Hey, I'm going to get something to drink from medical. Do you want one?"

"Nah, I'm okay, but thanks."

I'm dying for some caffeine, though, and a Coke sounds perfect.

A lack of ready cash was my problem. Then I remembered the spare dollar tucked into my body alarm case.

Yes! I can get a soda after all!

Preston had already left the wing and was on his way down the walk when I ran to catch up to him. I handed him the dollar.

"Get me a Coke. If they're out of that, a Dr. Pepper will do."

I walked back to the education wing. As I reached for the door, a noise caught my attention.

Boing, boing, boing.

A blue handball sailed over the thirty-foot fence, bounding a few feet away from me. The inmate recreational ball courts sat directly across from the education wing door, separated by thirty-foot chain link fence and razor wire.

"Hey, Ma'am, can you throw our ball back to us?"

"Sure."

I grew up playing baseball with my older brother. Looking at the height and angle of the fence, clearly, I had to throw it just right to avoid the awning that extended over the sidewalk.

I've thrown thousands of pop flies. Piece of cake.

My first throw fell short and dropped back at my feet.

Just a little more juice on this throw and it should go over.

My second throw barely missed going over. By now, several men had stopped to watch.

I'd better throw a little harder this time.

On my third heave, the ball sailed over the top of the fence and into the waiting hands of the man standing across from me on the handball court. As I threw the ball, something else happened, too.

Snap!

My foot landed in the groove separating the concrete panels of the sidewalk. Something akin to a cracking wishbone broke loose in my right knee. I stood, one-legged and in agonizing pain as inmates stopped and stared. None of them laughed.

Damn. I can't believe how much this hurts! How did I hurt my knee throwing a ball?

I balanced, wobbling precariously back and forth. I couldn't put weight on my right leg, but I wasn't going to fall in front of all those people. I willed myself to teeter on my left leg as pain overwhelmed me.

An inmate stepped towards me, tentatively. "Ma'am are you okay?"

Then I noticed all the inmates on the walk. They held their hands in the air, as though they were under arrest. They didn't dare touch me; not because I'd be mad and not because they would try to hurt me. Policy banned physical contact between inmates and staff, regardless of the circumstances. They'd be written up for assault on staff according to prison policy.

I'm stranded out here in the middle of the sidewalk and no one, even though they want to, can help me get back inside.

"You know, I don't think I am okay," I responded through clenched teeth. "Could someone please go inside the education wing and get me some help?"

"I'll go get a guard now, Ma'am!"

I'm so grateful for that young man.

His simple gesture was more complicated—and risky— than it sounded because he jeopardized himself for my sake. The prison considered him "out of bounds" once he entered the education door.

He wasn't a student and technically had no business walking into the wing. Inmates who went unauthorized places faced write-ups and disciplinary action. At that moment, when I needed help, a man who didn't know me risked himself to make sure I was okay.

A moment later, the Good Samaritan and Officer Presley came through the door, making a beeline for me. Using Presley's shoulder as a crutch, I hobbled into education.

I was like the kid who wrecked his bike in front of the whole neighborhood. I desperately tried to shake off the pain as though it wasn't all that bad.

It's just a sprain. Walk it off.

After about fifteen minutes of standing at the office area counter, I gimped my way down the hall to Classroom 10.

171

My students waited for me, and Keith recognized something was wrong by the pain in my face.

"Are you, all right? What happened?"

"I'm okay. I just did something stupid to my knee out there on the walk. I feel like an idiot. Everyone was staring at me."

"Don't worry about what other people think. Tell me what happened?"

I gave Keith the details and then sat for twenty minutes willing myself to be okay. The pain radiated from my leg and wouldn't let me fool myself. Finally, I gave into the pain.

Maybe I need an aspirin. Yes, an aspirin will make this all better.

"I'll be back in a few minutes. I'm headed for Barb's office to see if she has any pain relievers in her desk."

Keith looked at me with a twinkle in his eye. "Be careful. Don't hurt yourself."

I laughed out loud as pain shot from my knee to my toes and then up to my hip.

I hobbled through Barb's doorway. "Hey, do you have any aspirin I could take?"

"Sure. Do you have a headache?"

"No, it's my knee."

"Your knee? What's wrong with it?"

Mortified, I retold my mishap as Barb's eyes widened.

"I need to call the safety officer and you need to fill out an accident report."

"Really? I just twisted my knee. It's no big deal."

Barb broke into a flurry of activity. An hour, a visit with the safety officer, and several phone calls by Barb later, I was given orders.

The safety officer told me, "You can either go to the Work Comp emergency room in Salem, or you can seek medical care on your own."

I don't want to drive an hour to Salem. That's the opposite direction from home. Really, all I want to do is go to bed and try to sleep away this pain.

The ache overwhelmed me, and since Mike wasn't at work that day, driving home meant driving myself with a bad right leg.

"I'll just go home and see if it's better by the time I get there. If it's not, I'll go to the emergency room in Springfield. I don't want to add two more hours of driving to my day by going to Salem."

Both Barb and Richard Blake strongly suggested that I go home early. By now, sick with pain, I didn't argue. I limped down the hall to tell Kelly and then stopped by Classroom 10 to tell Keith I was leaving.

"I'll pray you get relief and that you feel better by tomorrow."

"Thank you. I don't think it's anything serious, but it does hurt. I'll see you tomorrow."

I gritted my teeth as Richard Blake escorted me out of the prison. As I drove home, a trip to the emergency room in Springfield seemed like a good idea. This "sprain" worsened.

Why did it have to be my driving leg? This hurts like hell.

Instead of turning off Highway 60 to go to my farm, I continued westward to Mercy Hospital in Springfield. I dreaded the additional time in the car, but my knee wasn't getting any better on its own.

I need to go to work tomorrow, so I'd better get whatever this is fixed now.

Once at the hospital, I waited an hour for a nurse to see me. Finally, a radiology tech took me back for x-rays, and another half hour passed while I waited for results. The night dragged on, I was tired, and throbbing pain consumed me.

Finally, the doctor entered my room with x-rays in hand.

"You don't have any broken bones."

"I know I don't have any broken bones. I didn't fall or hit my knee, and it doesn't feel like a bone issue. Something inside snapped. Can you tell me what did happen to it?"

"I'm sorry, but since this is a Worker's Compensation injury, you have to see a Work Comp doctor. I can't do anything for you. I'm not allowed to tell you any more than that you don't have any broken bones."

"You can't tell me anything?"

"No. I'm discharging you."

Nifty.

I drove home, discouraged, and dragged myself into bed after midnight.

There's no reason to miss work. Nothing is really wrong with my knee. It's just a sprain.

I double-checked my alarm and fell asleep. When the singsong tones of my phone went off at four o'clock, I wasn't ready for a day at the prison.

My leg feels like it's on the wrong end of a flamethrower. I'm not going to miss any days right now, though. I need to see Kevin before he deploys to Afghanistan.

Once at SCCC, the first half hour seemed uneventful. Barb asked what the doctor said, then I filled Kelly and Keith in on the useless trip to the hospital.

Suddenly, Barb screamed down the hallway. "Caroline, Get out of the prison! Right now! The wardens called, and you have to go! Get out of here!"

Barb barked orders like a drill sergeant addressing a new recruit. Everyone in the education wing stopped in their tracks. I moved as quickly as possible, but she wouldn't stop yelling.

"I talked to the wardens and they said it's against DOC policy for you to be here. You haven't seen a Work Comp doctor. Get out!"

"Barb, if I'd known that, I wouldn't have gotten up at four to drive all the way to the prison. I went to the emergency room last night. Isn't that good enough? You know I'm trying to save up my leave to see Kevin. I don't want to miss a day of work."

"No, the emergency room isn't good enough! You have to see a Work Comp doctor and you can't set foot inside the prison until you do. Get out of here. Right now!"

Less than an hour after I arrived at work, I drove myself the hour and a half back to Mansfield. Along the way, I played phone tag with doctors' offices who took Work Comp patients, hoping to find one who had an open appointment that day.

After several calls and a lot of frustration, I made an appointment for late in the afternoon with Dr. Fenster in Seymour. I arrived home, and the pain and lack of sleep caught up with me, so I slept until it was time to leave.

I wasn't familiar with Seymour, but my car's GPS system directed me as I wound my way through the side streets to the Seymour Medical Clinic. Dr. Fenster examined my knee, checked for mobility, and asked exactly what happened and where it hurt the most.

"My best guess, without having access to an MRI or CT Scan, is that you've torn your meniscus. If that's what it is, the surgery is pretty easy."

"How much time would I have to miss at work?"

"Not much at all. Recovery time is quick with a meniscus surgery. The biggest hurdle is going to be getting through the Work Comp red tape to have your MRI done. Until you get one, just try to rest your knee as much as possible."

"Can I return to work?"

"Yes, I'll write you a doctor's note. We won't know anything for certain until we get the test results back. I'll have my nurse set an appointment up in Springfield. Once you have the MRI, it'll take another week to ten days for me to get the results. We'll let you know as soon as we can get one scheduled for you."

When I returned to prison the next day, everyone wanted to know what the doctor said, but I didn't have much news for them. I repeated what Dr. Fenster told me, over and over, as I faced the same questions from everyone.

"That's painful, but easily fixed," Doris said. "Make sure you use the elevator at the administration building."

I'm not going to use the elevator.

The prison reserved an elevator for those physically injured and unable to use the stairs. A stigma was attached to the elevator, though. People assumed that anyone using it faked injury to get a disability claim. Some employees did work the system to get payouts or early retirements.

Being lumped in with scammers is mortifying. No way am I using that elevator!

Doris McGeehon was, in most people's opinions, an employee who tried to milk the disability cow. Some days, she used a walker on wheels that doubled as a chair.

When she thinks no one is looking, she walks just fine.

Her behavior ruffled feathers.

Kelly confided one day, "My friend, Donna, who used to teach here, saw Doris at Silver Dollar City last weekend. She said Doris was walking up those steep hills with no problem. She didn't have that walker with her either!"

It wasn't uncommon for employees working in the bubble to "forget" to open the exit doors for Doris. Sometimes they stranded her for half an hour or more.

Even though it hurt like hell, I climbed every one of those stairs.

After all, there's nothing wrong with my knee. It's sprained or has a minor tear in the meniscus.

It took two and a half weeks to get the MRI approved and scheduled. In the meantime, I went to work every day, limping like Igor from Frankenstein. I wasn't going to miss work, no matter what. Every leave day was precious. I wouldn't allow a little pain to interfere with my trip to see Kevin.

On the day of the MRI, I held my breath—literally. I'm claustrophobic and being stuck inside a tube for forty-five minutes was nerve-racking. The technician sensed my anxiety.

"Try to relax as much as possible. If you move, we may have to do the MRI all over again."

Exhausted from working through the pain, I let the hum of the machine and the dim lights lull me. I didn't quite fall asleep, but I did relax. Time passed quickly as I shut out the stress and pain while I remained motionless.

The waiting game for results began. I continued teaching— and climbing the stairs—while I fought through the pain to save my vacation days. One Wednesday afternoon, a week and a half after my MRI, I sat in my car after returning from lunch. Just as I opened my door to get out, my phone rang.

"Hello, Caroline, this is Dr. Fenster. I've received the results of your MRI."

"Oh good, how did it look? Is it my meniscus?"

He paused. "No, it's not your meniscus. According to the MRI results, you have torn your Anterior Cruciate Ligament. The Anterior Cru—"

My heart went cold. "That's my ACL," I said in disbelief.

Dr. Fenster paused. "Yes, that's your ACL. I'm sorry. When I examined your knee, you didn't seem like you were in enough pain for it to be your ACL. I don't know how you're walking around on it, but your entire ACL is gone. It's not even torn. It's just gone."

"Does this mean I have to have surgery?"

"I'm afraid it does, and it's not a minor surgery like the meniscus. The ACL is more complex. NFL players get this sort of injury. You need to plan for a few months off work and for several months of therapy afterwards."

"Thanks for letting me know, Dr. Fenster. I don't even know what to say."

"Get the surgery you need. You won't ever walk normally without it. Let me know if I can do anything else. My nurse is already working on getting an appointment for you with an orthopedic surgeon. We'll let you know when we have that set up."

This can't be happening.

I hadn't cried when I hurt my knee. I hadn't cried when pain shot through my leg day after day and week after week. When my trip to see Kevin went up in smoke because of a major knee surgery, I cried. My heart broke. I cried in my car.

I cried in my classroom. I cried at home. The injury ruined my chance to see my son, possibly for the last time.

Weeks went by, and I continued to work every day except for the pre-surgery consultation with the orthopedic surgeon, Dr. Webber, who agreed with Dr. Fenster. "If you want to walk normally, skipping the surgery isn't an option," he said. Put in those terms, I didn't have a choice. Work Comp set the surgery for May 23.

Already stressed, the reaction I received from the DOC was insult to injury. "I'm telling you right now, Work Comp won't cover this surgery," Barb snipped.

Richard Blake chimed in. "I've researched it, and your injury doesn't qualify for Work Comp coverage. They won't pay for the surgery or the lost pay if you choose to take time off."

Day after day they made their nasty remarks.

Are they right? If they are, I can't afford surgery or the time off work. Will I be permanently crippled?

A few weeks later, a letter I received from the state Worker's Compensation office proved Barb and Blake wrong. In writing, and then over the phone, the Work Comp representative assured me that my injury and recovery were covered. Even so, after I told Richard and Barb what Work Comp said, their naysaying continued.

Do they enjoy raising my stress level?

I decided to take the day before surgery off as a day of rest.

All my leave is going to be used anyway, so there's no sense not using the time I have.

Many people told me ACL replacement was a doozy. Since I'd never had surgery before, my anxiety mounted. The antagonism I faced at work didn't help.

On May 21, the head of personnel, Sheila Stokes, called me during work. "I understand you have requested six weeks off work for surgery, starting tomorrow. Is that correct?"

"Yeah, my surgery is on Wednesday."

She hesitated. "I don't know how to explain this, but Jefferson City has denied your leave request."

"How can they do that? This isn't elective plastic surgery. This is a Work Comp injury that's already been approved by the state. If I don't have the surgery, Work Comp might say I didn't follow through on my end and then they won't cover my injury at all."

"You're probably right," Sheila said, sounding worried about the ramifications.

"Why is this happening? I put my leave request in weeks ago, as soon as the orthopedic surgeon gave me the date. Why would they wait until my last day at work to reject my request?"

"I don't understand Central Office's decision at all. How about if I call Mary Castor and talk to her myself? Would that be okay with you?"

"Yes, Sheila, that would be great. Any help you can give me, I'm grateful for."

"Come to my office in a few minutes and I'll put it on speaker phone. Don't say anything at first and let's see what Mary says before she knows you're listening in on the conversation. Then you can hear for yourself what she says, and you can know for certain that I am fighting for you. You can ask her questions directly, too, to make her justify their decision."

"I'm going to the administration building," I told Barb. I didn't go into any details as to why I was headed there. Within ten minutes, I hobbled into Sheila Stokes's office.

"Sheila, I don't understand this. Ever since I hurt my knee, Barb Mason and Richard Blake have been telling me it's not going to be covered. Almost every day they tell me the sky is falling and that my surgery won't happen. It's been so stressful."

"Let's see what we can do about proving them wrong," Sheila said as she dialed Mary Castor's office in Jefferson City.

Sheila fought for me, and we caught Mary in an indefensible position as I began asking questions and countering her claims.

"We weren't aware of this surgery and there isn't enough time for us to approve it."

"I have a dated copy of the leave form I submitted three weeks ago, Mary."

"We didn't know you were going to be gone so long. We weren't aware you had an injury."

"Now, Mary, I know that the day Caroline was injured the safety officer, Bill Schumer, contacted your office to inform you of her accident. I have copies of the papers Bill filled out," Sheila interjected.

"Uh, I don't remember that. Let me check my paperwork." The distinct sound of flipping pages came over the speaker phone. "Oh, wait, why here is his report. Yes, I see what you're saying. And here is Caroline's leave request, signed by her supervisor. I guess you're right, Sheila."

"So, you're telling me, Mrs. Castor, that you are approving Caroline's six weeks of leave—starting tomorrow—for her surgery?"

"Well, yes, I guess I am."

"Thank you, Mrs. Castor. Caroline and I will document that we had this conversation with you, and Caroline, you are approved to take your leave starting tomorrow."

Sheila hung up the phone. "That was some conversation, wasn't it? I have no idea what they were trying to pull on you, but that was just ridiculous."

"Sheila, thank you so much for helping. I don't understand this last-minute craziness."

"There's no reason for your own department to treat you this way. I wish you the best on your surgery, and please look at this as a break from the people who have been making your life miserable."

I left work that day, fearful of the surgery ahead, but grateful for Sheila's intervention.

Surgery was dreadful, but I was relieved it was over, even though recovery was on my own. My sons weren't nearby, and no other family lived in the area.

My estranged husband (who lived at the farmhouse too, but our lives ran on different shifts normally) took little interest in either my surgery or recovery and even referred to ACL replacement as "the same as getting a root canal." His version of helping meant leaving a box of crackers, some fruit, and a sports drink on the bed as he left for work.

While help would be nice, I'm used to dealing with life and its obstacles on my own,

I plugged ahead. Simple things like going to the bathroom were monumental tasks. Getting back into bed was tricky. I couldn't lift my leg, which was in a full-leg brace.

I used one of Kevin's fishing stringers as a pulley that I connected to one of the metal brackets on the brace.

Country girl ingenuity prevails!

The room I slept in didn't have a television, but I enjoyed the peace and quiet. To keep my mind occupied, I read a collection of books I bought at Barnes and Noble before surgery. While bedridden, I spent hours each day with my leg strapped in the "perpetual motion machine" the surgeon sent home with me as part of my rehabilitation. It slowly bent my knee, forcing it to become mobile.

People warned me about the pain of ACL surgery. No one warned me that my knee wouldn't bend.

The fear this caused me fueled my obsession to spend extra time in the machine each day.

A week after surgery, my phone rang. "Caroline, this is Mary Castor from Central Office. How are you doing?"

"Hi, Mary. Thanks for checking on me. I'm still in a lot of pain, and I can't put any weight on my leg, so getting around is tough. To make matters worse, I'm allergic to the pain medication they gave me, so right now they're trying to figure out something that will work."

"Oh, that sounds awful. Where are you?"

"I'm at home."

"At home?"

"Yes."

"According to the Worker's Compensation paperwork your doctor signed, you were supposed to be back at work yesterday."

"What? There's no way I can be at work, Mary. My leave is for six weeks, and I only had surgery a week ago. I'm barely able to get to the bathroom."

"All I know is that you've been released by your doctor to work, and you need to either come back or resign your position. You'll have to work this out with Worker's

Compensation. Otherwise, we expect to see you at work on Monday."

Already woozy from the pain, I almost passed out. In tears, I called Marcy Baker, the Work Comp case manager assigned to my case. She was dumbstruck.

"I don't know what happened, but even I know you can't go to work this quickly after ACL surgery."

I sobbed. "Marcy, I don't know what to do. I can't lose my job."

"Don't panic. I'm going to call our attorney right now and see what can be done."

After consulting their legal department, Work Comp overrode the paperwork signed by Dr. Webber. The agency, maligned by so many, made sure I still received my paychecks, my therapy, and my six weeks of leave. My employer, the people I'd known for over a year, made my life as difficult as possible. For the second time since I began working at the Department of Corrections, the system made it clear they didn't value me or my well-being.

FEELINGS AND
FILING CABINETS

After six weeks of recovery at home, Worker's Compensation and Dr. Webber released me to return to work.

After weeks stuck in bed, it's great to get out of the house—even if it's to go to a maximum-security prison. I can finally drive again!

I didn't miss most of the people at the prison, but I did miss Keith, Kelly, and Mike. When I returned to work, Keith and Bryson surprised me by having organized the room. The floors were waxed, and they'd put posters up on the walls. They sorted, gave away, and threw away boxes of miscellaneous junk that had collected dust in my room from previous teachers. First, they cleared out my room by giving teachers a chance to take what they wanted, and then—with permission—they threw away the leftovers.

"I'm always too busy teaching to plow through the stacks. My room looks fresh and new, and I'm so grateful to you guys."

"We were happy to do it, Ma'am, and we're glad you're here again," Bryson replied.

Josephson stopped me in the hallway and said, "It's great to have you back, Ma'am. We've been praying for your recovery each week at Catholic services."

"Thank you! That was so sweet of you to have them pray for me."

"Don't thank me. It was your tutor who asked the Father to pray for you."

Keith, in his usual humble way, hadn't said a word to me about it.

During the break between first and second sessions, Christy Massey looked my leg brace up and down. "How on earth did you get *that* in here?"

"I have to wear my brace twenty-four hours a day."

"I understand that, but how did you get in here? Security should have stopped you."

"I came in the same way everyone else does—through the front door."

"You do realize that if inmates get you down and take the metal plate out of your brace, you're going to be in big trouble."

"Christy, if inmates get me down on the ground, my brace will be the least of my worries."

Shaking my head, I tottered off.

I'm vulnerable in here. I can't walk, let alone run, if hell breaks loose.

While released back to work, my recovery was far from over. I attended physical therapy three afternoons a week until early October; for sixteen weeks in all. To accommodate the time I took off, Barb and Blake canceled my third session class. On therapy days, I left work at 1:45 and the prison docked my pay for the lost time. Worker's Compensation covered therapy, but not the time I missed at work. Nothing about ACL replacement surgery came without a price.

Before I left for my appointments, Keith and I visited and prepared assignments in the classroom.

The extra time with him is a silver lining to my new schedule. We never run out of things to talk about.

One day, our conversation turned to what his life would be like once he was released. We discussed the stigma faced by former inmates, even from their loved ones. His sister and brother-in-law already treated Keith like a second-class citizen. His other sister hadn't contacted him since the day he was arrested. He went from being the "go-to guy" in his family to something less than fully human in their eyes.

Sitting at our desks, I swiveled in my chair to face Keith.

"I hope you never end up in a relationship with someone who won't let you forget prison. I'd hate to think that if you were late getting home from work or if you took a little longer getting back from the store that you'd have 'I hope you weren't out robbing a bank' thrown in your face."

"I do too," Keith said glumly. "I couldn't stay in a relationship like that. I'll have done my time. I'm not going to live with this hanging over my head for the rest of my life."

Keith stood behind my desk, putting assignments in the filing cabinet. As I rose to leave for the day's therapy session, I turned to look at him. Papers in one hand and his other arm resting on the opened top drawer of the filing cabinet, Keith and I stared at each other. We exchanged no words, but I sensed he wanted to say something to me.

After a moment, my rehab session demanded I leave. "Well, I'd better get going. I'll see you tomorrow."

"Yes, I'll see you tomorrow." A look mixed with sadness and happiness filled his eyes.

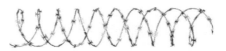

THAT'S WHAT SHE SAID

A round this time, Rick came home on leave from the Netherlands. Nearly a year had passed since I'd seen him, and we were eager to spend as much time as possible together. That included taking him on a tour of the prison. As a security officer in the military, he was familiar with jails and prisons, so it wasn't such an odd outing for the two of us. I filled out a visitor request that was promptly approved.

"No problem, Mom. I'd like to see where you work."

Having him meet Kelly, Mike, Keith, and a few other friends at the prison is important, but I also want him to meet the not-so-nice people like Barbara Mason.

"I want you to put faces to names after all the stories, good and bad, that you've heard."

The drive on that October day was picture perfect. Every turn of the road blazed with oranges, reds, and yellows in one of the best displays the Ozarks put on in years. The brilliant colors lifted my spirits but, more than anything, laughing with Rick made some of the darkness of the previous year disappear.

I've missed his quick wit and contagious laugh.

His transfer to the Netherlands left an emptiness in my heart. As we talked and joked in the car, I was happy again. Arriving at the prison parking lot, we entered the visiting area where Tracy Parr worked in the glass-enclosed bubble.

"I'd like you to meet my oldest son, Rick. He's the one in the Air Force, and he's home on leave."

"I've heard a lot of good things about you, Rick. Your mom sure is proud of you." She reached out her hand to shake his.

"Thank you, Ma'am. It's nice to meet you, and it sure is good to be home for a while."

"Tracy's daughter has been in the service for about six months now. We compare notes on our kids' military journeys."

"Which branch is your daughter in?"

"She's in the Army, like your little brother."

After visiting with Tracy, we climbed the stairs and passed through the metal detector. We stopped to say hello to Paul Grants, the officer assigned to the security checkpoint. Paul was one of the nicest people at SCCC, and we spoke every day as Kelly and I came and went at lunchtime.

The two of them shook hands. "Rick, I've been hearing about your trip back home for weeks. Your mom sure is excited about having you here. She loves you boys very much."

"I love her very much too, and it's great to be back home. I'm glad I got to meet you, Paul."

Rick and I turned the corner to the offices of the warden and assistant wardens. Kyle McMasters wasn't in, but Assistant Warden Eleanor Heath was.

"Well, who's this you've got with you?"

"This is my son, Rick. He's home on leave from the Air Force." They shook hands.

"That's wonderful. So where are you stationed and what do you do in the Air Force?"

"I work security forces at a base in the Netherlands."

Their five or ten minute conversation compared the similarities and differences between American and European prisons.

I stood listening as they talked shop.

"About the longest anyone in Europe is sent to prison is seventeen years. Unless it's a mass murderer, they believe they can rehabilitate people."

At this, Eleanor let out a cackle. "We don't even try to fix anyone here!"

This stopped me cold.

A warden just said it's funny to think we'd rehabilitate anyone in the "Corrections" Department.

Corrections officers laughed about harassing inmates as well as lying to them for the sake of lying.

Human beings, both staff and inmate, were used as sources of entertainment by corrupt staff members.

Dangerous, vile people are locked up in prisons, but isn't it our job to make them better? Don't we owe it to our communities to "fix" the people we are paid to supervise in the Corrections Department? Is her attitude the reason why teachers and non-custody staff are endangered? We don't wear blue; we are here to "fix" inmates, so that makes us less valuable as employees and coworkers?

After we walked out of the administration building and onto the prison yard, I turned to Rick. "I can't believe she laughed about fixing people in here."

"Yeah, that surprised me too. I've seen the way the Europeans run their prisons, and we do it totally different over here."

We shook our heads at her remark and continued on our way. Our tour of the prison amounted to an extended visit in the education wing.

As we entered the school, Bryson passed us in the hallway.

"I'm on my way to a Restorative Justice meeting right now. I'm sorry I can't stay, but it sure is good to meet you. Your mom is very proud of you." Bryson gave a wide smile and offered an outstretched hand.

Rick shook it. "Thanks, man. It's a pleasure to meet you, too."

Keith worked at his desk, entering grades on the classroom computer, as we walked into Classroom 10. Stiff and uptight, he was visibly nervous about meeting my son.

We both wanted Rick to have a good first impression of him

They immediately hit it off. Keith relaxed while they joked and talked sports. The two of them talked for ten or fifteen minutes before I took Rick down the hall to meet Kelly and Mike. As we made our way to the office area, we made one more stop in my classroom. I told Keith what Eleanor Heath said earlier.

Keith rolled his eyes. "Why am I not surprised?"

"I can tell you one thing. She said it in front of the wrong person. Some day she is going to be sorry she said that."

Before we left the education wing, Rick met Barb in all her glory. "Mom, that secretary seems a little manly...and a little off her rocker."

That's my boy.

His visit went by far too quickly, but I soaked up all the good times I could.

I'VE HAD MY ASS KICKED SO MANY TIMES I DON'T EVEN CARE ANYMORE

After Rick returned to the Netherlands, I went back to working around a host of unusual characters. I dealt with some odd coworkers, but the inmates created their own circus. The atmosphere inside the death fences was always tense on some level. Even during jovial times, the threat of violence was ever-present. Confrontations erupted because of a sideways glance or an offhand comment. Classroom 10 saw its share of strange and uncomfortable moments.

Ronald Jimenez, in my third session, not only behaved strangely, but his breath reeked so badly we smelled it feet away. That alone made him a pariah, but his behavior ostracized him from the other inmates. Jimenez was one of those "off the chain" guys who asked inappropriate questions, agitated other inmates, and possessed a complete lack of personal hygiene. Men sat five at a table to avoid having to be near him.

He gives off a vibe that no one wants to be around.

One day, out of the blue, Jimenez looked up from his assignment and stared at me. "What would you do if you came home and found me in your living room?"

Fifteen grown men paused at the brashness of Jimenez's question. I looked back at him. "What do you mean by that?"

"Just what I said. What would you do if you came home and I was sitting in your living room."

Everyone stared at me. I stared at Jimenez. "I'd shoot you."

Gasps and chuckles spread through the classroom.

"You'd shoot me?" Jimenez said, mouth agape.

"Yes, I would."

"Why would you shoot me for being in your living room?

"Because you wouldn't be invited. The only way you'd be in my house would be if you broke in. So, I'd shoot you."

Nodding heads bobbed across the room. Jimenez asked classmate after classmate the same question. "What would you do if you came home and I was in your living room?"

To a man, each answered, "I'd shoot you."

He couldn't comprehend why no one would be happy to find him, uninvited, in their homes. He kept insisting that one man, Parker, explain his response.

Finally, Parker made his reasons plain. "Listen man. I've got a thirteen-year-old sister. You wouldn't be welcome in my home if I was there, but if I came home and found you in my living room that would mean you were there with my little sister. She might have been taking a shower or something. I don't want you around her. I would definitely shoot you."

Jimenez leaned back, completely baffled. The men shook their heads and muttered.

I desperately want him out of my class, but school policy says we can only remove a student if we trade with another teacher. I don't see anyone volunteering to take him off my hands.

The moment did arrive, however, and sooner than I expected.

Kelly and I left on our way out the door for lunch the next day. Normally bubbly and fun-loving, an angry shadow hung over her.

"What's wrong?"

"It's that Morgan jerk! I'm so sick of his attitude. He won't work and just sits there in a mood all day, every day. If I could trade Morgan for someone else, I wouldn't even care who it was. I'd trade him for anyone!"

Sorry to do this to you, Kelly.

"Consider it done!"

"Really? You aren't going to want Morgan. He's awful."

"Don't worry about that, Kelly. I have someone I'll trade you for him."

Her face lit up. When we came back from lunch, Kelly went to Barb's office to make the switch on our class rosters.

When Keith returned from lunch, I filled him in on the trade. He raised one eyebrow and grinned.

"This isn't the first good deal you've negotiated for our classroom. I'm as relieved as you are to get Jimenez out of our room.

"Thanks, I wasn't sure I could pull it off."

"I'm going to have to start calling you the General Manager because you're so good at trades. I'm proud of you!" We laughed. "I do feel bad that Mrs. Rainer is the one we stuck with Jimenez."

"Yeah, me too, but she did say she would trade Morgan for *anyone*, and I wasn't sure when the next opportunity would come along."

Keith leaned back in his chair. "Well played."

The next day, student Roger Atkinson asked, "Where's Jimenez at? Did he go to the hole for something?"

"No, he's in Mrs. Rainer's classroom now."

Men looked at me in surprise. Atkinson said, "You mean he's not going to be in here anymore?"

"Nope."

Some "hell yeahs" and "hallelujahs" flew around the room.

I asked Kelly how Jimenez was fitting into her class as we left for lunch.

"Oh, he's great! He's no problem at all. Thanks for getting Morgan out of my room. You're going to be sorry you took him, but I'm glad he's gone. I'm sorry it's you I passed him off on, but I'm glad we made the trade."

"Don't feel sorry for me yet, Kelly."

She gave me a puzzled look. She looked relaxed and happy, though, and nothing was going to dampen her spirits.

After work the next day, I posed the same question as we walked down the sidewalk.

"Oh, he was fine. He's a little odd, though."

"That he is."

The following day, I asked again.

Her eyes flew wide open. "Oh my God! Jimenez is a freak! He's awful. Now I know why you wanted him out of your room."

"I'm sorry about that."

"I can't be angry with you because I stuck you with Morgan. I have to congratulate you, though, because hands down you made the best deal in the trade."

We laughed, glad there were no hard feelings.

Other interesting characters came and went through Classroom 10 with each passing week. Edmund Clancy, a middle-aged man who loved to stir trouble, was one. He swaggered around the camp, always involving himself in prison gossip.

He thinks it gives him power and it makes him feel important.

Clancy sought drama one afternoon by asking an open question to the class.

"Would you be a good citizen and tell the authorities if you saw someone breaking the law?"

"Are you asking us if we'd snitch? Hell no!"

Several men bristled at his comments. Snitching was a capital offense, both inside the prison and on the streets.

Clancy tried to bait other students. At first, he got no reaction from anyone. Then he changed tactics and called out individual students. He turned his attention to Brice Mitchell, a quiet young man serving a life sentence for murder. Brice wasn't a troublemaker in class, but he didn't like to play games.

"What about you, Brice? Would you do your civic duty and report it?"

"No, I wouldn't. I don't mess with other people's business."

No one in his right mind admits to being a snitch. That kind of talk causes you to wake up dead, or at the very least to seek protective custody.

Clancy persisted, turning his question into an interrogation. The class sat flabbergasted.

"If you were a good man, Mitchell, you'd tell the cops if you saw someone break the law."

"No, I wouldn't do that."

"Well, you should. Don't you want to be a good citizen? I've turned people in before. What's wrong with you?"

In the process of trying to get Brice Mitchell to lose his cool, Clancy outed himself as a snitch in a room full of maximum-security inmates. Still, some of the things Clancy said stung Mitchell.

He's obviously uncomfortable in the spotlight, but I'm going to give Mitchell plenty of time to deal with the situation on his own.

After a few moments, Clancy's rant ended. A half hour later, Mitchell sat stewing at his table, completely unfocused instead of working on his assignments.

I motioned for Mitchell to come to my desk. He took the seat across from me. "Don't let that guy get to you. Think about what he just did. He must have a death wish."

Mitchell gave me a relieved little smile. "Thank you, Ma'am. I needed to hear that."

"Go on back to your seat and keep working on your assignments. You know who Clancy is now. We all know who Clancy is now. Just concentrate on getting your GED and forget about someone who's so stupid that he'd admit he's a snitch inside a prison. The best revenge you can have is to act as though nothing he said matters."

Mitchell cocked his chin up. "That's exactly what I'm going to do."

Brice Mitchell walked back to his table, sat down, opened his assignment notebook, and began in earnest to complete his work. Clancy stared at him, hoping to catch a reaction, but he went unrewarded.

We just avoided a fight because a twenty-three-year-old showed more sense than a man in his fifties did. Clancy's lucky that Mitchell is as composed as he is. Another inmate might have snapped.

Violence swirled in the undercurrents of the prison and needed little to unleash it. A combination of young hotheads and the mentally ill, imprisoned in great numbers, concocted a sure-fire recipe for confrontation and bloodshed.

A month or so after Jimenez left Classroom 10, another student with rough social edges transferred into my class. DeMondre Moore, in his own world for the most part, made rude comments that his classmates seldom appreciated. In his late forties, Moore had spent more time behind bars than he did on the streets. Even after all those years, he hadn't learned to keep his mouth shut.

Moore interjected himself into a conversation better left alone one afternoon. Three men talked amongst themselves when Moore spouted off.

"Man, you're full of shit. You know you ain't never done that, fool."

"Old man, you need to shut the fuck up," snarled Rashad Gibson, one of the seething young men who passed daily through my classroom.

"Oh yeah? Well, I think you're full of shit. I'm from that neighborhood in St. Louis, and I don't think that happened."

Nothing stopped activity in a room faster than an impending fight.

The confrontational exchange continued between the two until Gibson, a six-foot-two-inch hulk of a man stood up from the table, kicking his chair away. Everyone held his breath and shot nervous glances around the room as the situation escalated.

"Old man, I told you to shut the fuck up! I'm going to beat your ass," Gibson bellowed as he moved towards Moore.

Then the unexpected happened. Moore grinned as though he'd heard the funniest joke in the world. He began chuckling. Gibson stopped, just like the rest of us, and stared at Moore in disbelief.

Moore should be afraid, but instead he's laughing.

Moore tipped his chair back against the wall. "I've had my ass kicked so many times I don't even care anymore. So, young man, if you feel the need to beat my ass, go ahead and do it. It's fine with me."

A nervous giggle engulfed the room. Gibson, who lifted his fist preparing to swing, stopped. Shaking his head in wonderment, he lowered his fist and returned to his seat. Sometimes quirky comments evoked violence, and sometimes they were the only way to avoid it.

Prison brought every imaginable personality together in close confines. Mental illness, short tempers, and a lack of social skills combined to create a dangerous brew of hostility. Many inmates did their best to avoid conflict, but sometimes trouble was impossible to steer clear of for those too angry or too delusional to use common sense.

Between the harassment by coworkers and the tensions among inmates, this is a terrible job.

WATER LEAKS AND OTHER LIES

In spite of the difficult surroundings, the friendship Keith Giammanco and I shared grew. We talked about politics, current news events, literature, and travel. Few people inside the prison, including employees, had intellectual conversations. Television series or sports comprised their favorite topics. Keith and I talked about those too, but we craved meaningful discussions. Our talks were the only bright spots in my days. I needed some bright spots.

Life at work worsened for me as Randy's six-month absence extended once again. I faced Barb alone, and our boss wouldn't return any time soon—if at all—to right the ship. The screws put on me at the prison continued, unchecked.

How much longer can I put up with Barb, Presley, and spineless "leaders" like Blake?

A sign hung above the entryway to the prison grounds, reminding employees that our behavior set an example for the inmates.

I don't know if some employees can't read or if they just don't care about what example they set, but my guess is the latter. After the way Stan Baker "trains" people at the Academy, a lot of these employees think they are supposed to set bad examples. They're rude, use inmates as entertainment, lie, and are intentionally cruel. Stan would be proud.

Both staff and inmates were lied to, creating an environment where no one knew who to believe or trust. Lies ranged from trivial comments to coordinated snow jobs told by several employees to multiple inmates or staff members. Some came straight from the wardens themselves, while others were perpetrated by run-of-the-mill employees. Sometimes those lies set other employees up for failure.

Without advanced notice, one morning the prison conducted a lockdown and emergency preparedness drill. Teachers and other morning shift employees waited for a few hours to enter the prison until the drill ended. Classes didn't begin until mid-morning. As students arrived in my classroom, I was puzzled by their comments.

Lyle Martin, was geared up when he came into class.

"It's off the chain that they just now released us. The COs in my housing unit said the midnight shift screwed things up so bad that they had to lock the whole camp down to fix it."

I looked at Keith in disbelief. He nodded.

"They said the same thing in my housing unit this morning."

"What are you talking about, Martin?"

"The lockdown. The guards in my housing unit said it's because the night shift screwed things up. I'm not sure what they messed up, but it must have been bad. We're running almost three hours late today."

Keith threw up his hands as if to say, "I don't even know what to tell the guy."

"This had nothing to do with the midnight shift. It was a planned emergency drill," I said to Martin and the class at large.

"What? Really?"

"Yes, really. I don't know why they blamed it on other staff members."

"Ah, hell. If I'd known that I would have been willing to take part in the drill. I'd like to know what to do if there's an emergency too."

The emergency plans for riots, floods, fires, hazardous spills, and nuclear war call for employees to lock inmates down and then leave. I don't have the heart to tell you, Martin, but your part in any emergency is to die.

Keith shook his head. "I knew it had to be a lie. That's what guards were telling the guys, though."

"Why do they lie, and why would they blame other employees? The only thing we have going for us as staff is maintaining some level of respect and authority. If other guards say the night shift is incompetent, the inmates will prey on that."

"Yeah, but you and I know they do that kind of stuff all the time around here."

Keith was right. A few months after the emergency drill, the teaching faculty attended a mandatory in-service at the training trailer, so school shut down for the day. Some of us told our tutors, and others did not.

The next morning, Patton, Kelly's other tutor, walked around the office area. He looked at the floor and surveyed the hallway. "Wow! They did a great job getting this place cleaned up."

"What do you mean?" I asked as he continued to walk around the office area.

"You'd never know this place was flooded yesterday."

"What?"

"Yeah, because of the water main break."

"Water main break? What are you talking about?"

"The guards told us there was a water main break at the school and that's why we didn't have work yesterday."

"Patton, that's not why we canceled school. All of the teachers went to a training."

He stopped in mid-stride and shot me an incredulous look.

"A training? Why would they tell us there was a water main break if you were all at a training?"

"I don't know, but that's a good question."

What's gained by lying to inmates about something so inconsequential as a training?

Later that morning, I stopped by Kelly's room.

"Did you hear what the guards told Patton about the day off work yesterday?"

"No, what did they tell him?"

I repeated my conversation with him to her.

"What the heck? I told Josephson we had a training, but Patton was at medical, so I just didn't think to let him know. Why would guards lie?"

"I don't know, but it's teaching inmates all the wrong lessons. If we expect them to become better people, do we really want them learning that as long as you have the upper hand you can lie all you want to?"

Kelly shook her head. "It makes no sense, does it?"

On the way home from work, Mike and I talked about it.

He sighed. "They do that nonsense all the time, and I don't get it. It's happened for as long as I've worked at the prison."

"It's not hard to do our jobs without lying. These guards purposely come up with wild stories to tell the inmates just for entertainment."

"That's true." Mike pensively stared out the window as we drove. "The guards laugh while they watch the inmates spread rumors that the guards started."

"No joke. They're going to get out of prison thinking that's normal."

Some staff began noticing how often the wardens lied to employees, too. Giselle Braun, a lovely German-born woman who worked as the unit manager for Housing Unit 3, noticed what went on. She often left for lunch at the same time I did, and we frequently walked back into the prison together. A few weeks after the water main break incident, we met in the administration building and walked back to work. I shared my concerns.

Giselle lowered her voice to avoid eavesdroppers. "The wardens use a divide and conquer approach. They always tell us that other employees are watching our every move. They make us paranoid."

"You're right. We're so fearful of our coworkers that it makes the job miserable."

"Not only that, it makes me wonder what the wardens are up to. What are they pulling while they have the staff busy turning on each other?"

We slowed to a stop on the sidewalk, cautious, even though we were the only ones within yards. We couldn't talk about such a thing around others. Our conversation equated treason in the eyes of the wardens. The administrators treated employees as their puppets, and we weren't supposed to question their motives or actions. We also weren't supposed to wonder what their lies diverted us from noticing.

I looked around, making sure no one stood in earshot.

"Sort of like what Kyle McMasters announced at the training I was at last week. He told us that seven dirty employees were caught bringing drugs into the prison. He claimed that we could all breathe easier because those seven were the cause of the low morale here."

Giselle gave a quick chuckle. "Low morale isn't because of a few drug runners. It's because of the corruption we work around every day. Their plan is to keep us fighting amongst ourselves, so no one notices."

"Do you know of anyone being fired lately? McMasters said the dirty seven were removed immediately, but I can't think of anyone who's gone, can you?"

"Now that you mention it, I can't."

"Giselle let's keep our eyes and ears open to see if we can figure out who these seven employees are."

"Let's do. I have to get back to work right now, but let's put out some feelers."

"I'll ask Kelly to do the same. She's worked here a long time and knows more people than I do around the camp."

Giselle and I checked in with each other a week later. "One cook is gone, but she's out for a surgery. I haven't heard of anyone else who isn't at work," Giselle confided.

"Me neither. I've even asked my students if they noticed any guards who'd been fired or quit in their housing units. I didn't tell them why, but surely one of them would notice if a guard was gone—let alone seven. Not a single employee has shown up missing."

"If they want to get rid of low staff morale, then they need to stop playing games with us. To be honest, Caroline, it frightens me."

"It does me, too."

Mike and I frequently talked about the head games the wardens played with the employees. Making our way down the walk one evening after work, we looked up at the large windows of the warden's office.

"I've heard that McMasters stands at his window and watches all of us." Mike gestured toward the administration building.

"I bet he has toy soldiers with our names on them, and he moves them around some board."

"I bet you're right. He's just sick and twisted enough to do that."

"Yeah, he's the big psychology professor on the outside. He uses us as one big experiment. This place is messed up."

We stopped our conversation as we reached the outside door of the admin building. We never knew when someone would report us for speaking up, so we had to be careful when and where we talked about problems at the prison. Paranoia ruled the prison system, and the administrators liked it that way. We continued our conversation in the car, free from prying onlookers.

Mike steamed the more we talked about it. "You know how sometimes. when the news beats a story to death, everyone starts to wonder if something bigger is going on behind the scenes? What bill is getting pushed through in the middle of the night while the rest of the world is focused on a plane crash?

"Yeah, I see where you're heading with this. It makes sense, doesn't it?"

"It does. I've been at the prison long enough and have heard too many red herrings spread by the wardens. I wonder what they are up to. Why do they feel like they need to keep everyone on edge?"

We recognized that the wardens manipulated the staff, but we couldn't quite put our fingers on what happened behind the scenes. What were they wanting to hide? We were used as pawns, and the divide and conquer atmosphere of the prison kept most employees too afraid of their own shadows to question why it was happening.

Only a few things—money, drugs, and power—cause this level of perversity.

UNDER THE WEATHER

K nee surgery ruined my chances to see Kevin before he deployed, but once my physical therapy ended, I had a mission.

I'm determined to save leave time, so I can be at Fort Drum when Kevin and his unit return from Afghanistan in September.

I hit a few roadblocks on the way, though. One literal; the other figurative. My farm, nestled deep in Prairie Hollow, was at the lowest point in all of Douglas County. The hollow—another word for "valley"—encompassed part of the Bryant Creek watershed. While beautiful and peaceful, my farm's location made it susceptible to flooding.

A few times a year, Bryant Creek and its tributaries devastated the area. The county road department fortified the roadways by dumping truck-loads of gravel on them, and they improved the water crossings by installing large culverts secured with concrete. Sometimes the county's efforts weren't enough, though, and the roads, culverts and all, simply disappeared as rampaging flood waters rushed through. The damage left people living in Prairie Hollow stranded until county workers rebuilt the roads.

Torrential rains hit that spring, and for three days I was land-locked. I drove a small passenger car, but not even a four-wheel-drive pickup could have navigated the six-foot-deep channel cut into County Road 109 where the culvert used to be.

I'm back to square one on leave.

A mother's love is highly motivational, though. Once the roads were fixed, I worked through migraines and bronchitis to build my leave up again. What I didn't anticipate was an outbreak of norovirus, the same intestinal disease that plagues cruise ships. It hit the prison hard.

Norovirus spread through contaminated water or food but, unlike cruise ships, when this disease ravaged prisons, it didn't make the nightly news. Out of sight from citizens, hundreds of men at SCCC dropped, vomiting and writhing with severe stomach cramps. Violently ill inmates overran the prison's medical hallway.

Between the four o'clock alarm and the ten-hour days and three-hour commute, I was always tired, but one morning I awoke especially exhausted. I tried to shake it off, but my head spun as I took my shower.

No calling in sick for this girl. Just drink some caffeine and you'll be fine.

Mike took the day off for a dental appointment, so I hit the road alone. When I arrived at work, I felt like a whirlpool drained my energy. I was unsteady on my feet, and by the time Keith walked into my classroom, queasiness hit.

As always, he smiled when he saw me. "Hey! How are you this morning?"

"Okay."

Keith chattered away. I only mustered one-word responses.

Keith stopped sorting papers and frowned. "Are you mad at me?"

"No, I'm not mad at you. I feel sick. I have a fever, and my stomach feels awful. I think I'm going home at lunch."

Keith eyed me carefully. "You're looking worse by the minute. Are you sure sticking around until lunch is a good idea?"

"Maybe I'll go home at the end of first session." My fever rose, and my head hurt. My stomach flipped and spun.

"You sure?"

"Yeah, I can make it." Within ten minutes, I changed my mind.

Dejected, I told Keith goodbye and went to the office to tell Barb I was leaving immediately. Before I left the education wing, I threw up in the bathroom, then I stopped in the administration building to vomit once again. Once to my car, I barely made it to the gas station in town before I stopped again. The ride home was miserable. I became acquainted with every public bathroom between the prison and my farm, turning what should have been an hour-and-a-half drive into nearly three hours.

Thank God Mike didn't go to work today. At least I'm not dragging him along on this trip.

Burning with fever, I arrived home and crawled into bed where I remained for three days. I lived on frozen popsicles, left from when Kevin last visited. As quickly as I could manage to stand and drive, however, I returned to work.

Thanks to the norovirus, I'm in the hole again on leave time.

Surrounded by illness, somehow Keith never caught it. Joe Bryson was sick, Keith's cellmate was sick, most of our students were sick, and he sat next to me when I was contagious.

"How on earth have you managed to be around this stuff and not get it?"

Keith's explanation was simple. "I don't drink the tap water here."

I don't see how that could help.

"Yeah, but you've been around, living with, people who were sick.

"I know, but I only drink melted ice because it goes through a filter. I don't trust the water in this place."

I thought he was a little paranoid until I read up on norovirus.

"I think you have a point. I bet there's a problem with the water or there's a source in the kitchen. That's the only reason why so many people across the camp would get sick."

"I'm telling you, it's the water."

I had to admit that he managed to not get sick when the rest of us felt like we'd stared death in the eye.

Angry, frustrated, and depressed, I forced myself to work, no matter what, to earn back lost leave time.

I doubt I can earn as much leave as I need, but I'm bound and determined to try.

A month after my norovirus attack, some of us, including Kelly and Doris, received letters from the DOC Central Office chastising us for going over our leave limit. Unlike my coworkers, however, I received something else: a phone call summoning me to meet with the wardens—immediately—to discuss my leave time. I was unnerved and went straight to Kelly's room.

"Kelly, you know the letters we got about our leave?"

"Oh, yeah, don't worry about it. I've gotten them before," she said nonchalantly.

"I just got a phone call saying the wardens want to talk to me."

"What the heck?"

"I don't get it. I'm not the only one who's used too much leave. Why am I the only one who was called up there?"

"They don't want to talk to Doris? Or me?"

I shook my head no.

"I've never heard of this happening. When are you supposed to see the wardens?"

"Now."

Kelly paused with a worried expression. "Let me know what they have to say as soon as you get back."

"I will."

My heart sank, and my knees became a little weak as I headed for the door and stepped out onto the walk. My fear turned to anger the farther I went.

I'm tired of the lies and manipulation—the mind games—of the wardens. I'm going to turn the tables.

A plan formed as I climbed the stairs in the administration building. When I reached the warden's office area, Angie Pike, secretary to Kyle McMasters, told me to sit in the waiting area. Angie and I shared a mutual friend, Lucy Carver, who worked for the Community Blood Center of the Ozarks. Angie and I had spoken a few times in the past, most recently after the death of Lucy's husband.

Angie is a good woman with a kind heart.

I'd sat in the waiting room for a few minutes when Tom Starkey appeared in the doorway with a dour expression on his face. "Follow me to Warden McMasters's office," he said sternly.

I did as he said and took a seat at the conference table.

He sat across from me without a word, then said, "Mr. McMasters will be here shortly."

I'm not worried about my job, so if they think I'm going to beg for it, they're mistaken. My absences are due to unforeseen circumstances, one directly related to unclean practices by the prison. I'm trying to save leave, and they aren't going to bully me into feeling guilty. I'm not going to be their game piece this time.

Tom Starkey excused himself from the table and a few moments later reappeared with Kyle McMasters. Both seated themselves across from me, giving stern looks to each other and to me.

"Do you know why you've been called into my office today?" McMasters began.

"No, sir, I don't." I let my voice waver.

"You're here because of something very serious."

My eyes welled with tears. I could tell he was pleased with himself. I wrung my hands.

"It is?" My voice was shaky.

Tom Starkey joined in with, "Yes, a very serious matter."

"You're here," McMasters said, "because you have exceeded the amount of leave you accrued, and this is a very serious situation. Didn't you receive a letter? It was necessary for me to—"

Tears rolled down my face. "Oh, is that what this is about? I'm so relieved!"

Perplexed, both men stared at me.

Tom Starkey said, "What do you mean you are 'relieved' about being called to the warden's office?"

"You know my husband works here, too?" I wiped tears off my cheeks.

McMasters looked puzzled. "I believe I knew that, yes."

"And my son is at war in Afghanistan."

"I wasn't aware that your son was in the military."

"Uh, no, I didn't know that either," Starkey added.

"I was so afraid when I was called up here. The only thing I could think of that you'd call me to your office for—to tell me in person—was if something terrible had happened. I thought someone had died. Other teachers received letters, but none of them were called up here, so it never even entered my mind that it could be because of leave."

Starkey and McMasters glanced anxiously at each other, trying to maintain their composure.

I see cracks in their facade.

"Because your educational supervisor is away on military duty, we had to discuss this with you here, in this office.

"Why only me? Other teachers got letters too."

Neither wanted to answer that question.

I continued. "You have no idea how scared I was that something had happened to my husband or son,"

My tears flowed. My voice caught. My breathing shuddered. Both men looked uneasy. Neither said a word.

"We have such a long commute to get to work, and now's when my husband would be on the road. I was sure you were going to tell me he'd been in a car accident."

Tears and more tears.

"No, your husband is fine," Starkey reassured me.

McMasters stood and paced around the room. Starkey rose and lingered on the other side of the table from me. He tried to regain his composure.

"Well, you have overdrawn your leave, and that is serious."

"I feel terrible about that, too. Believe me, I don't want to miss any days at all. I'm trying to save leave, not use it. Because of my knee surgery, I didn't get to see my son before he deployed. I want to be there when he comes home from war."

McMasters found something fascinating to stare at on the wall—anything to avoid eye contact with the tearful woman in his office.

I explained about the roads washing away and my terrible bout of norovirus.

"But you were gone for three days when you were sick, and that seems excessive especially when you'd already exhausted your leave," McMasters said, still trying to take control of the situation.

Out of the corner of my eye, I noticed Angie Pike standing in the doorway, witnessing everything unfold.

I know Angie got sick during the outbreak.

I turned to her. "Angie, you had it, right? It was terrible."

"Oh, Lord, it wasn't just terrible. I thought I was going to die! I had to miss an entire week of work. If Caroline was able to come back to work after just three days, I don't know how she did it. It took me until the fourth day to even be able to walk across a room. Terrible stuff!"

I had the wardens on the hot seat. Not only did I give them a hefty guilt trip, but now their own secretary spoke up in my defense. With Angie eyeing them, they quickly backtracked.

"I'm sorry. I hadn't meant to upset you."

"We never meant for you to be afraid."

"I'm glad you are feeling better now."

"We hope things go well for your son in Afghanistan."

"This was just a chance for you to explain your absences. Thank you so much for coming in. Sorry to have worried you."

The apologies kept flowing, and they looked guilty as hell.

This little toy soldier just pushed back.

Heartened by my success, I shook their hands. "If you ever feel like slumming, come on down to the education department. We'd love to see you there."

Everyone at the prison knows McMasters rarely sets foot inside the yard, and even then, it's under very controlled circumstances. He's terrified of the prisoners. The only time I've seen him in the education department was when he lectured us about staff-inmate interactions on Keith's first day of work. McMasters isn't much of a general to his toy soldiers.

As promised, I filled Kelly in when I got back to the school.

"You did not really do that, did you?"

"I most certainly did! It was time they got a dose of their own medicine."

In Classroom 10, I told Keith what transpired with the wardens.

"I'm proud of you. It's about time someone put them in a corner, even if it was just for a few minutes."

That evening, Mike Vaughn had tears of his own during my story, but his tears came from laughing too hard.

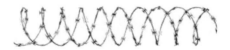

CERTAINTY

The friendly confines of Classroom 10 were my safe-haven in an otherwise dull and hostile environment. With Keith beside me, my days rolled by much easier than if I was alone. He was funny, smart, and trustworthy—all traits most of my coworkers lacked. His steady demeanor kept my blood pressure down and a smile on my face while I faced Barb's daily onslaughts.

One Monday morning, normally upbeat Keith came to work in a terrible mood. Quiet, withdrawn, and deep in thought, it was impossible to miss the change in his disposition.

I'm worried.

"Are you okay? Did something happen in the housing unit?"

"Nothing's wrong. Nothing happened. I'm fine."

I don't want to push it. He is, after all, able to have a life that doesn't include my nose in it.

After about an hour, Keith excused himself to go to the restroom.

I turned to Joe Bryson. "Is he okay? Did something happen to upset him?"

"There's nothing wrong. He's just all up in his feelings."

I'm not quite sure what Joe means, but I'm relieved nothing is wrong in Keith's world.

After he came back, we busied ourselves assembling assignment notebooks. Several students transferred out of SCCC in the past week, including one of our classroom favorites, Leroy Miller. He was a thorn in the side of every SCCC teacher who ever taught him, and he had plenty of rough edges, but he achieved for us.

Miller's knack for mentoring the younger men and encouraging them to improve themselves scored points with us. More than once, he'd given students a verbal kick in the pants to get them back in line. He liked and respected us, too. Leroy earned a soft place in our hearts because he also was a victim of Barb Mason.

For his parole hearing in February, I completed the required educational report.

"You better not give him a good report. I hate him. He's not getting parole," Barb barked on more than one occasion.

I always responded with, "I'm giving him an honest review."

Considering how much Barb hates Miller, you should make an extra copy of his report, just in case," Keith suggested.

I did, and he was right. The parole board denied Leroy Miller's parole, and he came to school angry.

"You said you were giving me a positive report, but you didn't. The board said they would have given me parole if it wasn't for the bad education report you put in my file."

"Mr. Miller, I swear I gave you a good review." He looked doubtful, so I pulled the copy out of my desk drawer. As he read it, a series of emotions swept his face.

"This isn't the report that was in my file at the hearing."

Barb switched my report for a negative one that she wrote, forging my signature. Making matters worse, Richard Blake signed the report too, so he is complicit.

When I asked the office for a copy of the report, they couldn't produce one. The next time Miller was eligible for a parole hearing was in three years.

Three years of a man's life was wasted because of a hate-filled, deceitful employee who let her own emotions get in the way of the process.

Miller may have been a doofus in the past, but he proved to be a valued member of Classroom 10. He continued to work hard on his coursework and to mentor the younger men. We were shocked when he, without warning, transferred to another prison. One day he was in class, and the next day he was gone.

"I don't think they even gave him any advanced notice," Keith told me.

"I live in his housing unit," Bryson said. "Yesterday morning they just showed up at his cell and told him to pack. He didn't know it was coming."

A change in the way the DOC leveled prisons brought about the rash of sudden transfers. Changing from a five-tiered system (Level 1 was minimum-security, and Level 5 was maximum-security), all prisons became low-medium or medium-high.

In the short term, reshuffling inmates wreaked havoc and expense. In the long term, however, the department saved in transportation costs.

Under the new system, inmates stayed put longer in a facility, even if their security levels dropped, since the new classifications were broader and more inclusive.

Thanks to the flood of transfers, our hands were full keeping up with students as they left and arrived in our room. I could tell Keith was in bad spirits, but we had too much to do and there was no time for conversations.

Keith's negative attitude worries me because prison life is difficult, even with Bryson's reassurance, I hate to see him miserable.

I breathed a sigh of relief when his mood improved by the time we finished the stack of assignment notebooks.

A few days later, he came to work uptight again. This wasn't the Keith I'd known for a year.

What could be wrong?

Bryson left for a Restorative Justice meeting, giving us some time between classes with no students around to talk about what bothered him.

Keith wasted no time. "There's something I've been needing to say to you."

I hope he isn't quitting.

"What is it? Is everything okay?"

"Everything's okay, but I've needed to tell you this since the first day we worked together." He paused. I held my breath.

"I love you, Caroline. I've known it since the first time I ever laid eyes on you, and every conversation we've had, every moment we've spent together, has made that feeling stronger and more certain. I know this takes you by surprise, but please hear me out."

I froze in my seat. *Did he just say what I think he said?*

For the next five or ten minutes, Keith's feelings poured out. He ended with, "I love you, and I will never, ever stop."

I sat motionless and overwhelmed.

"You're not responsible for my emotions. These are my feelings, and I don't expect you to feel the same way. Take as much time as you need to respond and—no matter what— I'm okay with it."

"Thank you."

Keith smiled. "I know I just put a lot on you that you weren't expecting or asking for today. Take as much time to think this over as you need."

Second session began, and I managed to make it through class, but minutes passed in a blur. At lunchtime, I left the prison to sit in my car. I didn't eat. I couldn't. A million thoughts raced through my mind as I carefully considered every possible outcome.

I love Keith, too, even if it's frightening to admit, given the circumstances.

The ramifications of a relationship with an inmate were many, and most held serious consequences.

I'm already on the outs with the prison. The wardens threatened my job a few months into my employment. Barb Mason constantly attacks me. No one cares when my life is threatened or when I have a major work-related injury. I'm unsheltered in the system and my job's tenuous as it is.

The added element of loving an inmate made me more vulnerable to my enemies. I had other concerns, too.

What will others think of me? Will my family be angry? Will I lose my friends? Loving an inmate will come with some social costs.

Then I considered what a relationship would do to Keith. His first four years in prison were uneventful. Keith, an introvert, managed to stay under the radar without embroiling himself in prison drama.

I don't want the fallout of a relationship with me to harm him.

I considered all the worst-case scenarios, but each time I came back to the same question.

If I go back in my classroom and lie—if I tell him I don't love him—and he walks out the door, can I face life without him?

No, I couldn't live without him in my universe. Tiptoeing around my love for him wasn't going to work anymore. Through my pain, I'd built up walls against the world.

Keith is already inside those walls. It's time to be honest with him—and myself.

I collected my thoughts and steadied my emotions before going back into the prison. Keith had an expectant look on his face when he entered the classroom, but he was patient.

I have an answer for him, but we can't talk, not yet. Not with all these people around.

As the class filled with students, I told him, "We both want the same things."

His eyes brightened, and energy returned to his face. "Okay!"

For the moment, that was enough. With jobs to do and students to teach, class took precedence over our personal needs. After school, we talked for a few moments.

"I'm sorry that all I said was 'thank you' at first. That's so dreadfully inadequate. I love you too. This is scary and complicated, but I love you. We'll have to be careful, and we need ground rules. No physical contact. No contraband. No favors."

"Agreed."

"We'll pretend we belong to a really strict religious sect that doesn't allow physical contact until marriage." We both laughed, relieved to be on the same page.

The next day, offered us more time to talk. "You're a lot braver than I am, Keith."

"Why do you say that?"

"I love you, but I wouldn't have had the nerve to tell you."

"I've never been more afraid to do anything in my entire life."

"What? You robbed twelve banks. You thought telling me you loved me was more frightening than robbing banks?"

"Absolutely! It's all about risk versus reward. Did I need money, and was robbing a bank dangerous? Yes. But nothing meant more to me, nothing was more valuable, than having you love me in return."

The scars of the past still weighed heavily on my heart.

"Why do you love me? I'm shattered into a million pieces. I'm like a mirror that's been broken and will never be the same. I've glued the pieces back together, and I'm functioning, but nothing changes the fact that I'm broken. Are you sure I'm what you want?"

"You aren't broken. You're perfect. You just haven't been able to see it."

My heart and spirit began to heal. "So, you really love me?"

"Yes, I really love you."

"I didn't even have to try."

"No, you didn't even have to try." Keith gave me a warm smile.

"Why did you choose now to tell me? Miller's transfer shook you up, didn't it?"

"Yeah, it did. So many men have transferred out of the blue. It worried me. What if I was transferred? What if I left here without ever telling you how I felt? I couldn't live with that. I had to tell you."

My mind floated back in time over important moments we'd shared during the past year.

"Do you remember that day when you stood at the filing cabinet before I left to go to physical therapy?"

"Of course, I do."

"I've always thought you wanted to say something to me while we looked at each other."

"Oh, I did. I definitely wanted to tell you something."

"Really? What was it?"

"I wanted to tell you, 'Someday I'm going to marry you.' I didn't want to freak you out, so I didn't say it. We'd only known each other a matter of weeks, but I knew in that moment that someday you'd be my wife."

Dreams Do Come True

O ur relationship took both of us by surprise. Neither Keith nor I intended to fall in love inside prison walls. Regardless, the moment we met our lives changed forever.

When Keith told me he loved me, I was stunned, but not completely unprepared for it. I'm not a mystic or New Age sort of person, but I had a vivid dream a week and a half earlier that put the idea on my radar.

In it, I showed up for work and instead of teaching, the prison asked me to be a transport officer for the day. Keith had a court appearance in St. Louis, and they needed me to take him to it. In real life, that would never happen, but dreams don't always follow logical paths. Nightfall forced us to stop at a rinky-dink motel along the route.

Nothing sexual happened, but as Keith drifted to sleep in the cramped hotel room, he murmured, "I love you."

In my dream, my eyes flew open. *Oh my gosh! He loves me!*

Then, in real life, my eyes flew open. *Oh my gosh! I think he really does love me!*

Maybe it was God's way of preparing me. Maybe my subconscious forced me to come to grips with what I knew but was unwilling to admit. A few days after Keith told me he loved me, I told Keith about my dream. He smiled and told me about the anxiety he experienced in the days and weeks before he'd spilled his heart to me.

"Remember the bad mood I was in?"

"Yeah, I even asked Bryson if you were okay."

"I was okay, but I was so stressed about telling you. I couldn't relax. I wasn't very pleasant to be around."

"I'm glad I have that effect on you."

Keith chuckled. "The night before, I tossed and turned for hours. I was afraid to risk losing our friendship, but I had to tell you. I spent those wakeful hours organizing my thoughts and planning what I'd say. Your dream was right. I loved you then, and I will always love you."

"Your presentation sounded more like a business plan. That college module paid off for you." We laughed.

Now with the truth out, a weight lifted from our hearts. Our relationship brought complications, but life was easier knowing Keith loved me.

For the first time in our lives, we have real partners.

STEPS FORWARD

N ot long before Keith's revelation, the prison held an event to celebrate the Puppies for Parole program which rescued dogs from local kill shelters. Inmates trained the dogs to make them adoptable. Participants spent twenty-four hours a day giving dogs a second chance at life. Without this program, they were certain to be euthanized. Just as the men in prison hoped for a second chance, these dogs needed a reprieve.

As a dog lover, I think it's a wonderful idea. I'm proud of SCCC for taking part in something so positive.

The dogs scampered and played on the prison yard, creating a happy scene in a dull and dreary environment. Thanks to Puppies for Parole, the dogs had futures, and the men thrived too. Gaining responsibility and developing trust and compassion were valuable lessons for the inmates.

Puppies for Parole was a win-win.

Along with hundreds of other employees, I attended the celebration held for the 1,000th adoption of a dog. We gathered in the prison visiting room while an emotional slide show of happy endings brought tears to the eyes of many. Some canine graduates, we found out, helped the disabled, while others gained love and security with families. It was a feel-good moment for the institution, and those moments didn't happen often inside the death fences.

Every warden and assistant warden at SCCC attended the ceremony, and the administration expected every staff member who could to stop by the event. Local dignitaries attended, and Kyle McMasters beamed as he shared happy stories. I left the party in good spirits.

Another celebration, this one meant for inmates, was scheduled for a few weeks later. Keith and Joe Bryson took part in a successful college business program offered by Missouri State University. It was a popular program, and the waiting list to be accepted was long. The college classes embraced all the positive aspects of rehabilitation.

At the end of each module, the prison held a graduation ceremony. As a teacher, I loved when students found success. Since Keith was one of the graduates, the upcoming ceremony held special significance for me.

Unfortunately, Keith, Bryson, and their classmates were the last group to go through the program at SCCC. Funding, which came from private sources, dried up, and the prison made no effort to find other options. Rumors swirled that hard feelings developed between the prison and Missouri State University.

A week after Keith told me he loved me, graduation day arrived. Nearly thirty men completed the module, and all of them invited family members to the ceremony. Keith's daughter, Elise, and her boyfriend drove down from Wisconsin, taking a break from their own college studies, to share in Keith's big day. He was excited to see Elise, and we were both eager for me to meet her.

This graduation wasn't like the ones that came before, however. Since the money faded away, the prison lost its enthusiasm. Barb, who always organized the graduation ceremonies, treated this final event as an annoyance.

She was foul and bitter on the morning of the graduation, and Joe Bryson faced the brunt of her sullen mood. He came into Classroom 10 shaking his head, and Keith and I asked he what was wrong.

"Holy cow. I went to the office to ask Ms. Mason if she needed me to help her with any last-minute details for the ceremony, and she bit my head off!"

"When isn't she biting someone's head off?" I asked and we all laughed.

"She's usually nice to me though, and she's always enjoyed graduation days. Normally she walks on air. This time she acts like she hates it."

"I'll say she's usually nice to you. Remember the time she came in here looking for you, wanting to know where her 'buddy' was?" Keith asked.

Joe Bryson rolled his eyes and sighed. "Yeah, I remember when you told me about that. I don't think she really sees me as her buddy. She just likes the help I give her. But today she acts like it's my fault that there's a graduation."

"Why is she being so ugly about it?" I asked.

"She knows this is the last one, so she doesn't care anymore. There's nothing in it for her now. I don't think she even got a speaker."

I frowned. "I'm sorry she's taking out her frustration on you."

"Thank you." Joe then put on his emotional armor and went back to the office area to help with what he could.

I know how much Keith enjoys going through the program. Nearly every day we talk about his classes, his professors, and how rewarding it is to stretch his business legs once again. He lights up whenever he talks about the stock market or business in general. Those classes put him back in his element. It's bitter-sweet for him to finish the module.

I had some worries about the ceremony, though. Meeting his daughter for the first time put my nerves on edge. I became a blur of activity, hoping to burn off enough energy to calm down and relax once I finally met Elise.

Keith smiled. "Don't worry. She's going to love you."

"I sure hope so."

One o'clock arrived, and we headed to the administration building for the ceremony. Gathered in the prison visiting room, students, their families, two professors from Missouri State University, and a handful of staff members milled around.

This graduation looks nothing like the gala for the dog program.

No slide shows or decorations adorned the room, and it lacked a buzz of excitement from prison officials.

Something is missing. Five things are missing, in fact: Kyle McMasters and the four assistant wardens.

They attended the dog program event but were nowhere in sight when inmates celebrated success. Eleanor Heath's cackle about "not fixing anyone here" rang in my ears.

Few staff members showed up, a glaring difference from the Puppies for Parole event. Those employees who did were custody staff on duty for the event. Their expressions groaned, "Do we really have to be here?"

Barb didn't bother to schedule a guest speaker, as Joe Bryson feared. Three inmates, including Joe, gave speeches. Inspiring words from the men society deemed worthless fell on a woefully small crowd.

The hope and promise men gained through those four college courses were lost on the wardens.

The graduates would be better off if they were treated like dogs. At least dogs are valued at SCCC.

After the ceremony, students and family members socialized. Both professors met the mothers, wives, grandmothers, and children of their students. Smiles, handshakes, hugs, and laughter filled the room.

In the dismal prison experience, families finally found cause to celebrate.

I spent time visiting with Joe Bryson's wife and mother.

"My son has told me how much he enjoys working for you," Mrs. Bryson said as she warmly shook my hand.

"He's a great addition to my classroom and he's such a nice guy. I'm happy to have him working in my room. He talks about both of you often."

"Thank you for seeing that he is a good man," his wife said. She smiled, but tears crept to the edges of her eyes.

"I do see it. He's worked hard in these classes, and I'm very proud of him. I'm so glad you were here to share this moment with him."

I joined Keith where he sat next to Elise and her boyfriend. By now, my nerves had subsided, although I was still a jumble on the inside. The three rose to greet me.

"You must be Elise."

"Yes, I am. It's so good to be here for Dad's big day."

"He's been eager to see you, Elise. Thank you for making the drive down from Beloit."

Elise is bright and thoughtful, and I like her!

Keith pulled a chair up for me to sit with them.

"Dad tells me that you used to teach on the Navajo Reservation."

"Yeah, I did. I taught there for four years, but I taught Navajo students off the reservation too. I also spent a year in Arizona teaching Apaches."

Stay calm. Make a good impression.

Keith's wink and smile told me I succeeded.

"It must've been fascinating working with Native Americans."

We talked about the differences between the Navajo and Apache people. She asked great questions, and I enjoyed sharing experiences. Our conversation was going well.

Suddenly, Elise stopped talking and stared at Keith.

"Dad are you okay?"

"Yeah, I'm fine."

Keith looked tense. She looked at him doubtfully. "You just seem a little 'off' today."

He glanced my way, gave a smile, and said, "Nah, I'm fine."

He's been as nervous about me meeting Elise as I've been.

Twenty minutes after the ceremony ended, the event came to an abrupt close.

"This is over!" barked a guard.

People stopped in mid-sentence, startled by the sudden, jolting words of the officer.

"Time is up! Get out of here!"

The guard yelled at grandmothers and small children as though they were criminals. His gruffness took everyone by surprise.

"Once again, time is up! You need to leave now!"

The guard meant business, and everyone got up to leave.

This is a staggering public relations blunder by the prison. The appropriate thing to say is, "Thank you for attending today. We are as proud of your graduates as you are. We hope you enjoyed your time and can visit your loved one soon." Instead, the prison is being aggressive. It's a demoralizing end to a day already over-shadowed by a lack of interest by the administrators.

Even if Keith wasn't an honoree, I would have been appalled. Because he was involved, I took it to heart.

I know exactly how those mothers, grandmothers, children, and wives feel. How much effort was it for any one of the five wardens to make an appearance? Family members, many of whom traveled hours to be here, could have been treated with respect.

I walked back to the education wing upset. As a teacher, my job was to give inmates an appreciation for education. Maybe the real trick was getting the wardens to appreciate it.

Later, Keith and I talked. "I'm angry that the wardens made a big deal about dogs but couldn't bother to show up when people achieved good things."

"I know, but you know they don't care about inmates."

He's right. Most employees view inmates as just a reason to have a job, but nothing more. Eleanor Heath and the other wardens don't care about improving inmates, and they certainly aren't going to celebrate their successes.

As disheartening as the ceremony was, the day wasn't a total loss. Keith and I shared our day with his daughter, and it went well. We made one more step forward.

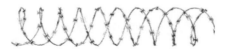

Copy Machines are Dangerous

O nce the dust settled from the disappointments of graduation day, we returned to the normal abnormality inside a prison. Many disturbing events happened on a daily basis at the school, and some of them revolved around something as mundane as the copy machine.

The temptation to use the school copier for unofficial business was strong for many tutors and porters. Some chose to run contraband copies. Pornography, betting slips, and other items not easily found inside a prison were moneymakers. Inmates forced others to run contraband to avoid a beating or to pay off a debt.

Yes, sometimes my tutors weren't in my classroom, but since I ran my own copies, I never worried about them getting into trouble.

Keith left on Tuesday afternoons for church services, and during softball season he'd leave for games and practices. He alternated on Tuesdays between going to church and playing ball. I teased him on softball weeks that he attended "Our Lady of the Fields."

"I've even told the Father that's what you call it."

"What did he say?"

"He said, 'Well, if you aren't going to be in church, I can't think of a better way for you to spend a Tuesday afternoon.' He got a good laugh out of it."

Bryson worked closely with the Restorative Justice program, and sometimes he left for meetings with the Inmate Activities Coordinator, Julie Redding. One afternoon, he said, "Ma'am, I have a meeting with Mrs. Redding. Is it okay if I go now?"

"Of course. Go ahead and go."

Julie Redding more than once told me how much she appreciated Bryson's help. I thought nothing of it when he asked to go to her office a few times a week, and that afternoon was no different. Keith and I busied ourselves working with students, so I gave Bryson the thumbs up to leave and forgot about it.

Not long after Bryson left my classroom, Barb threw another one of her blowups in the office. All of us stopped working, partly out of curiosity and partly out of fear of her wrath.

"Get out of here! You're fired!" Her shouts rang down the hallway from the office area.

A few of my students got up to step into the hallway to catch a view of the ruckus.

"We don't need her coming unglued at anyone in here, guys, so just sit down and do your work."

I gave them a look that stopped them in their tracks. Looking dejected, they sat.

Bryson was at his Restorative Justice meeting for at least half an hour when he walked into my room with Barb in tow. Neither looked happy.

He seems so distressed. I hope a family tragedy hasn't struck.

Keith and I glanced at each other, wondering what was wrong.

Bryson approached my desk. "Ma'am, I just wanted to tell you I'm terribly sorry and that I've enjoyed working in your classroom." Struggling to hold himself together, he extended his hand, which I shook.

"Wait, are you quitting?"

"No, I'm not quitting. I was fired."

"Fired? Who fired you?"

"I was written up and can't work here any longer. I'm so sorry. I wanted to come tell you myself. Thank you again for letting me work for you."

With that, Joe Bryson turned and walked out, escorted by Barb.

"What just happened?" I asked Keith.

"I have no idea. He was with Mrs. Redding. If something happened in her office, why didn't they just take him to the hole from there?"

"That's a good question. I can't imagine Bryson doing anything wrong. He's always a goody two shoes, and he's in tight with the IAC. This is strange."

Class demanded that we keep our minds on our work. Before long, Carlson, a tutor from Sandra's classroom, knocked at my door.

He motioned for me to speak with him in the hallway. He kept looking over his shoulder, making sure no one listened in on our conversation.

"What's up, Carlson?"

"Ma'am, do you know what happened with Bryson?"

"I know that he said he was fired, but I don't know anything more than that."

"That's what I figured. I thought you should know what went down. I didn't want to say this in front of your class, but you have a right to know."

"Okay, what's going on?"

"Well, he was using the photocopier."

"The copier? That doesn't make any sense."

"And it wasn't for anything good," Carlson added.

"No, Bryson was at Mrs. Redding's office in a meeting. He was working on something for her."

"Bryson wasn't at any meeting."

"What was he doing?"

Lowering his voice and looking around once more to make sure we didn't have any eavesdroppers, Carlson whispered, "He was running off porn."

I hear his words, but I can't wrap my head around this.

"Porn? Straight-laced Bryson was running off porn?"

"Yes, Ma'am. Sets of ninety-three different pornographic pictures. Some were of men."

"Oh my God. How was he caught? Who caught him?"

"Ms. Mason. There was a paper jam, and when she went to fix it, there were the pictures. This wasn't the first time he's done it, either. It's just the first time he was caught."

"He didn't seem like the type."

"I know, Ma'am. Sometimes you don't know why people do these things."

"Thanks for letting me know. I'd better get back in class."

I entered my room, sat in my office chair, and scooted over to Keith to fill him in.

"Bryson's such a good Baptist. He always carries his Bible around and acts embarrassed if he hears a dirty joke. He was running hard-core porn on the school copier?"

"Carlson said it wasn't the only time Bryson had run porn off, either. How is that even possible?"

Keith's face lit up with an epiphany. "I think I know how. What if he hasn't really been going to meetings at the IAC office? We've never checked on him to see if that's where he's really gone. We took his word for it, and Mrs. Redding told you about how much help he was. Bryson must have used that as an excuse to get out of class because he knew you had no reason to doubt him."

"I think you're right. I don't even know what to say right now—except that it's poetic justice that Barb nearly insisted that I hire him, and she ran around here calling him her buddy. Now she's the one who caught her buddy running pornography in her office."

Between classes, I walked to her office. "I heard Bryson was caught running some things he wasn't supposed to."

Barb's eyes went wild with anger and she fumed. "Yes, he was. I don't want to talk about it. He knew better."

"Yes, he knew better, and he never had permission to use the copier in the first place. I've made it clear to my tutors that they aren't to run copies."

"Well, he's gone now."

Returning to the classroom, Keith and I continued our conversation. "I hope it was worth it for him because he's lost his job and now he's sitting in the hole," Keith said. We finished out the day, still in shock.

The next morning, Keith sat down at his desk and said, "You aren't going to believe this. I just saw Bryson out on the walk."

"What? They didn't put him in the hole?"

"No. He said Mrs. Redding interceded for him."

"She's keeping him from going to the hole? Staff isn't supposed to get in the middle of things like that."

"That's not all. Bryson wants all the Restorative Justice craft supplies that he keeps in his desk. Some are markers and scissors. He wants me to bring them to him. If I get caught with that stuff, I'll be written up for having contraband."

"You're not going to take it. We'll figure something out. I won't put you in danger of getting a write up. Mrs. Redding let him walk around with contraband, but I'm not sending anyone out of this room with it."

Two days later, student Robbie Wilson approached me. "Ma'am, I hate to ask, but Bryson saw me on the walk and wants me to get his craft supplies. He said Giammanco won't do it. I don't really feel right about it, but he insisted that I bring him his things. He said he has to have them, but he's not allowed to be in the education hallway."

"I know what was left in his desk drawer. I won't let Giammanco have those things, and I'm not going to put you in that position either. I'm not sending any inmate out of here with contraband."

"Can I tell Bryson that if he asks me? He says Mrs. Redding says it's okay if we bring it to him."

"You tell Bryson it's my fault that you, Giammanco, or any other inmates aren't bringing him that stuff. I'm not thrilled that he is trying to press you guys. You shouldn't be jeopardized because he got himself in trouble."

"Thank you, Ma'am."

"If Mrs. Redding is so eager for him to get his supplies, then she can come get them herself," I told Keith.

That afternoon, Keith passed the message on to Bryson while out on the walk.

After a week of back and forth, IAC Redding wrote a letter authorizing the release of the items in Bryson's desk. Normally staff members wouldn't ask for favors on behalf of an inmate—especially not an inmate who should be sitting in the hole. I shook my head as I read the letter.

Some people have more pull than others around here, and apparently Bryson knows who they are.

I gathered up the craft supplies and left them in the office area for Julie Redding to pick up.

We'd soon learn that Bryson and his contraband were child's play in the grand scheme of things at SCCC.

THE MAJOR'S GARDEN
HAS A PLANT

I was once again down to one tutor. Even though we were swamped with work, I wasn't going to rush into getting another employee.

Bryson's behavior burned me, both because of the pornography and because he put Keith and my students in harm's way by demanding that they take him contraband. I'm wasn't in a hurry to bring drama into Classroom 10. We went six weeks before I hired someone new.

Mark Crawford, quiet, hardworking, and good at math, was a good fit. He knew Keith from their housing unit, and Keith gave him the thumbs up when I interviewed candidates.

Life settled into a new routine and, except for Barb's attacks, life remained pretty good in the education department. Barb fired another porter, also for copying extracurricular materials, but otherwise the school ran smoothly.

We limped along for a few weeks without a porter until Major Joe Jenkins insisted that Barb hire a specific inmate, a man named Ron Kessler, as our new porter. She hired him on the spot.

Red flags popped up. The major wasn't in our direct chain of command, and he had no business involving himself in the education wing.

Something is up. Why is Barb suddenly so chummy with the major? Why is she letting him call the shots in our hallway?

It became a topic of conversation between my tutors and me. I brought it up to Keith and Crawford after observing Kessler in action for a few days.

"One of the flower beds on the yard is called the Major's Garden. I have a hunch that this guy is a plant in Major Jenkins's 'garden.' Why else would he care who works in our hallway?"

Both men nodded in agreement.

"There's something weird going on, that's for sure," Crawford said.

"Let's watch each other's backs because Kessler doesn't have a good reputation," Keith added.

Students told me that our new porter enjoyed free rein around the camp.

He was big, aggressive, and immune from consequences—a dangerous combination in a maximum security prison—thanks to his cozy relationship with Jenkins. He made the most of his protected status.

"I saw Kessler walk into the major's office and have Bo Jeffreys thrown in the hole just because he said so," a student said in the middle of class one day.

An inmate with too much power and the major's blessing roaming freely in the education department concerned nearly everyone. His arrival in the school unnerved the students.

"I live in 5 House, same as Kessler, and he gets to stay out in the wing after all the rest of us have to lock down," Marcus Pike, a first session student, said.

"What do you mean? How long is he out of the wing after lock down?" Men wanted to know.

"He's out in the wing for an hour or longer than the rest of us. When some of us ask why, the guards tell us that it's major's orders," Jones explained.

"That's not the half of it," added Edgar Crisp, another student from Housing Unit 5.

"What do you mean?"

"He's not just out in the wing. They let him go from cell to cell to cell."

"Sounds like business is being conducted." I said.

"It sure does, Ma'am."

Matt Carter told me this same thing in the parking lot after work the other day. These guys are telling the truth.

Finding anything nice to say about our new porter was difficult. A violent man serving a life sentence for murder, he made a great strong arm for the major. From the get-go, Kessler caused turmoil in the school.

"I work for the major and not the education department," he bragged.

He got into fights and the major kept him out of the hole, and that wasn't all. The major gave him food from luncheons, allowed him to go anywhere on the camp, and gave him the power to send other inmates to ad seg. While he didn't sign his name on the paperwork, all Kessler had to do was rat on an inmate to the major, and it was a done deal. Staff members couldn't give our inmate employees a stick of gum, yet Kessler received all sorts of perks.

Officer Ballard, the education officer who replaced Underwood, frequently told inmates, "If you come to school out of uniform, I'll write you up!"

The prison required all inmates, workers included, to wear a complete gray uniform—no shorts or t-shirts allowed—no matter how hot the weather. Kessler, however, came to work out of uniform daily, and neither of the officers batted an eye.

Everyone noticed. Students asked questions. "How does he get away with wearing a t-shirt to work, Ma'am?"

"I think we know why he gets away with it," replied other students.

Our voices lowered when discussing Kessler because everyone feared him.

Kelly and I sat in her room talking about his behavior one day. "Did you see what he did this morning? He sat in the CO's chair, drinking coffee—while Presley stood," I told her.

"What is up with that?"

"Yeah, since when do inmates sit in Presley's chair drinking coffee while he stands? This guy has an unhealthy amount of sway around here."

The scenario repeated itself, day in and day out. The major protected Kessler no matter what. His belligerent attitude was dangerous. Within his first few weeks in our hallway, the man hired to help us threatened students, tutors, and even staff.

"I told Richard Blake about how he threatened my tutor—and me—and that I wanted him fired," Doris confided. "Richard did nothing. I'm afraid."

The rest of us are afraid, too.

Unlike previous porters, Kessler didn't clean the classrooms. He maintained the hallway, the bathrooms, and the office area. The tutors were now responsible for cleaning classrooms. He didn't run copies, either. He did, however, stop by my classroom, often, to shoot the breeze.

Just like his boss, the major, he thinks he's a charming ladies' man. He isn't.

Even though it wasn't his job, about a week after he was hired he walked into Classroom 10 and asked, "Can I take out your trash?"

I worked with a student at my desk and was too busy to stop to talk, so Keith answered him. "Sure, if you want to."

Kessler bristled, took out the trash, and left my room.

A few minutes later, I went to the office to run a few copies. I returned to find him standing over Keith at his desk. All my students stared at the spectacle. Kessler and Keith's backs were turned to me, so they were unaware that I saw and heard everything.

"You shouldn't disrespect me like that. I'm going to beat your ass." Kessler's fists balled at his sides. At 6'5" and 350 pounds, Kessler formed a forceful presence.

"I didn't disrespect you. You asked if you could take out the trash, and I told you that you could if you wanted to." Keith was angry, but he kept his composure.

I'm ticked. He's pulled similar stunts with other tutors, but this time he's brought his aggression into my room.

"Mr. Kessler, I want to talk to you." I pointed at him, and he followed me out into the hallway. "Just what do you think you're doing threatening my employee?"

"He disrespected me."

"How?"

"When I came in earlier and asked you if you wanted me to take out the trash, he told me I could if I wanted to."

"Yeah, and what's wrong with that?"

"He thinks he's better than me. He was acting superior and thought he could tell me what to do. He embarrassed me and now people are going to talk about me."

"He answered you because I was busy and couldn't talk at the time. It's his job to clean my classroom. As far as I'm concerned, he's the one you needed to ask because you were trying to take over his job."

"No, Ma'am, he disrespected me."

"If you think someone politely saying you can empty the trash if you want to is disrespectful, you seriously need to change your way of thinking."

The conversation isn't going the way he wants it to.

"Furthermore, if you're worried about being embarrassed in front of other inmates, you did a fine job of that yourself."

"What do you mean?"

"You went into a room full of students and threatened my employee for a stupid reason. How do you think you look now? No one thought twice about what Giammanco said to you, but I can guarantee you that all fifteen of those men are going to spread it across the yard that you barged into my room and made a fool of yourself."

"I didn't think of it that way."

"No, you didn't think about anything at all. Don't come in my classroom again."

I left him in the hallway as I walked back into my room. My students squirmed, and Keith and Crawford shook their heads.

"Kessler is not welcome in my classroom."

"I know Giammanco feels the same way I do about this, but we aren't going to let you be alone with that guy from now on. There's something really wrong with him, and he's a big-time creep," Crawford said.

"Thank you because I don't want to be around him. He's a menace and needs to be removed from this hallway."

He wasn't removed, though. Richard Blake ignored the pleas, requests, and demands of staff members to remove him from the education department. Blake proved to be a kiss-ass to the major and Kessler served as the eyes, ears, and enforcer of Joe Jenkins.

THE NUTS AND BOLTS OF HAVING THE SCREWS PUT ON US

I t didn't take long for Kessler's nasty presence to impact my life directly.

Now that he sees I have no interest in him and that he needs to stay out of my classroom, his brutish behavior is getting worse.

He tried pushing boundaries any chance he got, and even stormed into my classroom early one day. Looking at Keith and Crawford, he said, "You're going to clean Mrs. Massey's classroom. I'll clean this one."

We gave "hell no" looks to each other. In unison, Crawford and Keith said, "No, we're not."

"Oh, yeah you are. I'm going to clean this room. Get out!"

I've had enough.

"No, they aren't going anywhere. This is my classroom. They are my employees, and you have no authority over them. You're the one who's unwelcome in this room. Leave now." He hesitated. "Get out, Mr. Kessler."

Within a few days, we found out that rumors swirled around the prison yard about us. Kessler and Reese, Richard Blake's tutor, said Keith and I held hands in class.

The accusations are absurd. Two security cameras and fifteen sets of eyes are on us constantly. We never leave the room together, nor do we spend any time together outside of class in the office or work room. It's impossible for us to have physical contact without being spotted.

The rumors, nonetheless, were serious in the prison environment. Kessler sought revenge, and he was intent on getting rid of Keith, me, or both. "I don't get why Reese would do this. He has no reason to attack us.," I said.

"Reese just wants to feel important," Crawford told us.

"Yeah, why is he even a tutor? Blake doesn't teach any classes now, so he doesn't need a tutor," Keith added.

"Believe me, teachers have been wondering the same thing. Reese has too much time on his hands, and now he's stirring up trouble for my classroom. I'm not happy."

"Oh, he has a reputation for being a drama king. He caused uproars in the church group last month. He even criticized the chaplain."

"Not only that, Keith, but he's bad-mouthed Mr. Turner while he's gone," Crawford added.

"You're right. He spreads discord everywhere. Kessler is a perfect ally for someone, like Reese, who wants to feel important. It's no accident that Reese cozied up to the major's pet." Keith's face showed our shared concern.

"I think both of you guys are right. Drama's the last thing I want around here."

Some coworkers told me to brush off the rumors.

"Don't worry about them, Caroline. They're only offenders. Who cares what gossipy inmates say?" Mike told me.

"It's not that simple. Kessler and Reese may be offenders, but they have the ears of Blake and Jenkins. That makes their comments more dangerous than the run-of-the-mill inmate talk on the walk."

"I'm sure it will blow over."

"I hope so because this isn't trouble I need."

Kelly, Doris, and Sandra also told me not to pay any attention to the rumors.

I can't shake the feeling that things are about to get ugly.

I called Randy and asked him how to handle the situation.

"You need to put a stop to it. You're staff. Let Reese know it."

Randy's right. I'll meet Reese head on.

The next morning, Reese walked into my classroom to deliver testing rosters,

There's no time like the present.

"I've heard there are rumors going around the yard about staff, Reese."

He stiffened. "Ma'am, there's always talk going on about teachers having sex with offenders. It's not just you."

Funny, I never mentioned offenders, sex, or me.

"The rumors need to stop."

He shifted back and forth nervously. "Now, Ma'am, I want you to know I'm doing everything I can to put a stop to those rumors."

Sure, you are. That's why several people say you're the one spreading the rumors, Reese.

"Making false accusations against staff is a serious offense. It can get an inmate thrown into the hole."

"Why, yes, Ma'am, it is serious. That's why I've been trying to stop the rumors."

"You need to tell 'whoever' is spreading these lies that I know. I know, Reese. It needs to stop or, as staff, I'll do something about it."

Reese broke my gaze and beat a hasty retreat from Classroom 10.

I turned to Keith. "Well, we'll see what happens now."

"It was obvious he knew exactly what you were talking about and that you know it's him."

"Everything he said proved his guilt."

At lunchtime, Richard Blake called me into his office.

"I heard you had an argument with Reese. Can you tell me why you're mad at him?"

"There was no argument."

"He went to your room to drop off papers, and when he returned he was very upset. He said you were mad at him."

"I didn't argue with him, and I never said I was mad at him. Was there anything else you needed to see me about?"

Richard motioned towards a chair for me to sit down, but I shook my head and remained standing.

He insisted on making excuses for his employee. "Reese hasn't been himself lately. He's going through a lot. You need to keep that in mind when you're talking with him."

"I'm sorry to hear he's having problems."

"Oh, he is. His mother is very sick, and you know he hasn't spoken to his brother for years. His sister is going through a bad time and they've been arguing. Reese just has so much going on. You need to give him some slack."

You should tell your employee to back off his gossip mongering. Don't tell me to 'give him some slack.'

I left his office and went to lunch. Days went by and nothing improved. No matter how hard I tried to move forward, the accusations seeped into my classroom.

"Kessler was bragging on the walk that he and the major are going to get you fired," one student told me.

"He's jealous because you won't give him the time of day, Ma'am," said another.

Daily, reports filtered in that Kessler, Reese, and the major set their sights on us.

Offender Teague, the tutor working across the hall from Classroom 10, told me in a hushed voice, "Kessler tells tutors every day that he's looking for a way to get Giammanco fired."

We weren't Kessler's only victims. He threatened students and tutors and made life uncomfortable for teachers. Doug Mathers, the newest member of the teaching staff, was physically confronted and verbally assaulted by Kessler several times. No one stopped him. Mike and I spoke to Blake, privately and in staff meetings, asking him to fire Kessler. He ignored us.

Any other worker would be sent to the hole for any of Kessler's stunts.

Our acting supervisor wasn't the only employee who catered to Kessler. The education officers witnessed his threatening behavior and did nothing. In fact, they joined in with him.

"Ma'am, Kessler is at the front desk right now laughing with Ballard and Presley," Marcus Wells told me as he walked into class.

"Okay."

"Ma'am, they're talking about you."

"What did they say?"

"Kessler said, 'Someday I'm going to get that bitch walked out of here,' and the officers laughed about it."

My stress level amped up a few more notches.

WAR ON MULTIPLE FRONTS

Meanwhile, Barb continued her assaults. More than a year passed since her blow up at the training trailer, and every day had been miserable. She hadn't ordered supplies for me since Randy Turner left on what now seemed like permanent leave. Other teachers received supply orders, but not me.

At a Friday staff meeting, I proposed a solution.

"Richard, could teachers have a supply allotment? If each teacher was budgeted fifty dollars or so, we'd know what we could spend throughout the year for our classrooms."

"Shut up! Shut up! I know what this is about! You aren't going to do this to me. You aren't going to do this. No, you can't have an allotment!"

Barb's having another meltdown.

Everyone sat in stunned silence.

"My question was for Richard."

Richard sat back and didn't say a word. Barb said plenty. She yelled with spit flying out of her mouth. She pounded the desk. During her ten-minute rant, she stood and pointed at the rest of the staff. "You tell her! You tell her what she's doing! You tell her she's wrong!"

Thankfully, my coworkers didn't join in with her, but no one spoke up in my defense either. No one wanted to cross her.

She cycled through her tirade, ending red-faced and breathing heavily. The meeting ended on that note.

After everyone left, I cornered Blake. "Are you going to let her continue to treat me that way?"

"You know how Barb is. She has mental issues and there's no sense in putting myself in her line of fire. She stopped after a while."

"She stopped when she'd screamed at me for ten minutes. She didn't stop because you—our boss—did anything to stop her."

"Just let it drop." He gave me a stern look and walked away.

And so, life went miserably on. Barb bullied and targeted me at will. Now Barb, Kessler, and Reese worked against me at the prison, and according to rumor, so did the major.

A hostile workplace was only half my struggle.

My youngest son's deployment in Afghanistan was a constant worry. Every lunch break I anxiously checked my phone for a Facebook message from him.

The stress inside the prison is terrible enough without the constant fear for my son's safety. I worry every moment of the day. I don't even watch the news because I can't bear to hear about war casualties.

As a gunner, Kevin served on the front lines, manning the turret atop a large artillery vehicle. He protected the bomb squad with his keen shooting skills. One Saturday, he called me after his first kill. It shook him, and he struggled emotionally.

"Mom, I know I killed a guy yesterday."

"Was he trying to kill your men?"

"Yeah, they were under fire, and after I shot him the shooting stopped. That's how I know I killed him."

"Then, Honey, you did your job. You kept your guys safe and alive, so they can come home to their families." I hoped my words helped.

I told Randy about my conversation with Kevin. He reassured me. "If it didn't bother him to kill someone, he wouldn't be a good man. If he didn't kill those he had to, he wouldn't be a good soldier. Kevin is both a good man and a good soldier."

Kevin's success on the battlefield made him a target for snipers. He didn't share much about the daily dangers in the Forward Operating Base (FOB) because he didn't want to cause me any more worry.

I pick up enough in his voice to know that he and the men he serves with are in dire circumstances.

Random artillery shells lobbed into the FOB. The constant threat of dumb luck—of simply standing in the wrong spot—was intense.

One of his most traumatizing experiences occurred when a suicide bomber attacked a market in the nearby village. My son, who didn't even like the sight of needles, assisted the medic.

"Mom, so many of them were children."

He always had a soft spot for kids.

I realized that nothing I, nor anyone else, said could ever take those images from Kevin's memory. Every day I prayed that the cruelties of war weren't overwhelming my brave but kind-hearted son. I prayed that he'd come home safely, and for the most part, I trusted that he would be fine.

On July 4, though, I couldn't shake a terrible sense that Kevin would be killed. I spent the entire day in a quiet panic.

The next morning, as usual, before I left for work I typed a Facebook message.

"Hey, Kev. I love you and hope you're okay." I hit send.

But I don't think you are.

In the carpool, I tried to push my fears away by listening to Mike share stories about his holiday get-together. No matter how hard I tried, though, persistent fear crept into my thoughts.

July 5th was a Friday and a planned professional development day. As chairperson of the PD committee, I led the workshops. Instead of mentally preparing for my presentation, my thoughts clouded with fear. Once we arrived at school, we went to Kelly's room to shoot the breeze before the meeting began.

At 7:20 A.M., Officer Robertson, filling in for the vacationing Presley, yelled down the hall, "Caroline, you have an emergency phone call!"

My heart stopped, and my blood ran cold. With each step down the hallway, an anchor of fear weighed down my legs.

Which one of my sons will it be?

Rick was in the Netherlands at what seemed like a safe base, but I couldn't rule out the possibility of a terrorist attack. I worried most, of course, about Kevin. A few weeks earlier, I confided to Rick that I dreaded phone calls from unknown numbers.

"My heart sinks every time I get one because I'm afraid it will be bad news about Kevin."

"Don't worry, Mom. If anything happens to Kevin, I'll call you. Since I'm in the military, I'll hear before you do. I won't let you find out your son was killed from a stranger."

Whose voice will I hear when I pick up the phone?

I reached the counter at the guard's desk, and Robertson handed me the phone with a sick look on his face.

"Hello?"

"Hey, Mom."

It's Rick.

My knees buckled, and I leaned on the counter to remain standing.

"Rick, what happened?"

Silence. Then, a shuddering breath.

"Rick, tell me what happened to Kevin."

"His vehicle was either blown up or was in an accident. I don't know. I don't know how many people were killed." Emotional and rambling, Rick spoke for a few minutes.

He's not saying what I need to hear.

"Rick, is Kevin alive or dead?"

"He was alive when he talked with Dad for about a minute on the medic's satellite phone, but he's hurt bad. I don't know if he's still alive, Mom." He broke into tears.

I stood in the middle of a maximum-security prison, doing my best to comfort my son from halfway around the world.

"Mom, if he does make it, they are going to fly him from Bagram to Landstuhl, Germany."

Ten or fifteen minutes into our conversation, Rick said, "Hey, Mom, Sergeant Miles is here. I'll let you know once I know anything more." We said our goodbyes.

I need to talk to Keith. I can barely breathe. I can't leave here without letting him know what's going on. Who knows how long I may have to be gone.

A new guard, a woman I'd never seen before, arrived at the education wing to help Robertson. In shock, standing at the counter as she set her things down at the desk, I asked, "Can you call Housing Unit 3? Ask them to send my tutor, Giammanco, to the education wing."

"I sure can. It'll be about another twenty minutes before the next movement window opens, but I'll call for him."

"Thank you." I stumbled back to my classroom.

What will the next days or weeks hold? Will I go to Germany? Will I claim a body? What are Kevin's injuries? How is my fun-loving, outdoorsy, and athletic son going to deal with traumatic injuries if he survives?

So many unknowns swam through my head, and all of them terrified me. I couldn't wrap my head around what awaited me outside the prison walls. My head was in a haze, my legs were weak, and my heart wanted to burst.

Keith is the only one who can help me hold myself together. I won't leave the prison until I talk with him.

He walked into Classroom 10, beaming about the chance to see me unexpectedly.

He thinks I called him up just to see him.

One look at me and his face sobered. "What's wrong?"

I broke down as Keith listened. "What will I do if Kevin is dead?"

"We don't know that he is, and right now we are going to focus on what we do know. What we know is that Kevin was alive and doing well enough that he could make a phone call, so we know he was conscious and able to talk. That's big. Let's not worry about the 'what ifs' until we have to face them."

"You are the only thing keeping me together right now."

"I'll always be here for you. We don't know what the next weeks or months bring, but more than anything I wish I could be there for you on the outside. If they'd let me go with you, I would come back. I'd make up any time I was gone. I just wish you didn't have to go through this without me by your side."

"I know you'd be with me if you could. You are with me, and having your love and support is what's going to keep me going."

"You know," as he leaned forward in his chair, putting his elbows on his knees, "something told me last night that I needed to pray for Kevin. I always pray for our kids, but I prayed for Kevin first last night. I had an urgent need to pray for him, and I asked for God's protection over him."

"Your faith is one of the things I love most about you. That's why he's alive right now—your faith and prayers were heard."

"You should probably make plans with Mr. Vaughn to leave, Honey. I know you don't want to face what awaits you out there, but Kevin may need to call you when he lands in Germany, and you can't get a call in here. You need to be able to answer that call when it comes."

"You're right, I need to go. I just couldn't leave without talking with you."

"Since it might be a while before you're back, is there anything you need me to do around here?"

"Not that I can think of. Just pray."

"I will. Non-stop."

Mike drove that day and held his keys in hand when I went to his room.

"I've been waiting for you to be ready. I knew you needed some time to pull yourself together, but I've already told them in the office that I'm taking off whenever you need to go home."

During our ride, Rick called with an update on Kevin. The specifics were sketchy, but Kevin was alive and on a plane to Germany. Rick's sergeant offered to take him to Landstuhl Air Force Base, allowing him to be there when his brother landed on the tarmac. Rick called me again from Germany. Kevin arrived, still covered in desert sand and in bad shape.

We still have him.

In the field, his vitals spiraled, and the medic gave him a shot to revive him. He was wide awake and in pain. While at Landstuhl, tests revealed three broken vertebrae, a shattered left knee, a traumatic brain injury, and a spleen on the verge of rupturing.

Both my sons spent a week in Germany awaiting a medical flight to the United States. Kevin stabilized, and the doctors continued to run tests. During that week, I returned to work at the prison.

Sitting at home for days on end, bouncing off the walls with my grief and worry, won't help me.

Arranging Family Medical Leave took time, and it was easier to fill out the paperwork from work than at home. The need for Keith's support also drew me back to the prison.

Finally, my boys flew together to Fort Belvoir, Virginia. The Army arranged flights and accommodations for my ex-husband, his wife, and me. At the hospital, everyone focused on Kevin's recovery, and disagreements from the past were shelved. Rick stayed by his brother's side without fail for as long as his emergency leave lasted, sleeping in the hospital room recliner.

The military treated us exceptionally well, and the staff at the hospital on Fort Belvoir was wonderful.

His dad and I agreed to switch off for as long as our son was hospitalized. I spent two weeks with Kevin before I returned to Missouri.

I boarded my return flight to Missouri, uncertain of what awaited me at the prison. Before I'd left for Virginia, whispers of death threats circulated against us. The major played for keeps, and some of his henchmen threatened Keith who, unlike me, was trapped inside those death fences. For two weeks, I'd had no contact with him.

Is he safe? There's no way for me to know until I return to work.

Kevin left the battlefield in Afghanistan, and now I returned to a different type of warfront.

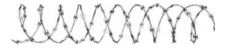

BLACKMAIL AND BRAVADO

S ome strange and unsettling events took place at SCCC during my stay in Virginia. Sandra Jennings, unhappy with the new developments, was determined to get answers. Normally laid back, Sandra became sick and tired of writing conduct violations that custody staff ignored.

"It never used to be this way," Sandra vented to me.

"No, usually if we write someone up, they go straight to the hole. What's been going on?"

"I've had students come back to class saying, 'I talked to the major and he told me not to worry about your write up. He sent me back to class, so here I am.' They laugh at me, Caroline. I'm not putting up with this any longer."

What Sandra described cut teachers off at the knees. No one, except Doris McGeehon, wrote students up for non-sensical reasons. If Sandra wrote a CDV, the inmate deserved it, plain and simple.

She has some goofy tendencies, but when it comes to fair and level-headed performance, she is a solid employee.

During the two weeks I was gone, the problem escalated, and Sandra refused to remain quiet. We already didn't wear blue. Now Major Jenkins backed inmates over teachers.

Since Richard proved useless as a supervisor, Sandra approached Major Joe Jenkins on her own, inviting him to meet with the faculty. He agreed to come to the education wing at lunchtime of the Wednesday after I returned from Fort Belvoir. We sat around a long conference table while Sandra explained our concerns. Other teachers chimed in with their experiences. Major Jenkins listened, along with Captain Keil who attended as the major's sidekick.

"This is a safety and security issue, and the prison is supposed to be all about safety and security," Sandra said as she sat down.

Standing slowly and deliberately, Jenkins looked across the room at us. "If you don't like me or the way I do things, that's okay. It's fine. But..." He paused for effect.

Everyone in the room waited to hear what he said next.

He took a moment to make eye contact with each of us and continued, "You should know that if you choose to complain about me or the way I do things, I've collected damning information on each of you."

We gasped.

He glared and let his comments sink in before he went on. "I will use the information I've collected against you if you complain about me. I thought you should know what I'll do before you say anything that crosses me."

A smug smile crossed his face. Captain Keil sneered.

The head of custody just blackmailed the entire teaching staff.

None of us, except Barb and Richard, seemed comfortable with what transpired. Richard sat beside me, smiling a kiss-ass smile. He understood the rules of the major's sick game.

The major's threats went beyond blackmail—which is a crime that puts people in prison. He also broke the department's duty to report policy. If an employee was aware that a coworker committed a crime or broke policy, he was required to report it to his superiors. Failure to report resulted in termination.

The major just admitted to collecting employee violations to cover his own misbehavior, and he should be fired.

Everyone in the room, except for Richard and Barb, sat stunned. Blake leaned back in his chair with a grin on his face as we teachers looked at each other in disbelief. The head of custody openly declared war on the teaching staff, and we were defenseless.

Blake is either a wimp, or he's in cahoots with the major.

CONNECTIONS

The major's threats shell-shocked the teachers, and I shared what happened at the meeting with Keith.

"Okay, this is getting nuts. Jenkins blackmailed the teachers. He's more of a criminal than most of us who are wearing gray in here. Where does he get off thinking he can threaten people—people who aren't doing anything wrong—when he plays favorites with a thug like Kessler?"

"I don't know, but I couldn't believe it when he said it."

"Did anybody say anything?"

"Blake sat there, saying nothing, of course. I told the major that I didn't feel threatened by his comments because I know I haven't done anything wrong."

"Good for you. Someone needs to stand up to him, but it's not surprising the spineless wonder of an educational supervisor we have around here kept quiet."

"Blake is worse than useless. I think he's involved with whatever the major is up to, or at the very least he has his own game he doesn't want the major to put an end to. He'll do anything to keep the heat off him. He should have protected his staff, but he sat there with a shit-eating grin instead."

"Things are only going to get worse around here. You need to quit. Get out of here. I will catch up with you later, but I don't want you in here. It's not safe."

"I'm not leaving you if I can help it."

"I know that you don't want to, but the reality is that too many cards are stacking up against us now. We both know that at some time they are going to make their move, and when they do I'll be thrown into the hole and I won't be able to protect you then."

I could quit, but I don't want to leave Keith alone in here. I don't want us to be apart, either. I appreciate that he wants me out of here, but I'm going to stick it out for as long as I can. We are safer together when we can watch each other's backs.

We tried our best to find silver linings, and our love carried both of us through the treachery surrounding us.

One morning Keith and I sat at our desks and talked about our first moments together. "I remember the first time I saw you, Keith. It felt like we'd known each other forever."

"I'll never forget it."

"When I walked into the hallway to call you for your interview, our eyes met. My heart leapt. It was the first time I'd ever seen you, but my heart knew you."

Keith paused, as though he wasn't certain if he should say something.

The last time he had that look I stood at the filing cabinet months earlier, on the day when he knew someday I'd be his wife.

"What is it, Keith?"

"The interview wasn't the first time we saw each other."

"What?"

"It wasn't the first time our eyes met. There was a time a few months earlier when we first saw each other."

"We did?"

"Yes, you probably don't remember it. I was at the library door, and you were running copies in the office area."

A memory I repressed came flooding back.

"That was you?"

"You remember?"

"I remember running copies, and a man stood in the library doorway. Our eyes met, and I had the most intense feeling in the world. I was overwhelmed and turned away. He, you I mean, ducked your head and stepped back into the library."

"You do remember!"

"I do now, but at the time I was so freaked out that I pushed it out of my mind. I thought I was going crazy."

"Some people would say that you are." He shot me a wink.

"It was you! No wonder we immediately clicked."

"I left here that day knowing I had to find a way to work with you. That's why I applied to be a tutor in the first place."

"You didn't talk to me that day, though."

"No, I didn't. I wanted to, believe me, but I was afraid you'd think I was just some creepy inmate hitting on you."

"That was a good call. I was in a bad place back then, and I probably would've thought that. Why haven't you said something to me before now? We've known each other over a year."

"I wanted to, lots of times, but I didn't think I should. Now we know we love each other, but, at first, I didn't want to pressure you or make you think I was stalking you. From the first time I saw you, I knew we were supposed to be together."

"That lightning bolt changed our lives."

"It saved both of us."

In the middle of hell, Keith and I have found our once in a lifetime love story.

"That's not the only connection we've had. I think there was another one before we ever met."

"What are you talking about?"

"We've talked about how difficult life was before I was arrested, and how miserable you were."

"Right."

"Remember when you told me you were suicidal on your birthday, September 10th, four years ago?"

"Yeah, that was a horrible day. I was so depressed."

"That was the same day I was sentenced to prison in state court."

"You were sentenced on my birthday?"

"Yeah, I hadn't mentioned it before because you always say your birthday is cursed."

"I think it is! If something bad can happen on my birthday, it does. The last time I had a good birthday was in 2001—and the next day 9-11 happened."

"Well, I hope your birthday isn't really cursed, and I promise from now on I'm going to do everything I can to make sure you have good ones."

"As connected as we are, the only thing that explains why I was so depressed that day, more so than I'd been in months, was that it was such a devastating day for you too."

"That's what I've thought all along. I've told you that I loved you before I even knew you, and I mean it."

LONDON BRIDGES

A fter a long and difficult summer, working conditions did not improve. In late September, Kessler crossed a line that brought me in direct opposition to Major Jenkins.

I'm not looking for a fight, but staff and inmates are endangered, and someone has to speak up.

Kessler acted like he ran the education department, and, in many ways, he did. His bullying permeated the school. As an inmate, he had no authority to order anyone around, but Richard Blake and the education officers forgot that.

I hadn't.

Tamara Wilson, who replaced Melanie Foster after she retired, worked directly across the hall from me. Quiet and professional, we all considered Tamara a welcome addition to the teaching staff. Her husband, Bill, served as the new prison chaplain. He'd worked at the prison for about a year before Tamara started teaching there.

The previous chaplain, Ed Henderson, left following a heated battle of wills with Major Jenkins, a pronounced Muslim. The major's meddling in religion on the camp undermined Chaplain Henderson, and he spoke out against the major. In retaliation, Jenkins assigned two violent ad seg inmates as the chaplain's employees. Jenkins upped the stakes when, according to friends of the chaplain, he personally ran Henderson off the road with his car one night.

Nothing happened to the major, so Ed Henderson resigned.

From personal experience, I was aware that the major pushed a religious agenda. One day, he insisted I run copies for him on the education copier while I ran some for my classes.

He has his own hallway and his own secretary, so he has no reason to come into our hallway and act like I'm his office staff.

I begrudgingly agreed, since Richard gave me the nod to do as the major asked. I ran my copies first, and I looked through his papers while I waited for mine to finish.

In a three-page memorandum to the custody staff, Jenkins ordered special privileges for Muslim inmates during Ramadan. According to his directive, inmates on room restriction could attend Ramadan services. They could eat off the special menu at the chow hall on demand. Muslim inmates in the hole would receive special meals as well.

The prison doesn't give any other religions special allowances. Suddenly it all makes sense. Now I understand why some inmates are the major's favorites and others are not.

Chaplain Bill Wilson took on a precarious role, and he did his best to avoid creating ripples in the prison pond. In late September, the Wilsons went on a family vacation. Tamara's tutor, Teague, planned a thorough cleaning of her room in her absence.

An easygoing fifty-year-old man, Teague was certainly no tough guy. When Tamara took off work, Teague asked for, and was granted, permission to wax the floors and disinfect the classroom—a normal occurrence when bosses went on vacation. On Tamara's first day off, Teague arrived for work and asked Officer Ballard to unlock the cleaning supply cabinet, so he could begin his project. With the officer's supervision, he gathered a bottle of cleaner, rags, a mop and a bucket then headed to Classroom 2.

A voice boomed in the hallway. "Who in the hell do you think you are getting those supplies without my permission?" Kessler loomed over Teague, with massive fists clenched.

"I got the supplies from Officer Ballard. He gave me permission. He unlocked the cabinet for me."

Teague tried to duck into the classroom, but Kessler shifted his enormous body to block the doorway.

"You didn't ask my permission. I'm the one in charge of the supply cabinet. I decide who can use my supplies."

Those aren't "your" supplies, and you aren't in charge of anything.

Everyone in the hallway stopped as the scene unfolded. Teague tried to step back, looking nervously around. Officer Ballard stood a few feet away, watching, while Kessler bullied Teague. His inaction was tacit confirmation that Kessler ran the show.

A foot and a half taller and at least one hundred and fifty pounds heavier than Teague, Kessler lifted his fist toward Teague's face, ready to swing.

"If you ever try this again, I'm going to punch you in the face!"

Teague looked at Ballard and realized no one was stepping in to save him. Frightened, Teague slipped past Kessler into Tamara Wilson's classroom. Kelly rushed to the office area to report the incident to Richard but, as usual, nothing happened. Kelly, Mike, and I over the course of days asked Blake to act. He didn't.

Nine days passed since Kessler's threats against Teague, and I approached Blake before school.

"Have you spoken to Teague yet about what happened with Kessler?"

"No, I've been too busy." Standing outside his office, he fumbled for his keys.

"Really? It's been nine days."

"I said I've been busy!" Richard stormed into his office, shaking his head.

At the end of the day, he still hadn't spoken to Teague. He never did. Tensions mounted as days passed.

Clearly Kessler can threaten anyone he wants to. He has power in the education hallway, and according to students and tutors, his reign of terror stretches across the camp.

Students became increasingly vocal about their fears.

"All it takes is one word from Kessler and the major has someone thrown in the hole."

"He beat a man up on the walk and never even got locked up, so I'm not surprised nothing happened to him when he threatened Teague."

Fear and anxiety reached a fever pitch as the days and weeks passed. In early October, Mike approached me. He'd left for lunch, so he'd passed through the administration building.

"I stopped by Eleanor's office when I came back from lunch. I told her what's been going on here with the porter. I told her we've tried to get Richard to do something, but he won't. Without Randy here, we really need help, and I asked if she would look into it."

"What did she say, Mike?"

"She told me she couldn't act on my word alone, and she wanted to know if there was anyone else who could back up what I'm saying. I told her you could. Is that okay with you?"

"Yeah, it's fine. I don't mind telling her what I've seen. Something needs to be done, and I'm glad you talked with her."

"Eleanor and I go back a long way, you know. She wants it in writing, so she'd like for you to send her an email, reporting everything you know."

We finally have someone who is willing to do something.

When I told Kelly what Eleanor Heath expected me to do, she said, "Be careful. You are going directly against the major, and he's going to be furious."

"I know, but we can't keep going on the way we have around here. The major is at the center of what Kessler's been doing, and Jenkins has basically declared war against us teachers already."

"That's true. I just worry about you. You're putting this in writing, and that takes it to a whole new level."

"Someone has to speak up, and an assistant warden has asked me to tell her what's going on. Thanks for being concerned, though. This could get ugly, and I'm worried too."

Using the computer in the staff workroom, the only one with even limited internet connection, that afternoon I wrote a lengthy email to Eleanor Heath, and her alone.

This is a sensitive issue, and there's no sense bringing anyone else into this, yet.

In the email, I gave example after example of Kessler's theft from the department and his aggressive behaviors that created a hostile work environment—all with no consequences.

I limited my report to incidents within the education department.

If the wardens want to investigate the major's favoritism or the aggression Kessler exhibits on the walk or in the housing units, they can do that on their own. I suspect the major uses Kessler as his drug deal enforcer, and if the wardens connect the dots, they'll come to that same conclusion. I'm just planting the seed.

Too many things added up: the major's overt protection of Kessler, the favors he did for him and the orders to allow him to go from cell to cell after everyone else locked down at night were sure signs that something illegal was happening.

When the prison fires staff members for sharing an earbud or giving an inmate a piece of candy, there is no legitimate reason for the major to treat Kessler as a pet.

My email was several pages long, even though I limited it to incidents inside education.

Eleanor has plenty to consider. I hope peace finally returns to our hallway.

I hit the send button.

The next morning, when I left my classroom to go to the office area to make copies, Major Joe Jenkins sat at the guard station.

Well, he obviously knows about the email. He looks like he wants to kill me with his bare hands.

Jenkins spent four or five hours sitting there, something he'd never done before. The school wasn't one of his normal hangouts. Anytime I stepped out of my room, he stared me down. After the major left, Richard Blake called me into his office.

"Shut the door and have a seat."

"Okay. What do you need to talk to me about?"

"I want to shake your hand and congratulate you." His eyes sparkled, and he could hardly contain himself.

"Congratulate me?"

"Yes! Whatever you said about the major sure got him in hot water."

"I didn't get the major in hot water. If he's in trouble, it's because of his actions, not mine. I didn't 'talk' to anyone, either. I was asked to write an email by a superior, so I did."

"Well, whatever you said sure had an impact. I wish you'd let me read your email."

I bet you do.

I just stared at him.

"Whatever you said sure made a difference. He's in a lot of trouble now."

"All I did was talk about safety and security issues in the education department. Kessler threatened to punch Teague in front of Ballard, and nothing happened to him."

You've done nothing to protect any of us, Blake.

"He's been put on unpaid leave, you know."

"Ballard?"

He grinned and scooted forward, like he was about to tell me a big secret. "No, the major. You got him in a lot of trouble. That's why I want to shake your hand."

"Like I said, if he's in trouble, it's not because of me, it's because of his own behavior."

"I'm your friend, Caroline. I want you to know how much I appreciate what you've done. I just want to help you. I hope in the future you'll come to me with any concerns you have."

"Richard, we have come to you with our concerns, and you've done nothing."

He jerked back in fake surprise, mouth open and hand across his chest. "I hope you don't think I'm the problem, do you?"

"All I know, Richard, is that I was asked to report what I knew to a warden, and that's what I did. I have to get back to class."

You're no friend of mine, Richard Blake.

For a few brief days, I felt relief. The atmosphere across the school relaxed.

Kessler will be out of the education department, and even the major's wings are clipped. I long for life to settle down and for the tension to go away. Staff, students, and tutors have held our breath since Kessler entered our world in the spring. Help is on the way.

The next week, however, Kessler still worked at the school, and Major Jenkins appeared on duty as usual. Before work five days following my email, I approached Richard Blake in the office area.

"I see the major is still walking around here."

Blake stared blankly. "Why wouldn't he be?"

"Because you told me last week he was suspended."

"Oh, *that.*" Richard batted the air with his hand dismissively. "Well, that suspension was a long time ago, like last month."

Then why did you ask to shake my hand and congratulate me for it?

I was terrified by the constant trail of lies.

I'm in worse danger now. Blake fished for information in his office last week, and he lied to me about the major's suspension. Now what?

Kessler wasn't removed until the following week, and he wasn't exactly fired. The prison advertised his porter position in the housing units, but otherwise he wasn't disciplined.

Relief swept the school, nonetheless, that he was gone.

At this point, we don't care how or why he's no longer terrorizing our hallway, we're just glad he's gone.

SEX, LIES, AND VIDEOTAPE

A few days after Kessler left the education department, I had a troubling conversation with Matt Carter, the same officer who shared the saga of Stacy McGraw and Willie Roseman.

He approached me after work.

"Caroline, remember when you told me that the porter in education walked around the housing unit wing after lockdown? They said it was because he worked in education and the major said he could be out longer."

"Yeah, I remember."

"It's true, even though he doesn't work in education anymore."

"No way."

"Last night I was in his housing unit. We locked everyone down and he was still out in the wing. I asked the guard assigned to 5 House why Kessler was still out. He said, 'It's per major's orders.'"

"So, he's still working for the major?"

"I played dumb. I asked him if Kessler still worked for the education department, but the guard said Kessler used to but doesn't anymore. Then he told me that now Kessler works for the major—and for Assistant Warden Eleanor Heath. I thought you should know."

Instead of being disciplined, Kessler was promoted? Now he works for the very warden who asked me to write the email. I'm in big trouble.

I worried all night. Unable to sleep, I spent about an hour texting Randy, getting his take on the situation.

"None of this looks or feels good, Caroline."

"I feel like I have a target on my back."

"You do."

Sleep came in fits.

Retaliation is a certainty. Kessler wields the power of the major and the wardens, and I'm on the losing end of this fight.

It was a holiday week, thanks to Columbus Day, so we worked the next day, a Friday. As soon as I reached the school, I stopped by Kelly's room to fill her in. I asked her to read the email which I saved on my classroom computer as a document.

"Yeah, I want to see what you said to Eleanor. I was afraid something like this would happen."

"Me too."

Kelly followed me down the hallway and took a seat at my desk. I sat in Keith's chair. As she read the email, Richard crept into my classroom and slipped behind Kelly to read over her shoulder. In disbelief, I watched him do it.

"Mr. Blake!" I said.

Kelly scrolled the screen up, jumped out of my chair, and left the room. Richard plopped himself down in a chair across from me on the other side of Keith's desk.

"You seem upset. What's wrong?"

I didn't answer him.

"Is there a problem? Did something happen? I'm your friend. You can talk to me."

I didn't respond. This continued for a few moments.

Holding my tongue, at this point, is useless.

Finally, I spoke. "Is something wrong, Richard? Yes, there's something wrong, but it's the same thing that's always wrong around here."

"What do you mean?"

"Oh, I think you know. The lies. The backstabbing. The retaliation. You know exactly what I'm talking about."

The look on his face told me he did.

"You want me to tell you what's wrong? Okay. It's wrong that you allowed an inmate to run roughshod over our hallway for months, even when people were threatened. It's wrong that Kessler now works for Eleanor Heath after she told me to tell her everything he does that threatens the safety and security here. It's wrong that good people are trampled on in this system. It's wrong that a man threatened to kill me when I first worked here, and the wardens threatened my job when I tried to get help. It's wrong that Barbara Mason has harassed and bullied me for two and a half years, and you did nothing. There is a hell of a lot that's wrong here, Richard, but it's the way it always is here."

"You're right, I haven't done a very good job of protecting you through this."

"Richard, you've been a part of the problem! You're the supervisor. You get the big pay to be the leader of the school. It's your job to stand up for the rest of us. You didn't. I was forced to. Now I have a target on my back."

"Yes, you do. I'm so sorry."

"You should be sorry. Your lack of leadership made me a target. You always claim you are my 'friend', but you haven't been much of a friend to any of us, Richard."

"I'm so sorry, Caroline. I was trying to protect myself. I should have protected you too." He sobbed and blubbered.

He's put a bulls-eye on my back, and I have to give him Kleenex?

"I'm going to be retaliated against."

"Yes, you are." Richard wiped his nose.

Our conversation ended after a few more moments, and I asked the officer at the guard station to call Keith up to my room.

He needs to know that the stakes have ramped up. His life depends on it.

Keith arrived in my classroom and I filled him in on the new developments.

"I didn't want you walking around here all weekend not knowing that trouble is on its way."

"Like I've said all along, when they move against you, they'll go after me first. They already have me and I'm easy to get to. Whatever happens, let's tell the truth, and we'll be fine."

"They are going to get rid of me, and you're going to end up in the hole or hurt. I'm so sorry you've been dragged into this mess."

"Don't be. We haven't done anything wrong, and you did the right thing trying to make this place safer. We will be okay. I haven't wanted you working here to begin with, and you know that. You've only stayed in this situation because of me. This is no time to regret anything. We'll deal with whatever happens. We love each other and that's not going to change. No matter what."

The weekend crept by. Monday passed, then Tuesday.

The tension is so thick I can almost reach out and touch it.

On Wednesday, Presley stormed into my room between the second and third sessions of class. He looked at Keith and barked, "Grab your coat and go up front!"

"I don't have a coat."

"Grab your coat and go up front!"

When a corrections officer tells an inmate to "go up front," it only means one thing: he's going to the hole.

They think he'll flip on me to get out of trouble. Keith isn't going to lie about me or anything else.

I wasn't going to be marched out of the prison in shame like Shannon Rafferty. I caught Richard Blake in the hallway and pointed at Keith's empty chair. "Richard, you and I both know what that's about. Last Friday you agreed that I have a target on my back, and now this is happening."

"Yeah, you're right."

"I'm done with this place. When I walk out of here today, I'm not coming back. I would appreciate it if you would write me a letter of recommendation."

"I completely understand. Give me your personal email address, and I'll get you the letter tonight."

I spent a few moments talking with Kelly, then I returned to Classroom 10. Rumors spread quickly. Sandra's tutor stopped me in the hallway. "Ma'am, the guards are telling guys that you and your tutor were caught having sex in your classroom," Carlson, told me.

"What? That didn't happen!"

"I don't think it did, but I thought you should know that's what they're telling people."

Dozens of inmates now lined the hallway looking at me, licking their chops.

If I'm putting out, they want a turn.

Thanks to Presley and Ballard's rumors, I became prey inside a maximum-security prison, and the guards knew exactly what they were doing. Presley stared at me and laughed.

He's set me up to be raped, and he wants to watch the show.

Angelo Jones a former student, walked up to me. "Ma'am what's going on? I heard they took your tutor out of your room."

"Yes, they did."

"What are you going to do?"

"I'm walking out of here today and never coming back."

"No, Ma'am. Don't leave. What can I do to help?"

"You? You're not going to do anything."

"Everyone thinks inmates don't have any power, but we can do a lot. You'd be surprised."

"Jones, I don't have time for this. There's nothing inmates can do about what's going on."

He continued to pester me, insisting that he could pull off whatever it took for me to stay at the prison. "Just tell me what I need to do, and I'll get it done. I have some power around here."

I laughed angrily and pointed to my classroom. "Really? Okay, get him out of the hole and back in the classroom. Oh, and fire the major. Can you do that?"

"No, Ma'am."

"I didn't think so. Now leave me alone."

As the last class ended, I gathered my personal belongings from my desk and locked Keith's glasses (which, in his haste, were left behind) in my desk along with his notebook.

Keith will need those, and I don't want them to disappear.

I then walked out of the prison for the last time.

The ride home was somber. Mike hugged me once we reached the commuter parking lot in Mountain Grove. "I'm going to miss working with you."

"I'm going to miss you too, Mike, but we know they're gunning for me."

That night, as promised, I received a glowing letter of recommendation from Richard. He raved about my work as the professional development chair and wrote a wonderful description of me as a teacher.

Then he blocked me on Facebook.

I wrote my letter of resignation, effective immediately, and put one copy in the mail to Mary Castor and one to Richard Blake. I also called the prison and left a message that I wouldn't be coming in the next day.

As soon as I left, I knew the character assassination would begin. The smear campaign grew quickly. Mike and Kelly kept me updated. Presley and Ballard continued their rumors which ran rampant across the camp. Presley said that my desk was full of love letters to and from multiple inmates.

As the education officer, people assume he knows what he's talking about.

Even officers in the administration bubble, that everyone passed through, added to the muck. Some rumors were more humiliating than others.

One night I called Mike. "What have they been saying about me?"

"Hold on just a second." He hushed his voice to a whisper. Doors opened and closed, then footsteps descended down a set of stairs. "Okay, I'm back. I had to go down to the basement. I don't want my wife to hear this."

"Oh my God, Mike. Is it that bad?"

"It's bad."

"What have they been saying?"

"I hate to even say it. It's awful."

"I need to know, Mike."

"The guards told people that you and your tutor were caught in your classroom. They said you were…"

"Were what?"

"Dry humping."

"Oh my God, Mike! Not only is that a lie, but it's sick and embarrassing. I can't believe they are saying that! No wonder you didn't want Ann to hear."

"They are saying that. I'm sorry."

Keith and I have the truth on our side. Two security cameras constantly filmed us, and those videotapes prove we did nothing wrong.

Mike called a few days later to tell me that the prison investigator, Jim Marshall, searched my room.

That's a relief. Neither Keith nor I fear a fair investigation.

"He went into your room with nothing but a notebook and a pen. He searched your desk and the whole classroom. He left with what he went in there with—just a notebook and a pen. If there were the letters Presley claimed there were, Jim Marshall would have had those in his hands when he left. I watched, and he took nothing. He also zip-tied the wall between our classrooms shut, so no one else can get in there."

"That's good to hear. There was nothing for him to find, and I'm glad the room is secure, so no one can plant evidence against me."

"True. There's one more thing you should know about today. While the investigator was in your room, all five of the wardens came down to the education department. They stood, watching, like they thought they were going to be there for the discovery of something big and damning against you. The looks on their faces when the investigator came out of your room empty-handed was a sight to behold."

"Now you see what I mean about this going all the way to the top of the prison. They were all after me because I upset whatever they and the major had going on with Kessler."

"This is big time trouble. Please watch your back and stay safe."

"Thanks for giving me the heads-up."

An ethical investigator will clear us of wrongdoing, but the investigation isn't our only worry. I'm not inside the death fences anymore, but Keith is.

The stress before I left the prison was horrendous, but what followed was its own form of hell.

What is happening to Keith? Is the investigator corrupt? If he is, what kind of fake charges will we face? Depending on the accusations, I could lose my teaching certificate. Keith could be injured or killed.

A lot of high stakes scenarios swirled through my head.

In Bad Standing

About a week after I walked out of SCCC, I received a letter from the Division of Offender Rehabilitation Services (DORS), the arm of the DOC the education program fell under. The department accepted my resignation, but I was considered "in bad standing" because I didn't give fifteen days' notice ahead of my departure. I called the DORS director's office.

I spoke to his administrative assistant, Lora, for over an hour. She explained that her boss was in an all-day meeting and wasn't available. She did, however, relay my information to the second in command, Curtis Rader, who called me back within half an hour.

There is no sense in mincing words.

I gave him details and named names. I told him about my concerns that Kessler acted as the major's enforcer.

"Are you aware that there's an investigation being conducted on you?"

"Considering that Mike Vaughn told me an investigator was in my room and that he went through my desk and classroom, yes, I'm aware there is an investigation."

"I wasn't sure if you knew or not."

"I know. I also know that I have nothing to hide. They can investigate me all they want to, and they won't find anything. I also know there are people like Major Joe Jenkins who are breaking policy, and possibly committing crimes. It's the major who has given special favors to an inmate, not me. If they want to investigate me, fine, but how about they investigate everyone involved in this?"

"After what you've told me today, I have to agree with you."

A few hours after our conversation, guards took Kessler to the hole under investigation. A few weeks later, SCCC transferred him to a prison three hours away. The major remained on staff, however.

During the next few months, I focused on finding work and on getting my head back on my shoulders. The trauma of working at the prison emotionally exhausted me. I moved to Kansas City to stay with my cousins who were kind enough to open their home to me.

I need a safe place to land while I put my frayed nerves and life back together.

Two months after I left the prison system, as I prepared to go to my temporary job at an educational service, my phone rang.

"This is Jim Marshall, an investigator from the South Central Correctional Center. Is this Caroline?"

"Hello, Mr. Marshall. Yes, I was wondering when I'd get this phone call."

"I spoke with Keith yesterday for over an hour. He's a very intelligent and articulate man, and I really enjoyed talking with him."

"Keith is smart and interesting."

"I couldn't get over how easy he is to talk to, in fact. He's a very honest guy, and I don't run across that very often in this job."

The conversation continued, and Jim repeated his comments about Keith's honesty and how personable he found him.

He's really laying this on thick. He doesn't realize that Keith and I are going to tell the truth, regardless of his tactics.

"Yeah, I think the world of Keith."

Sensing an opening, Jim said, "Well, he says he *loves* you."

"Yes, he does, and I love him too."

I just heard the air escape Jim Marshall's lungs.

"Most people aren't that honest. They tell me the inmate is lying or they say it was a one-sided infatuation. You've taken me by surprise."

"Keith and I believe in telling the truth. We aren't going to lie about our feelings or about anything, for that matter. I never brought in contraband, did special favors, or had physical contact with him. The DOC said we couldn't love each other, but they can't control emotions. It happens."

The conversation moved on. "I'm an experienced investigator. I found no evidence—zero—of any wrongdoing on either of your parts. No notes. No contraband. Nothing on the cameras. Even your coworkers who knew you best never saw you do or say anything that broke policy. I talked to Kelly Rainer and Michael Vaughn after I talked to Keith yesterday. They are credible witnesses, and they support everything you've told me."

Our phone call lasted over an hour. I told Jim about the email I wrote to Eleanor Heath and the fallout that followed.

"I want Keith transferred. Given the threats we both received, it's not safe for him at SCCC."

"Transferring inmates is out of my control. I investigate and write a report. I can't do anything about moving him."

"The major would be happy if Keith was dead, so he couldn't tell what he knows. I'm telling you right now, if anything happens to Keith Giammanco while he's at SCCC, I'll make sure that all the good people of Missouri know exactly what happens in that place."

Jim paused. "I'm going to recommend a transfer for Keith in my report to the warden. I can't guarantee anything, but I'm going to tell them a transfer is needed."

"Thank you, Jim."

He then brought the conversation full circle. "Keith sure is easy to talk to. I wish I could have talked to him longer."

I laughed. "Be careful. Look what happened to me because Keith's so easy to talk to."

"No, I don't think I should fall in love with him too!" We both chuckled.

Getting back to serious matters, I said, "How long do you think Keith will be in the hole? He's already been in there for two months, and I know it's awful."

"It shouldn't be long. You've both been cleared in my investigation, and there's no reason to continue punishing Keith."

"That's a relief. When can we write to each other?"

"You could have written to each other the moment your resignation took effect."

"Really? I wish we'd known that. Not talking to him has been awful. How long will it take for us to be able to visit each other?"

"I think the wait time is six months, but it could be a year. There's no reason why you can't visit after that."

That night I wrote Keith a long letter.

It's not as good as working next to him, but at least we can communicate openly, which is something we never could do in the prison. I can tell him I love him, catch him up on what happened since we last saw each other, and reassure him that we will get through whatever the prison system throws at us.

While Keith remained in the hole at SCCC, I didn't discuss everything in my letters. Too many people there looked at us as entertainment. Our personal business was ours, not something for them to twist into more rumors. On most days, I wrote Keith two letters. One I sent immediately. The other I held until he transferred.

A speedy transfer and Keith's rapid removal from the hole were wishful thinking. The transfer took two more months, and by the time they released Keith from the hole he was thirty pounds lighter and looked like he'd been in a concentration camp. Retaliation, threats, cold conditions, and poor food filled his four months in ad seg.

In the middle of winter, guards claimed they were one coat short when the men were taken outside for exercise. Keith was the one who didn't get a coat. They gave him sympathy cards, instead of Christmas cards (donated to the prison), to send out during the holidays. The sergeant who slid them into his cell laughed. He received death threats from other inmates, and from the looks on the officers' faces, they wouldn't have stopped it from happening. The hole was a dirty, loud, and chaotic place, and Keith needed out of there.

Finally, a few weeks after my conversation with Jim Marshall, Keith made a fifteen-minute phone call to me. It was the only one they allowed him per month.

"God's been with me, Caroline."

"God was with you, but the DOC was afraid hell would break loose if anything happened to you." We laughed.

"I had a feeling you were out there fighting for me."

"I was. Your safety is my top priority. We are going to get through this."

The call went by far too quickly. Before it ended, Keith said, "Just remember, I love you and I will never, ever stop."

By now, I was officially separated from and preparing to divorce my estranged husband. Money was tight, and in character, he insisted that I pay the entire cost of the divorce. This made finances difficult, but once finalized, a divorce would allow me to marry Keith.

I continued to search for a full-time teaching job while I worked part-time for a tutoring business. I finally landed a teaching job months after I left the South Central Correctional Center.

In mid-February, Keith transferred to the Southeastern Correctional Center, a facility 397-miles from where I lived in Kansas City.

The distance isn't accidental.

Shortly after he arrived at SECC, I called the prison to ask a few questions. Keith was in an honor house prior to the investigation, and now that he was cleared in the investigation, I wanted him placed back in an honor wing.

The switchboard operator transferred my call to assistant warden Cara Michaels, and it didn't go well.

"No, he was in administrative segregation before he transferred, so he will not be going into an honor wing," she said.

"I don't understand why not. He did nothing wrong."

"We don't reward bad behavior."

"He was cleared in the investigation, though, and he's never had a write up the entire time he's been in prison."

"Being cleared in an investigation doesn't mean there was no wrongdoing. Write ups aren't the only measure of bad behavior. I know all about your situation."

"I don't think you do. You only know what you were told. If something had happened between us, which it didn't, Keith would be considered the victim according to DOC policy."

"What's your point?"

"My point is that, as a victim, he wouldn't be guilty of wrongdoing and therefore shouldn't be kept out of an honor house."

"That's not going to happen!"

"So, you're telling me that it's DOC procedure to punish potential victims?"

"I'm not talking about this with you."

"I am only talking with you because he has transferred to your facility, and I'm trying to make sure he gets his honor status back now that we have both been cleared in the investigation."

"What makes you think you were cleared?"

"The investigator, Jim Marshall, from SCCC told me we were during the phone call interview we had."

"I don't believe an investigator would give you details of an investigation."

"Well, he did because we didn't do anything wrong. It's not right that Keith is being put in general population when he should have honor status, even though he transferred."

"The DOC makes transfers as convenient as possible for inmates and their families, but he will remain in general population."

"His placement at SECC is not convenient for Keith."

"Oh, that's right, you're in Kansas City, aren't you?" She let out a cackle.

I hadn't told her where I live.

"All I want is for you to answer some of my questions."

Our conversation went nowhere and was a sneak peek into the attitude we'd deal with at SECC.

We aren't on the DOC's Christmas card list, that's for sure. Anytime they can make life difficult for us, they're going to do it.

Six months after I left SCCC, two things of note happened. First, an outside drug task force arrested Major Joe Jenkins for the distribution of drugs.

This is sweet vindication. Those nightly cell visits Kessler made when everyone else locked down were business transactions, just as I suspected.

Joe Jenkins's arrest explained his refusal to go through the security checkpoints in the administration building.

While nothing changed my job loss or my separation from Keith, hearing the major's name on the news gave me satisfaction.

According to an ABC 17 report, a sheriff told Kyle McMasters a year ahead of Jenkins's arrest—while I still worked at the prison—that Jenkins was under investigation for drugs.

The prison protected Jenkins and allowed him free rein. Even after his arrest, he remained on the payroll for months.

Around the same time as the major's arrest, I applied for permission to visit Keith, but SECC denied my request. Six months or a year, as Jim Marshall had explained, was already a miserable amount of time to wait.

The news from the prison was worse than anything we expected: We were put on a five year visiting ban. DOC policy allowed any investigated employee to be banned for five years—even if cleared in the investigation.

SCCC knew they would separate us, at least physically, for years the moment they began the investigation.

I contacted Jim Marshall, who had told me to get in touch if I ever needed anything.

"I don't understand this. I found no wrongdoing on your part. There is no reason for you and Keith to be denied visits."

"Is there anything we can do? Could you send me a copy of your report, so I could show them?"

"I wish I could, but I don't keep copies of reports. Those are all sent to Jefferson City. What I can do, though, is give you the name and number of the person who does have the report. His name is Ed Chalmers. Tell him I told you to call him, and after you've talked to him, call me back to let me know what he says."

I thanked Jim and immediately dialed Mr. Chalmers's office in Jefferson City.

Ed Chalmers, in a display that would make the DOC proud, made it clear that he was not happy that I called. "There's no way I'm going to give you a copy of the report."

"Why not? I was cleared in the investigation. I should get to see what was said."

We went back and forth for a few minutes.

"Oh, I remember your case now. You told your supervisor that the only way you wouldn't resign was if your inmate employee was released from the hole. You demanded it. He refused, so you quit. No, I'm not going to help you."

"I never said that to my supervisor or any other DOC employee."

"Yes, you did. It's in the report."

Damn that Angelo Jones! He took the sarcastic comment I made to him and ran to Richard Blake. Then Blake claimed I said it to him.

"I didn't say that, but I still want a copy of the report."

"I don't give copies of reports to people who weren't under investigation."

"I was under investigation."

"No, you weren't."

"That's funny because the paperwork I got from SECC says I am denied visiting rights because I was under investigation. Curtis Rader told me I was under investigation. So did Jim Marshall."

"You're not getting a copy of this report."

"Okay, so if I wasn't under investigation, that means Keith was. Can he have a copy of it?"

"I don't give investigation reports to inmates."

I called Jim Marshall's office, as he had asked me to do, to let him know how the conversation with Chalmers played out. A woman answered his phone.

"Is Jim Marshall there? Jim asked me to call him."

"Is this Caroline?"

"Yes."

How does she know who I am when I haven't identified myself yet?

"I'll be taking all calls from you from now on."

"Jim asked me to call him."

"You won't ever speak to Jim Marshall again. Do you understand?"

"Yeah, I definitely understand."

A nagging curiosity never left me after that intercepted phone call. One night, months afterwards, I decided to contact Jim through social media.

"Chalmers told me he wouldn't give me a copy of the report because I wasn't under investigation."

"That's not right. You were under investigation."

"He also claimed your report said I told my supervisor that Keith had to be put back in my classroom or I'd quit."

"I did not say that in my report. I don't know where they got that from."

"I wanted to ask you about that, but I couldn't."

"Why not?"

Jim doesn't realize people in his office were running interference between us.

"Did you know they were intercepting my calls at your office? A woman answered your phone when I called back that day, and she told me from now on she'd take all calls from me. She said I'd never talk to you again."

"No, I didn't know that. I'm a little freaked out that they went behind my back that way."

"Stay safe, Jim. You're a good, honest man, and the prison doesn't like that."

"This is definitely disturbing, Caroline. I never avoided your calls."

"They don't want you to know the truth, Jim. At least now you know that they're watching you as closely as they're watching me."

As time went by, visiting rights weren't all we were denied by the prison system. They rejected our request to marry. SECC said they wouldn't allow it because I wasn't on Keith's visiting list.

You're the ones who won't let me on his list.

Department policy allowed couples to marry, even during visiting bans. I contacted a state legislator who helped me get approval. At first, the DOC Central Office in Jefferson City told us we could have a non-contact wedding, but neither Keith nor I accepted that. We wanted to exchange rings, hold hands, and have our first kiss. We wanted an actual ceremony, not one separated by glass.

The DOC relented and agreed to a contact wedding, but by then Keith transferred across the state, ironically to the Kansas City area, which I had moved from by now, and we had to start the process all over again.

As much as it hurt to not see Keith, there were some silver linings to being outside the prison system.

Blowing the whistle at SCCC cost me my job and kept me from seeing Keith, but it also gave me a freedom I hadn't had before. The DOC kept employees under a gag order. We couldn't complain about corruption nor support legislation or even reach out to legislators. If state laws or prison policies unduly cost taxpayers, if they fell short of rehabilitating inmates, or if DOC employees committed crimes, employees couldn't talk about it. By leaving SCCC, I wasn't under their thumb any longer. Legislators and tax-payers would now know about corruption and the short-comings of our criminal justice system. I would tell them.

Growing up with a deputy sheriff father, I was familiar with government and law enforcement. When I left home for college, I earned a degree in political science.

I understood how the system worked (or should work).

I felt driven to bring awareness and change. I met with legislators, spoke in front of organizations, appeared on radio and television programs, and developed a social media presence. I also began writing.

"Why don't you just leave the prison behind you and forget about it?" family members asked.

I couldn't walk away from the prison system and chalk it up as a bad dream.

Keith's still inside, for one thing.

Beyond that, I refused to ignore the experiences I had. Prison couldn't slip out of my consciousness.

Some people might walk away and never look back, but I can't.

For the next few years, I worked my regular teaching job and spent my free time writing and reaching out to leaders and community members. Some were receptive, but others weren't. Many bought into the lie that the "good guys" kept us safe in the Department of Corrections. Too many legislators relied on prosecutors to guide their voting habits, and they accepted anything the DOC told them. They turned blind eyes and closed minds to the revelations of a whistleblower.

I was not alone. Legislators marginalized or ignored problems raised by other people who came forward. Every time a former employee reached out, legislators treated him or her as though it was an isolated incident. Eventually, however, the cracks in the dam became too large to stop, and the truth started to trickle out.

In November 2016, a Kansas City news outlet, *The Pitch*, released a series called "Prison Broke," exposing the corruption in the Missouri DOC. Legislators ignored and isolated personal horror stories for years, but the $7.6 million paid to settle harassment and retaliation suits against the Department of Corrections caught their attention, and that of the public at large.

A special state litigation fund hid payouts from view. Settlements weren't listed in the Department of Corrections budget, so the cost of corruption was masked. Politicians, primarily motivated by votes and dollars, discovered, through breaking headlines, that millions of dollars were spent on their watch to settle lawsuits. The dirty little secret was out of the bag. Constituents now asked tough questions.

Speaker of the House, Todd Richardson, created a subcommittee to investigate the corruption allegations. Representative Jim Hansen chaired the Subcommittee on Corrections Workforce Environment and Conduct. By the time this committee formed, the Director of the Missouri Department of Corrections resigned. The weight of the news articles and the impending Missouri House investigation became too much for him.

I reached out to subcommittee members and received a call back from Representative Hansen's legislative assistant. He was dumbfounded by what I told him and connected me directly to Jim Hansen, who called me.

"I'd like to talk with you. Come see me on one of the days when we have hearings at the capitol."

"I'll make sure I get up there." I wasn't going to miss a chance to talk with the chairman.

Shortly after reaching out to the subcommittee, I received Twitter messages from another DOC whistleblower, Jon Griggs. A former Kentucky lawman, Jon worked as a drug task force officer for the Missouri DOC.

"How did you find out about me?" I asked during the two-hour phone conversation we arranged after exchanging several Twitter messages.

"I searched for Missouri DOC whistleblowers, and your name came up."

Jon and I talked often as we shared our experiences with one another. Death threats kept him in the shadows, and he was careful whom he confided in. I valued his trust, and I understood the high stakes he faced.

Jon's story wasn't an easy one to hear. While working at a prison in eastern Missouri, fellow employees set him up to be assaulted by two knife-wielding inmates in retaliation for uncovering drugs and radical terrorism. His quick thinking and combat skills saved his life.

The DOC fired him after he told an investigator, "God was with me or I would have died when they attacked me." The prison labeled him as "a religious fanatic" for mentioning God and terminated him.

Jon's pending case against the DOC didn't sit well with certain powerful people, and the death threats and break-ins began. Menacing calls even threatened his parents who lived out of state. Jon stayed out of the limelight until *The Pitch* articles, which detailed his lawsuit, were released, blowing the cover off the corruption fermenting in the prison system. Once his story became public, he was free to operate in the open.

Jon and I both wanted to testify, so we met at one of the first hearings at the state capitol. For me, this was an exploratory trip.

Is the subcommittee serious about ending corruption? Their body language and which questions they ask—and don't ask— will tell me a lot.

Sitting in the audience, we listened to testimony by the Director of Human Resources and the Inspector General, neither of whom provided adequate or cohesive answers to the questions posed by the subcommittee.

Chairman Hansen, exasperated by the lack of transparency by two key Department of Corrections leaders, threw up his hands and said, "This is starting to sound a whole lot like a shell game."

The legislative assistant for a Democratic representative sat in the row ahead of me. Speaking to his coworker beside him, he said, "Now they see what we go through. The DOC has never released any information to our office that we've requested. They won't even answer our phone calls."

I leaned forward and said, "I don't mean to eavesdrop, but I couldn't help but hear what you said."

"That's okay. I'm so fed up with the Corrections Department."

"I'm a former employee. If representatives can't get anything from them, imagine how employees are treated."

"It's insane. There's something really dirty going on in that department."

"Yes, there's a lot of corruption in the DOC. You see how the people at the top behave. Imagine how bad it is at ground level."

"I had no idea until, *The Pitch* articles came out. We'd heard whispers, but all of us are shocked by how pervasive this is."

As we listened to the witnesses testify, the lack of straightforward testimony stunned the audience. Finally, people outside the DOC witnessed the sliminess of the prison system. Disgust covered the faces of people in the crowd.

"What do you know? The politicians and reporters are finally seeing for themselves the run around that we get from the DOC," Jon said to me in a hushed voice.

I nodded, and we sat in silence as we listened to the rest of the opaque testimony. Both witnesses claimed nothing fell under their power, yet they were at the top of the personnel and investigative branches of the prison system. Somehow, the buck never stopped at their desks.

I spoke briefly with Chairman Hansen following the hearing. He was in a hurry to vote on the House floor, but he said, "Wait for me in my office. I want to talk with you."

Before I made my way to Representative Hansen's office, Jon Griggs and I spoke with reporters covering the hearings. I shared my contact information with a well-known journalist who covers legislative and political news.

Jon and I parted ways, and I wound my way through the hallways to Representative Hansen's office. Room 111 shared a waiting area with the office of Representative Paul Fitzwater, the chairman for the Corrections Committee, under which the subcommittee fell. Paul Fitzwater attended the morning's hearing, so he was aware of what happened during testimony.

Fitzwater has known about the corruption. I met with him last year, and all he did was give lip service. He didn't lift a finger to investigate anything, and I doubt I'm the only one he's blown off.

As I waited for Representative Hansen, Fitzwater entered from the hallway.

"Do you need to see me?"

"No, I'm waiting for Representative Hansen. He asked me to wait for him here."

"Weren't you in the audience at the hearing?"

"Yes, I was. That was some testimony."

"This," Fitzwater waved his arms in the air, "is taking up all of my committee time."

"Well, I worked for the DOC, and I'm glad the House is investigating the corruption."

I can tell he doesn't remember speaking to me before.

"Sure, there have been incidents here and there, but I'm losing all my committee time to this. I'm tired of it already." He stopped for a moment to get his messages from his legislative assistant.

"This investigation is important." I stared incredulously at the man at the helm of the Corrections Committee.

He turned around, facing me as he flipped through his stack of messages. "You know, by the time all is said and done, there could be a few wardens who lose their jobs over this."

Fitzwater's tone implied that would be the most significant result of the hearings.

"By the time all is said and done, if it's looked into far enough, there could be a few wardens who find themselves behind bars," I replied.

Fitzwater instantly bristled. "That's a very serious statement you've made!" He stormed into his office.

"It's a very accurate statement," I called after him.

Refusing to look at me as he left the office, Fitzwater stalked into the hallway.

Representative Hansen's assistant arrived, lunch in hand. Genuinely concerned about the corruption, he and I had a great conversation as I waited. After fifteen or twenty minutes, the representative arrived, and we went into his office to discuss the need for reform.

"I came here today to see if the subcommittee was serious."

"What do you think now?"

"Everything I saw in the hearing room tells me it is."

"This is my last term in office. If I accomplish nothing else in my years in Jefferson City, I want to fix this problem."

"I can't tell you what it means to me that you're taking this seriously."

"I am, and I want you to testify in front of the committee. We're starting at the top, and then eventually we'll have employees testify."

"I think you should do it the other way around."

"Oh?"

"Yes. If you have the talking heads at the top come in first, they'll give you the same run around you saw today. I think you're better off having employees testify first. Then you know what questions to ask the higher-ups. They'll have to answer to specifics."

"I'm going to have to think about that, but you may be right."

"I think you'll get to the bottom of things faster if you do."

"Let me ask you a question. Some people say the employees need pay raises. They claim that's why professionalism is lacking in the DOC. Would a pay raise have made a difference in what happened to you?"

"Right now, the focus has to be on cleaning out the corrupt employees. If you give everyone a pay raise now, you're just rewarding the corrupt employees. Clean house first."

"If you had made more, would you have stayed?"

"If I'd made $50,000 a year, I still would have been treated the same. It reached the point where I couldn't stay quiet and they got rid of me. No amount of money would have changed that."

"You're right. I promise you, I will do my best to clean up the system." We shook hands, then I left to speak with other legislators.

I posted about the hearings on social media before I drove home. Two nights later, a fellow prison wife contacted me in a chat. I knew Mandy through a mutual friend, and we'd talked a few times in the past. She lived in Paul Fitzwater's district and was also a former employee of the DOC who met her fiancé inside. "I had a conversation with Paul Fitzwater, and it worries me."

"What happened, Mandy?"

"I saw Fitzwater at a social gathering and told him I'd like to talk with him about *The Pitch* articles."

"What did he say?"

"He said, 'Now why would you have any interest in that?' He looked angry that I even brought it up."

"That's a strange response from someone heading the Corrections Committee, isn't it?"

"It sure is. I told him I'm a former DOC employee and that prison reform is important to anyone who pays taxes. I also told him I have a loved one in prison. I couldn't believe what he said next."

"What did he say?"

"You're a respected businesswoman in this community. You don't want to involve yourself in prison issues. You have a reputation to uphold. Stay out of this for your own good."

"That's bizarre."

"I'm really angry that he reacted that way."

"I had a conversation with him when I was at the capitol the other day. He made it clear he didn't like this investigation."

"I'm stunned that my representative, a man I've known for years, brushed my questions aside. He even criticized me for showing interest. Why shouldn't all of us care? What's my being a businesswoman have to do with it?"

"It's weird that he's discouraging you from asking questions." I described my conversation with him at the capitol.

"I never thought he'd be so indifferent. Why wouldn't he care about the corruption?"

"That's a good question. What's in it for him?"

Something tells me he has his reasons, and they aren't good.

Almost on cue, the next expose in *The Pitch* revealed that Fitzwater lied when he claimed he knew nothing about the corruption. Emails proved former employees warned him of the dangerous conditions festering within the department.

Fitzwater can deny all he wants to, but the emails are black and white proof that he's blowing smoke.

The evening after the latest article broke, the reporter I spoke to after the hearing, called me. "You realize that since you're involved with an inmate, if you testify, your testimony won't be considered credible?"

I've heard this too many times.

"I'm sick and tired of the stigma. Anyone attached to an inmate is devalued and dismissed. My testimony will be credible because I'm telling the truth. My relationship with Keith doesn't change the validity of what I experienced.

Someone may not approve of my personal life, but that doesn't negate the actual crimes committed by DOC employees. I've seen the corruption with my own eyes."

"I'm not saying you're wrong, but the legislators aren't going to believe you because you love an inmate."

"Most of them are friends of mine on Facebook. They know who I am. They know what I work on. They know about Keith. I'm pretty sure they already view me as credible."

Two weeks later, the subcommittee asked former employees to testify, and I was one of them. Representative Hansen decided to talk to employees before bringing in any more administrators.

Maybe he did listen to me.

A caseworker from northwestern Missouri testified ahead of me. He concentrated on better training for supervisors and on recommendations for handling hostile workplace situations.

"We need to make it easier for an employee to transfer to another facility if they're being harassed where they work."

Why should the victims have to transfer to another facility? Why don't they just get rid of the bad employees?

His testimony lasted about fifteen minutes. When my turn came, I placed my notes on the table and handed a legislative clerk packets of information for the legislators to review later. Included in that packet were copies of reports given to me by a current sergeant working in the system. He couldn't testify for fear of losing his job, but I could.

Sitting in the hard, plastic chair, looking up at the sub-committee in the tiered seating before me, I was unafraid. I kept my testimony direct and to the point. I put a face to the victims of corruption they had heard about but not experienced themselves.

This is no time to beat around the bush or to talk about esoteric policy changes. I want them to understand the corruption on a personal level.

"The harassment and retaliation of staff members directly relates to the department's failure to rehabilitate inmates. Corruption is so widespread that it's impossible for everyone, including inmates, to not see it. It's difficult to look at inmates and tell them to stop behaving like criminals when you, yourself, are acting like a criminal. Unfortunately, that's the situation we have in the current DOC."

The legislators nodded in agreement.

My testimony stretched for half an hour. "I provided you reports leaked by a current employee and copies of blogs I've written about corruption within the DOC. If there's anything else you'd like to know, I'm willing to talk in greater detail with you."

The legislators flipped through the packets I provided them, but during my testimony, their eyes remained glued on me. I wasn't talking in broad terms. I gave them first-hand testimony regarding shocking behavior.

"Before I end my testimony, I also want to address another topic. Most of you know me through social media and are aware that I am in a relationship with an inmate. That's not a secret, and it's nothing I hide."

They nodded in agreement.

"Some people may try to discount what I have to say because I love an inmate. What I have explained to you today—everything from the prison's failure to protect me when an inmate threatened to rape and kill me to the major of a maximum security prison blackmailing the teaching staff—has nothing to do with my personal life. Agree or disagree with my relationship, but the criminal and unethical behavior of my coworkers and supervisors cannot be excused by my perceived wrongdoings."

The hearing adjourned, and I stood to leave. Two subcommittee members, John McCaherty and Tim Remole, stepped down to the hearing room floor and shook my hand.

"Thank you for your testimony. I was moved by what you had to say," Tim Remole said.

"Yes, I was shocked by the things you went through. I'm sorry you had to put up with it, and we're doing what we can to make sure it doesn't happen to others," John McCaherty added.

"Thank you. I understand that the caseworker before me was trying to support the department as much as possible, but we must do better than transferring the people who are harassed at work. Why should the victim and his or her family have to move to escape harassment? The perpetrators need to be removed, and retraining isn't enough."

"We agree."

A third legislator, Bruce Franks, Jr., made his way to the witness table. I reached out my hand to shake his, and he waved my hand away. Instead, Bruce shook his head, outstretched his arms, and gave me a hug.

"Thank you for having the courage to tell the truth."

"You're welcome. I just want the system to change, and the legislature needs to know what's going on."

As I walked through the hearing room, the reporter I'd spoken with over the phone looked on. As I walked past, I made eye contact with him.

"Well, it looks like they thought I was credible after all."

"Yeah, you did great!"

"That's because I know what I'm talking about."

The hearings continued. While the director, Jack Morelli, resigned, the second in command, James Jordan, was still in office. His testimony took place a few weeks after mine. Prior to his testimony, a subcommittee member contacted me, asking for questions I believed should be asked of the outgoing department leader. I sent a list of six questions, including where did he believe responsibility fell for the corruption and what had he done to end it?

Pending lawsuits against the department named James Jordan specifically. Accusations stemmed from his time as a warden. As the deputy director of the DOC, he oversaw the investigations, cover-ups, and lawsuits resulting from corruption. Shortly before his testimony, he resigned.

I'd love to be in the audience during his testimony, but I can't miss another day of work.

A friend of mine, Jamie Stephens, however, went to all the hearings. She said, "I'll send you Facebook messages to keep you in the loop. This should be good."

It was. Jordan's performance was so bad that the audience laughed out loud at some of his answers. "I've never seen anything like this," Jamie messaged me. "He was the laughing stock of the entire hearing room. I'd have felt sorry for him if he didn't deserve the ridicule."

"Oh, I wish I could've been there to see it myself."

"Some of the questions the committee asked were brutal, and Jordan had no good answers for any of them. If he hadn't resigned already, he wouldn't have a choice after this. That's how bad his performance was this morning."

Finally, the politicians are seeing for themselves what DOC employees have dealt with for years.

Looking for Leadership

A new governor and the resignation of Jack Morelli meant a new director for the DOC. Instead of promoting from within, the governor tapped an outsider, a former probation and parole administrator from North Carolina named Camila Mosley, to fill the vacancy.

Three months after my testimony before the subcommittee, a meeting between Ms. Mosely, Jim Hansen, and me was scheduled. We met in Representative Hansen's office. Seated on the brown leather couch across from me, Camila Mosely made herself comfortable while I sat on a hard, wooden chair.

"Would it be okay with you if I sat next to you on the couch? This chair hurts my back, and it sort of feels like I'm in a job interview."

Not exactly thrilled with the idea, she nodded yes as I settled into the couch to begin our conversation.

"Thank you for meeting with me."

"I'm not quite sure why you wanted to talk with me." Her sweet Southern drawl hung in the air.

"I worked in the trenches of your department. I faced a hostile workplace, and it would help you to hear what I have to say." I began telling her of my experiences.

She interrupted me, repeatedly. "You aren't telling me anything I haven't heard before. That was years ago."

"I think her experiences are important," Jim Hansen interjected.

"What happened to me may have been a few years ago, but it's still pertinent. These same things happen today inside your department. The corruption hasn't gone away."

"You and I both know that the people at the bottom of the system and the people at the top know there are problems. I'm working to bring those in the middle back into line."

Her dismissive tone is irritating.

"There are people at all levels who are corrupt."

She countered by saying that there were "a few bad actors" in the system. "You're preaching to the choir."

"There are more than 'a few bad actors' in the system."

"The number is very low, and I can assure you that I have already addressed every issue you've brought up."

"You've only been in the department for a few months."

Her face took on a hardened look, as though she had tired of the meeting already. She said, "I understand you are in a relationship with an inmate. There is no way you were harassed or retaliated against. You're the one who is at fault."

She's trying to put me on the defensive. Nice try, but it's not going to work.

"When my life was threatened, and the wardens responded by threatening my job, I didn't even know Keith. Most of what happened to me had no connection to my personal life. Major Joe Jenkins blackmailed the teachers. The school secretary was a workplace bully. That had nothing to do with anything other than corruption in your department."

"But you became romantically involved with an inmate."

I placed my elbow on the back of the couch and leaned forward. "Keith and I acknowledge that we fell in love someplace the DOC doesn't approve of, but we didn't act on our feelings."

"But you crossed lines you shouldn't have. You have no leg to stand on when talking about retaliation."

"Crossing lines? Keith and I are honest and upfront about our relationship, but I never did favors for him or compromised the safety and security of the institution. I had coworkers openly say they hated and despised certain inmates. They made inmate lives hell and even had their buddies on staff join in. And do you know what happened to them?"

I stopped to look Jim Hansen in the eye.

"They were patted on the back and told they were great employees." Jim Hansen's eyes widened.

I turned back to Mosley. "Do I love an inmate? Yes, I do. In the end, love or hate, those are just emotions. Whether or not I acted on those emotions is what matters. According to you, nothing that happened to me counts because I love Keith, but if I hated him I'd be a good employee."

I struck a chord with Jim Hansen. Camila Mosley shifted nervously in her seat.

"I'm telling you about real problems inside the department. I'm trying to help you."

"You aren't telling me anything new," she said, digging in her heels.

"You should talk with my husband. He sees things that you could learn from."

"I'm not going to talk to an inmate!"

"Really? Because you just got through telling me that the people at ground level see what is going on. You don't get any lower than being an inmate in the system. He could give you insight."

She looked as though I'd just flung a bag of urine at her.

I shifted gears. "How do you feel about shaming as part of a rehabilitation program?"

"Shaming is never allowed."

"Well, the ITC program requires inmates to wear signs that say they are nothing but criminals. Inmates in some rehabilitative programs are told that they are criminals and will never be anything other than that."

She jotted down notes. "That shouldn't be happening."

"It is. Here's another thing you may not already know about. You know those white transport vans that are used to take inmates from place to place?"

"Yes."

"If you look at them, you'll see that none of them are handicap accessible."

"Oh, is that what this is about? Is your inmate disabled?"

"No, he isn't. He did have a surgery last year, though, and a disabled inmate rode in the van with him to the doctor. Do you know how they loaded that man onto the van?"

Both Mosley and Hansen shook their heads no.

"The guard picked him up out of his wheelchair and tossed him into the back seat of the van. Federal law is broken—and federal funding is risked—when disabled people are treated that way."

More frantic note-taking took place. "Thank you for letting me know about this."

"I figured you'd want to know about it before the feds find out. I'd like to work with you to make the department run better."

Camila Mosley met my offer with a blank stare.

Instead of accepting my offer she said, "There are so many good things about our department, and if all people hear about are the bad things, how are we supposed to make the system better? You need to do your part and tell people about the good things and not the bad. After all, the problems come from just a handful of bad actors."

"I'm more than happy to be a cheerleader for good news, but I need good news to tell. Before *The Pitch* stories broke about the corruption and the payouts, the public never even thought about the prison system. They assumed the good guys were keeping us safe. Representative Hansen's subcommittee would never have been formed. If no one talks about the problems, they'll never be fixed."

She sat stone-faced.

I continued, "I actually like you. I even bragged about you during an interview on KTRS, a major St. Louis radio outlet, saying I was heartened by your appointment because you come from North Carolina, a state with a proven record of criminal justice reform."

"That's true, North Carolina does have a good reputation, and I appreciate you saying that about me."

"I want to talk about good things. I even like North Carolina—except when they try to beat my Arizona Wildcats in basketball."

She gave a smirking smile, "*Try*? We don't *try*. We beat them,"

Jim Hansen tilted forward, elbows on knees. "I played basketball for the University of Arizona Wildcats."

Holy cow. Neither one of us saw that coming from Hansen.

Her glib remark backfired. Jim Hansen and I shook hands and laughed at our newfound connection. I said, "I went to school with Steve Kerr and Sean Elliott."

"Back in the Lute Olsen days," Jim Hansen said, his face lighting up. It was a pleasant break in the strain of the moment.

Possibly, the most telling moment of the conversation came when the three of us discussed how to get the corrections staff to behave professionally.

"You're going to have to retrain 11,000 employees. That's a big job, and we realize it's going to take time," Jim Hansen said as he looked at Mosley.

She reached her hand out and put it on Jim's arm. In her breathy drawl, she exclaimed, "Oh, no, Jim. It's more like 4,000 that need to be retrained. They are the problem employees."

"4,000 employees?" Hansen and I looked at each other in shock.

That's far more than a few bad actors.

"No, I think Representative Hansen is correct. All 11,000 employees need to be retrained. The 4,000 you mentioned need to either learn how to be professional or they need to be removed. The rest of the 11,000 need to learn that it's okay to be professional. They need to know what to do when they see corruption. All DOC employees need reprogramming."

We sat in awkward silence for a moment.

Jim Hansen then said, "We brought up basketball. Remember that she isn't replacing Lute Olsen or Dean Smith. She's coming in after the guy who was 0 and 21."

"I agree it's a tough job, but she needs to be open to input from people who are trying to help her."

Camila Mosley didn't realize it that day, but she defined our role. Keith and I were willing to work with them, but the leadership of the department wouldn't listen. Everyone is safer when prisons run correctly, but the system likes the status quo. We will continue to be watchdogs for the citizens.

For as long as Keith is inside, he will be the eyes and ears watching out for the rest of us. I will be the public voice for our cause.

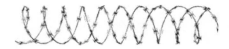

How Did This Happen?

C orruption doesn't happen by accident. It's groomed to exist. Even the physical placement of the facilities plays a role. Just as some inmates are chained to the prison through the "preschool to prison pipeline," employees are also chained to the system by their zip codes.

Missouri's prisons are predominantly placed in small, rural towns lacking economic opportunity. Often the main employer in the area, the prison owns its employees. Men and women are economically bound to the DOC if they wish to remain in their homes and near their families.

The DOC is so desperate for employees that it has lowered its hiring age to nineteen. No nineteen-year-old can be an effective authority figure to inmates, and they are easily swayed by veteran guards, some of whom are minions of Stan Baker. Employees no longer need to have a high school diploma or driver's license. People with criminal records and prison stints of their own are allowed to work as corrections officers. The lines have become even further blurred between the good guys and the inmates.

Subsistence pay from the only employer for miles around creates an atmosphere ripe with trouble. Officers earn $29,000 a year with benefits. That's a tempting figure when you are nineteen, but before long reality sets in. Car payments, rent, food, and utilities all take bites out of paychecks. Years go by, and the pay does not increase. Many officers support entire families on $29,000. What began as a dream paycheck for a young employee becomes a source of stress and worry for a thirty-year-old with three children to support. Bills mount, and prices go up, but the state paycheck doesn't. Still, it's the only "decent" job around.

Desperation to keep that prison paycheck creates blind eyes. Money, even in the form of low wage jobs at a dangerous worksite, is a powerful motivator. No one reports abuses. No one questions authority.

Personal integrity erodes as family budgets outweigh ethics. Too many employees decide to work the system, succumbing to the lucrative drug trade that runs rampant in the prisons.

While posters displayed in prison visiting rooms threaten family members with felony prosecution if they are caught with drugs, employees caught selling everything from marijuana to heroin and meth are either forgiven, protected, or at the worst fired. The risk is low versus the monetary reward, and employees can justify their illegal behavior in a hundred ways in their minds.

The culture of fear within the prison allows coworkers and superiors to behave terribly. Bullying, workplace hostility, sexual harassment, and sometimes physical assaults occur. Fearful people are easily manipulated. Every employee recognizes the consequences when a Stacy McGraw files a grievance. She wasn't the first nor the last employee made an example of to frighten other workers. If you say something, you'll be next.

In the big picture, Stacy got off easy. She lost her job. Lawsuits settled by the DOC revealed that some who rippled the DOC pond wound up poisoned or physically attacked. Corruption plays for keeps.

The need to bring awareness, to shine light in the dark corners of the prison complex continues. News of the corruption impacted the general public's mind. That original $7.6 million reported by *The Pitch* has ballooned to nearly $120 million in lawsuit settlements. As if the proven harassment and retaliation isn't a big enough black eye on the state, Missouri has dragged its feet in paying victims their court-ordered awards. Jon Griggs is one of the successful plaintiffs who still awaits his settlement.

In a Springfield, Missouri Walmart, a chance meeting with a young woman named Jenna Ramsey reminded me of the damaged reputation—albeit deserved—of the Department of Corrections.

"I'm entering my last semester of college," Jenna said as we chatted.

"What are you getting your degree in?"

"Criminal justice."

"What kind of job are you thinking of?"

"I applied with the Department of Corrections, thinking it would be a good experience to work as a corrections officer."

"Honestly, I can't encourage you to do that."

"Oh, I'm not. Once I read news stories about the corruption, there's no way I'd work there. I'll use my degree some other way."

"Until the system is cleaned up, I think you're making the right decision."

The headlines and lawsuits aren't the only negative impression the DOC has made in the public eye. The same employee behavior that I worried about during my time at the Academy leaves a black mark as well.

On a recent trip to Jefferson City, one spent meeting with legislators and testifying in front of another subcommittee on criminal justice reform, I stayed at the Capitol Plaza Hotel— the same hotel my cohorts and I stayed at during training.

In the middle of the night, I awoke to pounding on my hotel room door. I looked through the peephole, and a drunk man in a blue t-shirt was outside my room, demanding to come in. I said nothing, but slipped over to the phone and called the front desk.

"I'll be right up to check, Ma'am."

In between my call and the desk clerk's arrival, the man left but then returned to bang on my door once again.

A few minutes later, the clerk arrived from downstairs. The door banger had disappeared, but the clerk asked me to tell him again exactly what happened, which I did.

He rolled his eyes and said, "Well, the Department of Corrections has a group of employees staying here."

"What?"

"The DOC has people staying here for some sort of training."

"That's why a drunk man was banging on my door in the middle of the night? Does this sort of thing happen with DOC employees often?"

He paused. "Yeah, I hate to say it, but that's the best explanation for what happened to you. We deal with that sort of thing all the time from them."

When Department of Corrections employees are the first explanation for unruly behavior in the mind of an experienced hotel clerk, it's a pervasive pattern of behavior.

TRUTH CAN WIN

U nfortunately, since my meeting with Camila Mosley, circumstances have worsened. It's a crisis the department created itself. Mosley and her predecessors kicked the can down the road for so long that now a tipping point has been reached.

Under her command, staff shortages ballooned, impacting conditions for inmates and employees. Housing units have closed at some prisons because there simply aren't enough employees to man them, and inmates live in even more cramped conditions. Guards are asked to work double shifts multiple times a week, equaling a million hours of overtime in just six months. Caseworkers and other non-custody staff sometimes pull second shifts as guards because no one else is there to fill positions.

Morale is low, and stress is high. Imagine the demands a guard faces, working again after already logging in sixty hours that week, alone in a housing unit wing with seventy-two or more inmates. It happens often. They are tired, stressed, and resentful.

What Camila Mosely and the politicians haven't fully realized yet is that the resentment harbored by prison employees is directed towards them. Some employees envision a time when they have enough political clout to unseat legislators and other elected officials who ignore their pleas.

Go to nearly any corrections facility in this state, and you will hear employees openly complain about their jobs and the DOC. They will vent to inmates, visitors, and other staff members their long lists of grievances, unsolicited. Employees openly criticize the director, her administration, and the wardens in front of complete strangers. That didn't happen when I worked there, and I have witnessed a collapse of morale. Fear still pervades the system, but disgust with the working conditions overrides the filters employees used to have when talking about the department.

Workers exude an attitude of "I just want to get through my shift. I don't care what happens during it. I don't care what happens after I leave. I just need to survive." That makes prisons less safe, and the corruption continues. Inmates know they can skirt rules, or even openly defy them, and nothing will happen to them. When they see guards sleeping in housing unit bubbles, when guards routinely let violations slide, inmates gain the upper hand.

I still have friends inside the death fences. They contact me privately to share the frustrations, the stories of continued corruption, and the sheer exhaustion of working for a department that cannibalizes its good employees.

Some employees are coming forward publicly, although anonymously, by speaking to the press. In one news report, an employee said overworked employees are paid to become hostages in understaffed prisons. His warnings weren't exaggerated.

Wholesale riots have broken out in more than one facility, and there is fear, among employees and inmates, that more are on the horizon. Inmates are getting the upper-hand. A hundred straws are breaking the camel's back, and at any given moment one of those straws will ignite another riot.

The leadership of the Missouri Department of Corrections allowed corruption to reign for too long. State legislators and the governor carry blame as well. They ignored the pleas of staff and inmate alike and chose instead to believe the false narrative of the DOC leaders without questioning it. Truth has a hard time when people want to believe a lie.

The subcommittee led by Jim Hansen released a handful of changes for the DOC to make, but they fell far short. Most were already in place, but unused, within the DOC. The toothless recommendations did little to change what poisons our prison system from within.

The leadership changes Camila Mosley touts to politicians amount to little more than a shuffling of wardens from one prison to another. New blood and a renewed determination to end corruption has been lost.

It's easy for the DOC to claim success when it gags its employees from speaking the truth, then threatens them if they do. The hope that flickered in the hearts of employees has all but been extinguished by the lack of leadership and the legislature's failure to follow through on promises.

I continue to speak up in hopes that others will find their voices. Many current employees of the DOC would love to, but they still fear—for good reason—for their jobs and safety. Employees confide in me because I am free to confront the lies the DOC wants people to believe.

Max Donley, a longtime employee of the DOC, says Camila Mosley, herself, threatened to force his resignation because he reached out to a legislator. It wasn't just any legislator, either. It was Jim Hansen.

Max says that the DOC director laughed at him when he said he wanted legislators to know what goes on inside the prison system.

"You're wasting your time. I have the legislators' ears, and they won't care what you say."

Max claims he tape recorded this conversation, but fear and the advice of his attorney keep him from sharing the tape at this time. The same fear that persisted when I worked at SCCC pervades the system today, and the problem is statewide.

I asked Representative Hansen about Max's situation, carefully trying to protect his identity. Hansen's response was woefully indifferent. "I don't believe that anyone who tape records his boss is credible, so I don't believe any of what he says."

Camila Mosley has his ear. Because Max spoke up, he's targeted at work, and he's trying to hold on until his upcoming retirement. He has begun a lawsuit, and he's confident in the evidence he has against the department.

No one should live in fear because the truth is told. No one should worry that a lifetime of service to the state is endangered because they reached out to an elected official whose job it is to fight for citizens' best interests.

I sent him to Jim Hansen's office in good faith, and now my confidence in the legislators tasked with changing the system is damaged. I respectfully challenge state leaders to restore my faith in them.

Hundreds, perhaps thousands, of employees have been retaliated against, harassed, or driven out of the department, all victims of the culture of fear and intimidation that pervades the DOC. A dark curtain shrouds the department, and corruption grips the system.

In my meeting with the two of them, Jim Hansen defended Camila Mosely by saying, "You can't turn a big ship around overnight."

That might be true in the first few months, but valuable time has passed with no improvements. In fact, some things are worse now for employees, inmates, and ultimately tax-payers than they were before.

Even monumental tasks need to show progress—or at least a wholehearted commitment to improve. I haven't seen it happen yet, and people are suffering. $720 million of Missouri tax dollars are spent on a system that fails its citizens. In how many other states is the story the same? How many billions of dollars are spent unwisely in our country every year on a system that desperately needs to run more effectively, efficiently, and ethically?

Change is crucial. The system's continued business as usual approach is inadequate.

When news reports share the concerns of employees (most recorded in shadow with altered voices), the DOC official response has been to refute the men and women in the trenches. The Department of Corrections has turned on its own in a very public way, calling its employees liars. The divide is enormous between the administration which continues to cover up the problems within and the rank and file employees who live the nightmare daily.

Ironically, in many ways, inmates and employees have more in common now than either ever dreamed possible. The DOC leadership and its failure to respond to the needs of the people working and living in its facilities is now the common enemy of both.

Inmates aren't rehabilitated when conditions inside the prison are so dysfunctional, and communities are failed when inmates are not prepared for life outside the prison walls. Both inmates and employees are languishing inside prisons that are failing us all.

When our tax dollars support a state department that instills fear in ethical employees, something is terribly wrong. State employees should work in safe and transparent environments—in the kind of workplaces we would all be proud of as taxpayers. When it comes to the prison system, we are paying for a workplace that behaves criminally. We should never have to look at the color of their uniforms to know who is whom.

The subcommittee headed by Jim Hansen existed for a second year, but only two hearings were held, each with the same witness: Camila Mosley, who bragged about the sweeping changes she made within the department. No employees, past or present, were asked to testify. Clearly, no continued interest remained, and the Corrections Committee willingly accepted the rainbow and butterfly tales of the director.

Perhaps a horrific tragedy within the system will clear their heads, but that's not something we should have to rely upon.

It's frustrating to watch the system continue to erode, but all is not lost. While money and fear are motivators, truth is too. When people learn about the secretive prison system, there is hope. Change can happen. What I, and countless other employees, witnessed inside the death fences doesn't have to repeat itself.

Leaders and community members must understand what causes and contributes to the culture of fear, though, before change can happen. Missouri isn't an anomaly, and other prison systems need watchful eyes cast upon them. Right now, so much work must be done before our prisons are free from corruption, but it can happen if the public demands a better product for the money we spend.

Between the death fences, the violent inmates, and the corrupt employees, prison wasn't a pleasant place to be. I was inside those death fences for two and a half years, Keith remains behind them, and good people are trapped working there.

Sometimes it seems like nobody cares, but everyone should. Everyone's lives are endangered when broken systems don't produce rehabilitated inmates, and no one should work someplace where honesty is deadly.

I want Officer Duncan to be proven wrong someday. I want state employees to behave so professionally that there is no confusion over who the criminals are and who the good guys are inside the death fences.

Let's stop making it hard for truth to be heard. Stop believing the lie.

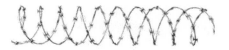

Acknowledgments

My love and thanks go to my husband, Keith. Your quest for truth to prevail is an inspiration, and we will continue to count all things joy. You are my anchor and my sail.

Deepest appreciation to our children, Rick, Kevin, Elise, and Marissa. Even when you haven't understood our need to tell the truth at our own expense, you have loved us.

Many friends helped me carry the torch and hone my craft while writing this book. Ruth Ramsey, Rochelle Wisoff Fields, and Mark Reynolds gave me guidance and provided extra sets of eyes to help me tell my story in the clearest possible way. Our friendships are invaluable.

To my friends whose personal lives are impacted by incarceration, including Debrah Falkenrath, Winona Carroll, Kathy Ray, and Debra Forehand, thank you for your strength and determination, and for the laughter and tears that we share on this journey.

To my friends still employed by the Corrections Department, whom I cannot name for your own safety, you are in the trenches fighting the good fight in a system that does its best to silence the truth. You know who you are, and I thank you for your willingness to help me bring light to the dark corners. Be brave and find your voice.

Thank you to my readers and social media friends. Your love and encouragement inspire me daily, and I am humbled and blessed by your continued support.

Special thanks to the good people at RhetAskew Publishing, who believed in this book.

ABOUT THE
AUTHOR

Caroline Giammanco is an author, educator, and criminal justice reform advocate. Born and raised in the Ozarks of southwest Missouri, she attended the University of Arizona where she earned a B.A. in Political Science and a post-baccalaureate certification in Secondary Education. She is invited to speaking engagements and book signings around the country, spreading the word about the need for criminal justice reform.

She teaches high school English in southern Missouri and lives on her favorite place on earth, her farm. She has two sons, Rick and Kevin; two step-daughters, Elise and Marissa; and she is married to the love of her life, Keith Giammanco.

Caroline's two previously published books, _Bank Notes: The True Story of the Boonie Hat Bandit_ and _Guilty Hearts: The World of Prison Romances_, also lift the corners on the world of incarceration.

Web:	http://www.booniehatbandit.com
Facebook:	https://www.facebook.com/BoonieHatBandit/
Twitter:	https://www.twitter.com/GiammancoBook
Email:	carolinegiammanco@gmail.com

WWW.RHETASKEWPUBLISHING.COM

9 781949 398052